D0778570

CHEFS' FRIDGES

CHEFS' FRIDGES

More Than 35 World-Renowned
Cooks Reveal What They Eat at Home

CARRIE SOLOMON AND ADRIAN MOORE

HARPER
DESIGN

An Imprint of HarperCollinsPublishers

Contents

INTRODUCTION

We got our first glimpse of chefs' refrigerators in Paris, a city whose food culture is protected by UNESCO, and the place that Adrian and I most often call home. Our day jobs (photographer-writer and head concierge at a Paris luxury hotel) as well as our after-work hours revolve around food. We each count a handful of chefs as friends, the kind who invite us over for simple dinners at home made with a few pinched items from the restaurant's reach-ins as well as ingredients from their home fridges. It got us thinking. What happens when the restaurant shuts down for the night, the chef's whites come off, and these culinary artists head home to grab something to eat? After we rummaged through a few fridges we knew we were on to something. And voilà! We had the makings for our first book, *Inside Chefs' Fridges, Europe*.

In that first book, we wanted to get behind the persona and the cult of that particular chef and drill down to the juicier, more honest bits. And what better way to do it than to peek at the stuff they keep inside their refrigerators and to get invited to a meal made from its contents? As we made our way across Europe, we were astonished by how many ketchup bottles, industrial cheese blocks, and tomatoes we found inside various fridges. We were even more surprised to find illegal foods (delicate birds, odd varieties of mushrooms). Sometimes we found ourselves in slightly precarious situations, such as the time an empty fridge caused one chef (known for a wild temper and boozy ways) to invite us on a raucous clay pigeon shoot in the quest to feed us dinner. But the real draw of our snooping was the fascinating, wow-can-you-believe-they-have-that-in-their-fridge voyeuristic element that came with turning up exotic, or even forbidden, goods and the odd supermarket products.

Despite being longtime Parisians, we were both raised in North America, so naturally our thoughts turned to our homeland for the next book. Would the refrigerators of chefs in the Americas be larger or more luxurious than their European counterparts? Would they have smart fridges that stock only local products, or would they reveal niche goods that come from far-flung places? Would there be Weight Watchers meals, sliced cheese, marijuana, or nonorganic eggs? While we mainly focused on North American chefs, we couldn't resist comparing their iceboxes with a few European fridges—and yes, they are indeed bigger. We would have liked to get to farther corners of the world—hopefully we will in the next book.

Our nosing around gleaned some pretty delectable truths: under those chef's whites was almost always a personality trait not visible in the restaurant dining rooms, TV shows, or cookbook pages. We got the inside dirt on the wild ways of South American vegetable smuggling and found out who was too honest to lie at the border. We saw chefs who had hit it too big, too quickly, make life changes that caused them to stock their shelves with non-alcoholic beer and kombucha. We learned how to store grains and seeds—in a cold refrigerator. We saw chefs who flew by the seat of their pants when it turned out their assistants had forgotten to give them a heads-up that they needed to cook for us—those were some of the best meals! We came across chefs who had no idea what was in their fridge. We put our hands inadvertently on prickly pears (real and metaphorical), face creams, snuff, and homemade marijuana gummy bears, listened to what it was like to grow up in an orphanage and how it felt to be nominated for a Nobel Peace Prize. We discussed mayonnaise (a lot!), turned down a taste of blue Kool-Aid, and listened to the merits of having three fridges.

There were definitely some overarching themes. There were condiments galore, experiments in fermentation, and different types of refrigerators—bachelor fridges, second-marriage fridges, refrigerators that had been spiffed up a little too much to be believable, and then those so sticky that we wiped them down a bit.

Almost all the chefs wanted to prepare us eggs, and when we pulled up to the table it was hard to say no; luckily for the book's sake, we started asking them to make something else. There was so much to find out; we wanted to get insider tips on everything: how to upgrade leftover takeout rice or boring condiments, pickle anything, make hot sauce, prepare freezer hash browns, get rid of fridge odors (surprise, it's not baking soda!), and recycle vegetable stems into kimchi.

It's all in these pages—in close-up photographs and words, in the juxtaposition of the low-end supermarket-sourced and high-end niche products, in forgotten containers and foodstuffs pilfered from the chefs' respective restaurants, things familiar and strange, nostalgic and chaotic, freaky and fun. In the end, we discovered, peering inside these famous chefs' refrigerators and freezers was just another way of getting a peek into their creative minds.

HUGH ACHESON

Hugh Acheson grew up in Canada, but discovered his passion for food in Georgia. He spent his early childhood with his dad, an economics professor with a basic dinner repertoire: "Dad made us fish sticks, burnt rice, and canned yellow wax beans. He tried, but the culinary arc of an economist was limited," Acheson recalls. When Acheson moved to Georgia (and later South Carolina) to live with his mom and stepdad, he got a taste for Southern food and life—fried okra, his stepfather's collard greens, barbecue, as well as a healthy dose of football and tailgating.

Back in Canada a few years later, he spent his days "skipping school, playing pool, drinking" and, along the way, "cooking a lot." His first job came at fifteen, when he became a dishwasher at a bar/restaurant. He then cooked his way through college in Montreal and left school to focus on food. A stint with Rob McDonald at the famed Café Henry Burger in Ottawa taught Acheson the importance of poise in a busy kitchen as well as stylized French cuisine.

He followed his ex-wife, then a student, to Athens, Georgia, a college town made famous by the B52s and REM in the early 1980s, but not exactly known as a food mecca. That changed in 2002, two years after he opened his first restaurant, Five & Ten, when *Food & Wine* magazine named him one of the best new chefs. Acheson followed up that success with more restaurants in Athens and Atlanta. Today he's finding a creative outlet with his new podcast, *Hugh Stirs the Pot*. "I'm known for being a bit of a jackass and outspoken. So the podcast is me sitting in the restaurant talking with food critics and chefs about life and chefdom and all sorts of stuff."

When he's not managing his restaurants, podcasting, or writing cookbooks, you can find Acheson hanging out on his back porch at home or cooking with his daughters. His kitchen is cozy—shelves filled with cookbooks line its perimeter, there are worn Persian rugs on the wood floors, and a cast-iron kettle sits on his electric stove. Over in the corner, there's usually a terra-cotta kimchi pot filled with homemade vinegar, ready for making one of his favorite pickled sides. His fridge also contains multiple glass-jar experiments in fermenting and pickling; he's concentrated on kimchi after a few kombucha fails.

As he made plates of farro, which we ate outside on his porch with some cold kombucha, we talked about food—and the inside of his refrigerator.

CURRENT HOMETOWN:
Athens, Georgia

RESTAURANT THAT MADE HIS NAME: Five & Ten, Athens

SIGNATURE STYLE: Southern with a nod to French/Italian technique

BEST KNOWN FOR: His gig as a judge on *Top Chef*; four cookbooks; six James Beard Award nominations; and his slight unibrow, which he only shaves for charity events

FRIDGE: Kenmore

1. **BREW DR. KOMBUCHA**—"I tried to make my own but it's hard to do live culture when you travel a lot. Sometimes my kombucha experiments blew up in the fridge."

2. **ATHENA PARADISO BEER**—"They're from Creature Comforts Brewery, a wonderful locally owned brewery right here in Athens. They're very refreshing."

3. **HI-WIRE GOSE BEER**

4. **CHAMPAGNE / FRANCIACORTA SPARKLING WINE**

5. **VERDICCHIO**

6. **GOCHUJANG**

7. **BROWN MISO**

8. **HOMEMADE VINAIGRETTE**—"This is a classic French-style vinaigrette that I've been using for at least thirty years. It's made up of three parts olive oil, one part red wine vinegar, garlic, Dijon, salt, and pepper."

9. **PORK LOIN, BACON, MEXICAN CHORIZO**

10. **PICKLED OKRA**—"I started pickling when I was very young. In chefdom it's very important to understand the necessity of saving a season. My favorite things to pickle are probably wild ramps, okra, green tomatoes, green beans, and onions."

11. **HOMEMADE DAIKON GREEN KIMCHI**

12. **PICKLED HABANERO PEPPERS**

13. **RED MULE GRITS**—"These are great grits made nearby. The mill was built out of old transmission parts, and a mule powers it by walking in a circle."

14. **BOILED PEANUTS**—"They're a big Southern staple. I boil them in water with salt and spices like star anise and chili. I eat them as a snack, but they are also good in salads."

15. **PICKLED BEETS**

16. **HOMEMADE CHICKEN STOCK**—"I make soup probably once or twice a week. When I'm not in the restaurants, I work a lot from home, and soups are an easy, from-scratch meal to cook."

17. **BEEF SIRLOIN**

18. **TURMERIC, GALANGAL, FLAT-LEAF PARSLEY, FENNEL**

ON   OFF

1. **"MYSTERY MEATS**—
   "If I had to venture to
   guess I'd say oxtail,
   steaks, ground beef,
   and boneless lamb leg.
   I should probably get
   better at labeling my
   home fridge."

2. **CHESTNUTS**—"I roast
   them and use them in
   stuffings. I keep them in
   the freezer because they
   don't keep for very long
   after being roasted."

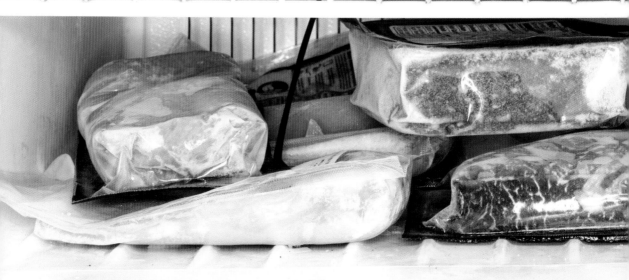

Q & A

What do you eat when coming home from a long day at work? Roast chicken, gravy, turnip greens, and rice.

Do you cook a lot at home? I do. We all should. It completes the day. I make soups. Salads. Food at home is about nourishment and simplicity—roast chicken, stews.

It looks like you have the quintessential bachelor's fridge. Divorced human fridge is more like it. Bachelor implies young and care-free. I am old and anxiety-ridden—but happy for the most part.

What do you do with kimchi at home? I fold it into cooked rice for a simple rice bowl or use it minced combined with cream for a simple sauce or for vinaigrettes. There is a ton of umami flavor going on.

How did you get started making it? I started making kimchi a number of years ago after eating it at Korean restaurants and reading about it. Folks like David Chang had a big influence on that. It is a chef's quest to take a global idea and make it in their own way. I make cabbage and radish kimchi in the classic way, but also sometimes use collard greens and stems, kale, Brussels sprouts, spring onions, and a number of other things. It's pretty much always in my fridge, whether it's homemade or store-bought. It just adds a lot of flavor to food.

Do you test new ideas at home? When you've got a number of restaurants I find you cook at the restaurants less. So you experiment a lot at home. But a lot of it is thought process before execution.

Why refrigerate your grains? A lot of grains are sprouted and they go rancid if not.

What do you cook for your daughters? I grilled some steak the other day, with stewed greens and pommes Anna. The kids meander over from their mom's house. They come for dinner a lot.

What would we never find in your fridge? Tomatoes. They should never live in the fridge.

What foods do you hate? Or what foods would you never eat? Not much really. I'm not a huge kidneys fan.

What is your favorite junk food? Arby's fast food.

Where do you go food shopping? Kroger. It ain't fancy but it is convenient. Also the local farmers market and a huge Korean store called H Mart.

What do you pick up there? I most often buy kimchi, Chinese greens, bok choy, lemongrass, lots of ginger, and galangal. I also buy a lot of fish there because they have a wonderful fish counter. My most recent trip I bought a bunch of ruby-red shrimp and Newfoundland snow crab.

What are some of your favorite local produce or products to use? About ten types of field peas, chilies of all shapes and sizes, tiny turnips, spring leeks, Vidalia onions, tender young collards, okra of all shapes and types. It's the South!

Poached Chicken Tartine with Crème Fraîche, Stilton, and Figs

I love tartines. They are simple and pretty and are easy to assemble if you have bread and a few things in the fridge. To me, it's sort of the sandwich for someone who doesn't eat as much bread as they used to.

2 tablespoons unsalted butter

¼ cup minced yellow onion

¼ cup minced celery

1 sprig thyme

2 bay leaves

2 cups chicken stock

2 chicken thighs, bone in but skin removed

1¼ teaspoons kosher salt

1 large round loaf of country bread (*pain de campagne*)

2 tablespoons olive oil

½ cup crème fraîche

½ teaspoon lemon zest

1 tablespoon lemon juice

1 tablespoon chopped fresh tarragon leaves

6 fresh figs, stemmed and quartered

4 ounces sliced Stilton

12 arugula leaves

Melt the butter in a medium-size pot over medium heat until it bubbles. Add the onion and celery, and cook for about 5 minutes, stirring occasionally. Add the thyme sprig, the bay leaves, and the chicken stock. Simmer. Season the chicken thighs with 1 teaspoon of the salt, then immerse them in the broth. Cover and cook for 20 minutes, until the chicken is tender. Remove the chicken from the pot and set aside. Keep simmering the broth.

Cut four slices of bread, ¾ inch thick, from the center of the loaf. (Save the rest for another meal.) Place a large heavy skillet over medium-high heat and heat the olive oil until just about smoking. Fry two slices of bread at a time for 2 minutes per side, or until each side is golden brown. Remove and place each slice on a paper towel.

Pull the chicken off the bone and place in a small bowl. In another small bowl, combine the crème fraîche with the lemon zest, lemon juice, tarragon, and remaining salt. Mix well.

Spread some lemon-tarragon crème fraîche on each slice of bread. Arrange the chicken evenly over the crème fraîche, then add figs, sliced cheese, and arugula leaves on each of the four tartines.

SERVES 4

Farro with Chorizo, Radishes, Daikon Kimchi, and Fennel

This is a variation on a dish I've been making for years. A nourishing meal that I can throw together quickly and serve to friends at the last minute.

3 tablespoons fruity olive oil

1 shallot, minced

1 cup farro

3 cups water

1½ teaspoons kosher salt

1 cup shaved fennel bulb

2 tablespoons lemon juice

½ cup sliced radishes

1 teaspoon canola oil

½ cup uncased Mexican red chorizo sausage

½ head radicchio, leaves only

1 tablespoon unsalted butter

2 tablespoons grated Parmesan cheese

¼ cup daikon kimchi (recipe follows)

Heat 1 tablespoon of the olive oil and the minced shallot in a 2-quart pot over medium heat. Cook for 2 minutes, until the shallots and the oil are slightly golden in color. Rinse the farro in cold water until the water runs clear. Drain the farro and add it to the pot. Stir well until the farro is slightly toasted. Then add the water and 1 teaspoon of the salt. Cover and cook for 20 minutes, until the farro is al dente. Shut off the heat and let the farro rest in the uncovered pot.

Put the shaved fennel in a bowl and season with ½ teaspoon of salt, the lemon juice, and the remaining olive oil. Add the sliced radishes and toss well. Let the mixture sit at room temperature until it softens.

Heat the canola oil in a frying pan over medium heat. Add the chorizo and crumble it. Cook for 5 minutes. Add the radicchio and sear it alongside the chorizo.

Warm the farro, stirring in the butter and Parmesan. Divide the farro among four bowls, and spoon on the cooked chorizo and radicchio. Top off with the fennel and radish salad and a heaping spoonful of kimchi.

SERVES 4

Daikon Kimchi

2 pounds daikon radishes, with tops

3 tablespoons kosher salt

2 tablespoons brown sugar

⅓ cup minced garlic

⅓ cup minced fresh ginger

¼ cup smoked paprika (*pimentón*)

¼ cup chili powder

1 tablespoon chili flakes

2 tablespoons lime juice

½ cup fish sauce

½ cup salted shrimp (measured before chopping), rinsed and finely chopped

2 bunches scallions, cut into ½-inch pieces

Cut the greens from the radishes and chop them into roughly 1-inch squares. Submerge the greens in cold water to dislodge the dirt and then drain the water. Repeat two more times. Spin the greens in a salad spinner or drain and place them on a clean dishcloth.

Rinse and peel the daikon radishes. Cut into thin, ⅛-inch rounds and place in a large mixing bowl. Add the daikon greens and salt with 1 tablespoon of the kosher salt. Place the daikon in a large bucket and let it soak in its own juices for 1 hour. Drain and rinse.

Combine the radishes and greens with the remaining 2 tablespoons salt and all other ingredients in a mixing bowl, toss, and then place in large container with a lid. Store in a cool, dark place for 3 days to ferment. The kimchi can be kept in the fridge for up to 2 months.

MAKES ABOUT 1 QUART

CURRENT HOMETOWN:
Bethesda, Maryland

RESTAURANT THAT MADE HIS NAME: Jaleo, Washington, D.C.

SIGNATURE STYLE: Tapas, or little plates

BEST KNOWN FOR: Minibar by José Andrés and nineteen other restaurants; World Central Kitchen, the NGO he started after the 2010 earthquake in Haiti; numerous James Beard Awards, including 2018 Humanitarian of the Year

FRIDGES: Sub-Zero and Hoshizaki

JOSÉ ANDRÉS

One of José Andrés's favorite impromptu lunches on busy days is jarred chickpeas, which he eats while standing, plate in hand and back against the fridge. Chickpeas and other simple dishes remind him of his childhood in Asturias, on the coast of northern Spain. Money was often tight for his parents, who were both nurses. At the end of the month, in between paychecks, his mother would make the most of what was left in the pantry: "If we had a little ham and cheese left over, she would bind them with béchamel and make *croquetas*," says Andrés.

"When my brothers and I were young, we would sneak into the fridge in the middle of the night and eat the croqueta mix with our fingers, and then try to smooth out the top to cover up the evidence. When my mother would see the mix with little finger marks—craggy like the surface of the moon—she would know we had been sneaking tastes!" he recalls.

That taste for croquetas may be why he's been interested in food since he was little. "I would watch my parents cooking, and was inspired to begin myself at the very young age of seven years old," he says. At fifteen, he went to culinary school in Barcelona. One of his first jobs was at a convention center there, where he met Josep Puig, whom Andrés calls "one of the best chefs in Spain. The food was not fancy but it was very good, and I had a lot of responsibility—I had to learn how to execute each of the dishes, classics such as Spanish tortillas, perfectly every time."

From there Andrés went to work for Ferran Adrià, who'd just opened El Bulli right outside Barcelona. Adrià became a mentor and, later, a great friend, but he also fired the twenty-one-year-old budding chef. A week later, Andrés landed in New York City with fifty dollars in his pocket. After a couple of gigs in New York, he went to Washington, D.C., and shortly thereafter turned Washingtonians on to tapas when he became the chef at Jaleo. From there, things moved quickly—Andrés opened restaurants throughout the country, wrote a cookbook, began teaching classes at Georgetown and Harvard, and, because of his humanitarian work serving more than 3.6 million meals in Puerto Rico after Hurricane Maria, became a Nobel Peace Prize nominee, among his many other awards and accolades. Not bad for someone who didn't graduate from high school or even culinary school.

Like his personality, Andrés's kitchen is expansive—it encompasses his indoor greenhouse, located downstairs from the kitchen, and a solar cooker next to the barbecue outside. His Sub-Zero is stacked with containers of leftovers, spreadable cheese, and homemade smoothies for his wife and three kids as well as experiments for his group of restaurants, ThinkFoodGroup. It's also replete with chef indulgences—specialty Spanish olives, small tins of caviar and bottarga (cured fish roe from Italy), as well as vegetables from his garden.

1. **LEFTOVER SMOOTHIE**

2. **DON BOCARTE ANCHOVIES**

3. **DUFOUR PUFF PASTRY**

4. **JOSÉ ANDRÉS MANZANILLA OLIVES**

5. **MAPLEBROOK FARM BURRATA**

6. **FARM EGGS**—"We buy them by the flat!"

7. **BLACK GARLIC**

8. **BRAISED OXTAIL**

9. **MAPLE SYRUP**

10. **PERSIMMONS**

11. **PADRÓN PEPPERS**

12. **LAUGHING COW CHEESE**

13. **NANTUCKET SCALLOPS**

14. **YOGURT**

15. **SASANIAN CAVIAR**

16. **TRIKALINOS BOTTARGA**

17. **GRAPE TOMATOES**

18. **POMEGRANATE SEEDS**

19. **LEFTOVER TOMATO SAUCE**

20. **CANELONES**

21. **HOMEMADE BÉCHAMEL**

22. **HOMEMADE HONEY**

23. *HUEVO HILADO*, a Spanish dish of whisked egg yolks cooked in a concentrated sugar-and-water solution—"I think it pairs great with smoked salmon or caviar."

24. **COOKED TURKEY**

25. **FRESH ORANGE JUICE**—"Whoever wakes up first will squeeze enough for everyone, whether it's me or my wife or one of the girls. My entire family loves it!"

26. **LOCAL APPLE CIDER,** from Black Rock Orchard in Maryland

27. **FENNEL, FROM HIS GARDEN**

28. **WHITE ASPARAGUS**

29. **ROMANESCO**

30. **BLOOD SAUSAGE, CHORIZO, AND PORK BELLY,** for cooking *fabada*, a Spanish stew

Q & A

How many refrigerators do you have?
We actually have two—one in the kitchen and one in my garage. The kitchen fridge is for our daily use—eggs, cheese, vegetables, you know. The Hoshizaki in the garage is for everything else. My team and I do a lot of R&D at my house, so we fill up the second fridge when we are working. It also makes a great backup when we are getting ready for hosting.

What do you always have in the refrigerator? Cheese—I love cheese and we always have local cheeses from Maryland, Pennsylvania, and Virginia, as well as from Spain. We will also have some ingredients like miso and kimchi to amplify dishes that I am cooking—a little bit of miso does some amazing things to stews, soups, sauces. And eggs . . . almost every meal I make has eggs in it. And we will always, always have leftovers in the fridge, no matter what.

Who does the food shopping in your house? We all like to go to the local farmers markets. I will get produce, cheese, eggs, and meat there. Nothing tells you more about how vibrant your region is than going to the farmers market.

What are some of the local products you use? The apples are amazing; Maryland has some very good cheese makers, too. We also have a Farmshelf—it's an indoor greenhouse— and we grow our own lettuces and herbs in there. In addition, we have a garden in our yard where we grow potatoes from all over the world, tomatoes, beans, herbs, lettuces, and carrots. And we have our own bees too, so we gather our own honey.

What is in your freezer? Some people might find it crazy, but I think peas are the best frozen vegetable imaginable! Most frozen vegetables can't hold up to the cold, but peas are special—as are fresh shelling beans, like cranberry beans. It is great to have them frozen when they are not in season. I also always keep good puff pastry in the freezer; you never know when you might need it. And my daughters, they love ice cream, so we have many different kinds.

Tell us about a "niche" product, something you just discovered. I just learned about this Jordanian dried yogurt called *jameed*. I brought some back from a trip to Jordan and keep it in the freezer. Jameed is used in *mansaf*, the national dish of Jordan. I believe that mansaf will be one of the next major dishes to come to the United States— it really is incredible and I love to experiment with it, to see what else we can do with it.

Describe your cooking style. I am always thinking of a different way to do things. Look at a tomato, an onion, and a bundle of herbs— and ask yourself, how can I extract the essence of this? How can I make it taste like the most perfect version of itself? It's important to look at history, seasonality, technique, and flavor.

What is your favorite food when coming home from a long day at work? I like to take some zucchini and cook them in water— cook them until they are al dente, then you add a little bit of miso and sesame oil to really bring out the amazing flavor of the vegetables, top with some *furikake* [a Japanese seasoning], and then eat it all with chopsticks. You eat the savory, tender zucchini first, and then the broth is amazing—it makes the best soup.

What do you cook for your family? I make the kinds of foods that I grew up eating, like *arroz a la cubana*. Tichi cooks a lot as well— I really love her spinach and garbanzo stew, it's my comfort food. The recipe is from her family in southern Spain; she learned it from her mother, who learned it from her mother, and so on for many generations. It actually was one of the first dishes that Tichi made for me when we were first married!

Burrata with Persimmons, Jamón, and Honey

For this recipe I use the honey that I harvest from the bees I raise at home in my backyard. I collect it myself. I believe it's been a remedy for my daughter's allergies. Greek honey is wonderful as well.

---

4 Fuyu persimmons

1 pound burrata

2 ounces sliced jamón serrano

½ cup lemon dressing (recipe follows)

Toasted hazelnuts, roughly chopped

Maldon salt

Freshly ground black pepper

Peel the persimmons and slice into ¼-inch-thick rounds. Arrange on a large serving plate or four individual plates.

Lightly break apart the burrata with a fork and place it on top of the persimmon slices, then top with the jamón serrano.

Drizzle the lemon dressing over the salad and garnish with hazelnuts, Maldon salt, and freshly ground pepper.

SERVES 4

....

Lemon Dressing

½ cup fresh lemon juice

1 tablespoon honey

½ cup neutral oil, like canola or grape

2 tablespoons extra virgin olive oil
    (I prefer Spanish olive oil)

1 teaspoon white pepper

Kosher salt

Whisk together the lemon juice and honey. Continue whisking as you slowly drizzle in both oils—the neutral one and the olive oil. Add the white pepper and kosher salt to taste. (Store extra dressing in the fridge for up to a week.)

MAKES 1½ CUPS

DAN BARBER

When you ask Dan Barber about what led him to start cooking, he cites his mother, but not in the way you might think. "My mother passed away when I was four, so the origins of my becoming a chef might start there—overcompensating for the void," Barber says. "I cooked a lot of grilled cheese sandwiches—English muffins with seven slices of Kraft cheese soaked in margarine. This was the seventies, after all."

Another reason Barber started cooking early on: his father wasn't adept in the kitchen. His go-to dish was scrambled eggs—made with margarine, no salt, and cooked to the point of no return. Barber thought that's how all eggs tasted until an aunt cooked some when he was sick in bed with strep throat. "I'll never forget the way she made them," Barber recalls: "Whisked over a double boiler, finished with French butter and tons of herbs. They were so soft they slid down my throat. To be fair, I owe this memory to my dad. Without his butchered eggs, my aunt's might never have made an impression."

Another early influence was Blue Hill Farm, his grandmother's farm in the Berkshires where he spent his summers. His job was to move the cows from field to field and make hay for the winter. One year cornfields replaced the pastures. "Riding the tractor, I never understood the importance of preserving a view like that until one summer, it was gone," says Barber. "It felt so foreign to me—this thing that disrupted not just the landscape but what I usually did for the summer. And you couldn't even eat it. It was grain corn!"

After college, Barber went to California to become a writer. "I thought cooking would be a good way to stay afloat. Write by day, cook by night. That was more or less my plan. At some point, the cooking just stuck." During his twenties, Barber staged at Chez Panisse, and then attended the French Culinary Institute in New York City. Shortly after graduation, he left to work for Michel Rostang in Paris. "I went to Paris because in those days, you went to France to learn how to cook. I still think there's no better training than the discipline of a French kitchen," he says.

In 2000, Barber and his brother, David, opened Blue Hill in New York City. Barber had an unwitting commitment to locally sourced ingredients—an ethos that brought Blue Hill into the spotlight when Jonathan Gold of the *Los Angeles Times* first dined there. It was spring and the restaurant had accidentally doubled up on their asparagus orders. Barber refused to toss the excess. Instead, he transformed the menu into an ode to asparagus. Gold loved it. He lauded Blue Hill as *the* "farm-to-table" restaurant and, seemingly overnight, it became a sensation.

Barber believes chefs are in a powerful position to influence not only their menu, but also food trends and what's sold in supermarkets and on TV. Last year, he launched Row 7 Seeds, a collaborative seed company. The project began when Barber met Michael Mazourek, a professor and vegetable breeder from Cornell University, and asked him why butternut squash doesn't taste very good. The question inspired Mazourek to develop a smaller, more flavorful Honeynut squash. Now the goal is to do that for a wider audience—to create seeds that are

CURRENT HOMETOWN:
New York City

RESTAURANT THAT MADE HIS NAME: Blue Hill, New York City

SIGNATURE STYLE: Farm-to-table cuisine

BEST KNOWN FOR: Blue Hill at Stone Barns; his book *The Third Plate*; James Beard Awards for Best Chef (2006) and Outstanding Chef (2009); and his seed company Row 7

FRIDGE: Sub-Zero

tasty and sustainable and accessible beyond the world of fine dining.

"More and more, I'm realizing that the recipe for a dish begins long before an ingredient even enters my kitchen," says Barber. "Really, it starts with the seed. With that in mind, we try to showcase the work of plant breeders and farmers by serving vegetables and grains unplugged and relying on the produce to speak for itself."

Seeds aren't far from Barber's thoughts as he prepares lunch for his two daughters in their sunny Manhattan kitchen, which has plenty of wood, mason jars, and kids' drawings—and

no fancy gadgets in sight. "I'm so much further beyond where I thought I would be in this business of cooking—beyond my wildest dreams, really. And yet, when I leave for work in the morning, my daughters give me this smothering hug, and no matter what I have ahead of me for the wonderful and grueling hours of cooking, I've already experienced the best part of the day. So there, that's a hint for me on where I want to go," he says. While we chatted, his wife, the novelist Aria Sloss, popped through the kitchen to put their youngest child down for a nap as Barber cajoled her sister to eat her sautéed broccoli, mushrooms, and bread.

1. **GRASS-FED RAW MILK FROM BLUE HILL—**
   "My wife and kids go back and forth from raw to
   pasteurized. But I only drink raw milk."

2. **KEFIR—**"I like it on my oats in the morning."

3. **PEPPER JAM—**"We make that pepper jam at the
   restaurant from all the excess peppers from the
   fall. I keep it around in the winter for an extra
   kick of heat and sweetness."

4. **FRESH MILLED WHOLE WHEAT FLOUR**

5. **HIS WIFE'S YOGURT AND SOAKED
   OATS WITH DATES**

6. **TOMATO SAUCE—**"I made it with my
   older daughter, Edith."

7. **COLD BREW COFFEE—**"My wife turned
   me on to cold brew, but it's fair to say she
   is the principal consumer."

8. **APRICOT PITS**

9. **GINGER AND TURMERIC—**"My wife ends her day with ginger and turmeric
   grated into hot water, so we get them fresh at the farmers market."

10. **RADISH KIMCHI—**"We make a lot of sauerkraut at the restaurant, but
    I tend to just love other people's kimchi."

11. **DILL PICKLE SPEARS**

12. **SOUR FARMHOUSE ALE—**"It's fermented with raw honey and conditioned
    in oak barrels for sixteen months. As I get older, I see the wisdom in always
    having a cold beer at the ready."

13. **WHITE MOUSTACHE PASSION FRUIT PROBIOTIC WHEY TONIC**

Q & A

You keep flour in your fridge? These are fresh milled whole-wheat flours. We need to get out of the habit of thinking about flours as staying on the shelf; they are alive and need to be chilled, almost like fruit. Taste this bread we make with it.

Wow, that is incredibly moist!
The difference is that it's fresh milled.

What do you usually eat for breakfast?
I just love oats. It's a nice thing to be able to eat something that you know is improving the health of the place where it comes from. Oats are a good example of a magic crop that adds nutrition to the soil instead of depleting it, like wheat, corn, and rice. We buy our oats from a friend and then get them malted. At the restaurant we ferment them with just a little salt and let them sit for a couple of days. Then we roast them.

Is that a jar of pits down on the lower shelf? I look at that every morning and get a little depressed as I was supposed to have done this project in the middle of summer with my daughter and we never got to. It's all of the pits from the apricots in late July. When you take the pits and crush them with a hammer you get this almond flavor. Then you can infuse the pits—I was going to do that with milk or cream and make a dessert topping. But it was fun to save the pits.

Where do you shop for food? I go to Whole Foods and the farmers market on the way to school with my daughter. We get pastured eggs from Stone Farms and cheese down the street from Murray's cheese shop.

What has been your biggest cooking fail at home? Lately it's been a consistent string of failures to get my daughters to eat anything other than the daily predictables, like pasta and bread.

What do you wish your children ate more of? It's more that my daughters go through these phases when they refuse to eat *one* thing in particular. Somehow, those phases have a way of aligning perfectly with when that one thing is in season. Like right now it's spring and we just got in the first of the ramps—it's such a small window when we can eat them. And of course, what does my daughter now suddenly hate? Ramps.

Why do you have so many live cultures like raw milk, kefir, and kombucha?
These days, more and more people are interested in fermented and live culture foods because of their ability to activate our microbiome and improve our health. But I'm also interested in the flavor. When you ferment something, you catalyze a series of reactions that breaks down proteins and completely transforms the flavor profile of that food.

Is that Halloween candy in your fridge door? Yes, I used to have a terrible sweet tooth but the last few years it hasn't been as sweet. I'm also a peanut butter junkie—but I don't consider that to be junk food.

Oat and Herb Tabbouleh

I make this with chopped herbs, lemon, and, in this case, whole oats gently cooked. I like to use oats because they are soil supporting—good for us, good for the landscape. They're especially delicious when served with fresh ricotta, made with grass-fed milk if you can find it.

1 cup rolled oats

2 cups water

4 shallots, minced

8 large bunches parsley, minced

4 bunches mint, minced

8 sun-dried tomatoes, finely chopped

1 teaspoon nutmeg

1 teaspoon cumin

½ cup lemon juice

¼ cup olive oil

Salt

Pepper

Homemade ricotta cheese (optional; recipe follows)

For the oats, warm a sauté pan over medium-high heat. Layer ½ cup of the oats evenly, and toast until golden brown, stirring constantly for 10 minutes. Let cool.

Heat the water in a saucepan over medium heat. Add the rest of the oats. Simmer for 5 minutes until the oats are cooked and fully tender. Strain the excess water and cool the oats at room temperature. Once cooled, mix the cooked and toasted oats together.

Combine the shallots, parsley, mint, sun-dried tomatoes, spices, lemon juice, and olive oil. Add to the oat mixture and mix well. Season with salt and pepper. Serve with or without the ricotta.

SERVES 4

Homemade Ricotta Cheese

1 gallon whole milk

1 quart buttermilk

Salt

White pepper

Heat the milk and buttermilk in a large, high-sided stainless-steel stockpot. Simmer over very low heat, scraping the bottom of the pot occasionally with a rubber spatula.

Once the curds have separated from the whey, between 20 and 25 minutes, remove from the heat and strain. Reserve the whey for another use. Season the curds with salt and white pepper. Serve immediately. Or keep them covered in the refrigerator for 1 to 2 days.

MAKES 1 QUART

PASCAL BARBOT

Pascal Barbot isn't just the chef of the Michelin-starred Astrance. He also serves as its culinary mentor, training some of the world's most celebrated chefs, including Magnus Nilsson, André Chiang, and Adeline Grattard. "When chefs come work for us, they learn not just how to cook, but how to order and meet the producers, run the front of house, and even sometimes how to park a car," he says. Cooks learn faster by doing everything, Barbot explains.

That hands-on approach came early. Barbot, who's from Vichy, had a "happy childhood." His father took him fishing and hunting and he picked vegetables and fruit from the garden, learning quickly that food has its seasons. From the age of ten he was preparing vinaigrettes at his mother's side and by the time he was a teenager he knew he wanted to cook for a living, even though he knew absolutely nothing about restaurants—and had never eaten in one. When he interviewed at a small cooking school near Vichy, Barbot had to lie to the board about his experiences dining out in order to be accepted, he recalls. Through contacts, he went to London for an apprenticeship at Les Saveurs ("the first Japanese-owned Michelin-starred restaurant in Europe"). There, he tasted such delicacies as caviar and sole for the first time—until then he had never seen fish that didn't come from a river.

When Barbot was called up for mandatory military service, his horizons expanded again. He became a cook on a French ship that toured the South Pacific. There he encountered Tahitian-style ceviche and such products as chayote, mangoes, and taro, all of which later influenced his own cuisine.

After his tour was over, Barbot furthered his education by working at L'Arpège with legendary chef Alain Passard, eventually running the kitchen and becoming friends with his future business partner, Christophe Rohat, and then going to Australia for two years to cook there. The laid-back Australian attitude made an impression on Barbot, and helped him realize that he wouldn't need such things as a maître d' or sommelier if he ever opened his own place.

Back in Paris, after a change in ownership jeopardized his chances to work as the head chef at the newly reopened restaurant Lapérouse, Barbot and Rohat decided to open their own place. "Better to own your own small place and be happy than unhappy running someone else's big business," Barbot explains.

Although they didn't have much money, friends and family pitched in, as did former mentor Alain Passard, who provided the Rolodex of his best clients. Astrance opened in the year 2000.

From the beginning, Astrance was different. Because the restaurant could fit only twenty diners at a time and the staff was small, Barbot decided to do away with the classic menu and focus instead on the freshest, most seasonal ingredients that his producers delivered each morning. By letting the producers decide what to bring, there was very little waste—the restaurant's refrigerators were left completely

CURRENT HOMETOWN:
Paris, France

RESTAURANT THAT MADE HIS NAME: Astrance, Paris

SIGNATURE STYLE: Classic French cuisine with an Asian twist

BEST KNOWN FOR: His three-Michelin-star restaurant; making the World's 50 Best Restaurants list multiple times; and his menu that changes each morning based on his deliveries

FRIDGE: Seimens

empty at the end of each evening. The result: iconic dishes such as mushroom and foie gras millefeuille marinated in verjus, and John Dory flavored with curry, mango, and papaya.

Barbot had found his style: French technique married to local products, inspired by the dishes he had tasted on his travels. No one had seen cooking like this in Paris before, and Astrance got its first star less than a year after it opened—and its third seven years later.

"It's funny everyone always calls my cooking fusion cuisine," says Barbot. "I'm not a fusion chef, whatever that means. It's just my education, the fact that I traveled to New Caledonia,

Fiji, and Tahiti when I was young. There are lots of French territories out there that, because of history, there is a mix of different styles and cultures—for them it's completely normal."

That mix of cultures also comes into play when Barbot cooks at home in his kitchen that overlooks his rooftop vegetable garden—as well as the rooftops of Paris. While he rarely eats there when the restaurant is open, on his days off, meals consist of fresh ingredients amped up by his well-chosen stock of condiments. But whether he's eating tomatoes and eggs or steamed rouget and seasonal veggies, there is always something sweet or spicy thrown in.

1. **REYNAUD FINE FOOD SARDINES**

2. **BUMBU SATE**—"My girlfriend loves this!"

3. **CHILI PASTE**

4. **REYNAUD FINE FOOD CAVIAR**

5. **COCONUT SUGAR,** to use with soy sauce to marinate different proteins

6. **BONNE MAMAN RICE PUDDING**—"I eat this in between lunch and dinner service."

7. **AROY-D RED CURRY PASTE**—"I mix this with coconut milk and combava (Kaffir lime) and use it to marinate shrimp."

8. **FERME DES PEUPLIERS YOGURT**

9. **CHICKEN BREASTS**

10. **SALAD**—"This is an example of mise en place that I do at home. I always wash, dry, and box up my salads so that they are ready to use."

11. **DRIED SCALLOPS**

12. **CHILI FLAKES**

13. **SESAME SEEDS, YUZU KOSHO, FERMENTED SHRIMP, COFFEE CREAMERS**

14. **XO SAUCE**

15. **SHELLFISH OIL,** left over from making XO sauce

16. **EL NAVARRICO CHILI OIL**—"From one of my chefs who wanted me to taste it."

17. **FRESH YUZU**

18. **ANATRA APOLLONIA (PEAR, PINEAPPLE, AND PASSION BERRY) JAM**

19. **HAM**

20. **BLACK CURRANT JAM**—"My mom made it for me."

21. **SOY SAUCE**

22. **CILANTRO**

23. **CHILI PEPPER PRESERVED LEMONS**

24. **TOFU**

25. **SEA BASS FILLET,** for ceviche

26. **GINGER**

27. **HUNDRED-YEAR-OLD EGGS**—"A friend brings these back from China. We eat them in a salad with tofu and vegetables."

Tahitian-Style Marinated Fish

This dish is similar to ceviche. In the original recipe for poisson cru there's no zucchini, but I like to add it. I also prefer to buy fish that is prepared using the Japanese ikejime technique, which paralyzes the fish and drains its blood and makes for a firmer flesh.

2 teaspoons preserved lemon, minced

2 tablespoons lemon juice

¾ cup coconut milk

1 cup julienned carrots

⅔ cup julienned zucchini

¾ pound sea bass, diced in ½-inch cubes

½ teaspoon salt

12 sprigs cilantro

Whisk together the preserved lemon, lemon juice, and coconut milk. Stir in the carrots, zucchini, and sea bass. Add salt. Refrigerate for 20 minutes.

Divide the marinated fish among four bowls, and add fresh cilantro to each one.

SERVES 4

Q & A

What do you always keep in your refrigerator? Condiments, citrus fruit, fresh vegetables from the local market. And always chili peppers!

Which condiments are your favorites? Asian, of course! Things I pick up on my trips, like Kamada ponzu sauce, Espelette pepper jelly, hazelnut oil, any kind of Japanese vinegar. Also, Korean red ginseng is great for a bit of a vitamin when I'm tired.

What do you tend to cook when you're at home? When I'm in a hurry, I'll throw some tomatoes and garlic in a frying pan with some olive oil, kind of Provençal style, then I'll crack in an egg. It only takes five minutes and it's delicious. I also love fried rice, and steam-cooking fish and vegetables. It's healthy.

What is a niche product you have that you are especially proud of? I have some artisanal nuoc mam that my girlfriend brought me from Thailand that is exceptional. I've also got some amazing preserved lemon from my friend chef Stefano Baiocco, who has a restaurant on Lake Garda in northern Italy.

What type of junk food do you crave? I've been known to eat a hot dog from time to time.

What would you never eat in the fridge? I'd never eat that tube of concentrated milk [in the fridge door]. It's my girlfriend's, not mine! I think she puts it in her coffee.

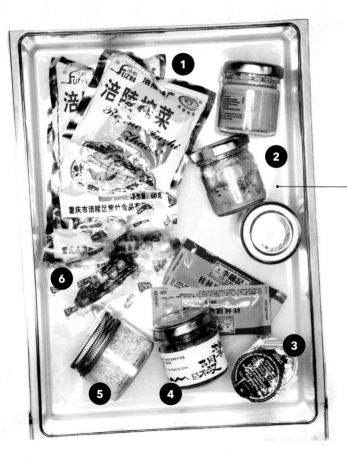

1. **PICKLED MUSTARD STEMS**

2. **FERMENTED SHRIMP**

3. **COFFEE CREAMERS**

4. **YUZU KOSHO—** fermented citrus-chili paste

5. **SESAME SEEDS**

6. **CHINESE SAUSAGE**

KRISTIAN BAUMANN

Born in Korea, adopted by a Danish couple, and raised in a Copenhagen suburb, Kristian Baumann was attracted to foraging and cooking from childhood. One early memory revolves around a twelve-inch puffball mushroom he discovered on a preschool field trip. He brought it back to class and strong-armed his teacher into cooking it up in butter. "Just so delicious!" he says, recalling the woodsy smell of the sautéed mushroom and the delight he took in discovering it.

Later, in boarding school, he pestered the elderly cooks every day to let him hang out in the kitchen. His schoolmates might have complained about peeling twenty pounds of potatoes and other kitchen chores, but Baumann loved it all, and soon graduated to sausage making and roasting the odd lamb or pork chop. "I had no talent at all but I was having a lot of fun!" he says.

The only thing he wanted to do was go to cooking school, which he did. After a couple of internships, he became an apprentice at Noma, under René Redzepi, and then a sous-chef with Christian Puglisi of Relae. Working with Redzepi opened Baumann's eyes to what he considers the foundations of the Copenhagen kitchen: foraging, farming, and collaboration. While at Relae, he learned how important it is to rethink the most basic ingredients. Take water, for instance. "There is a lot of calcium present in Copenhagen's water, but after we installed filters at Relae our stocks became much more flavorful." On trips to South Korea, Baumann noticed that the monks always brought water fresh from the mountains: "The cleaner the water, the better the rice," he says now.

Baumann had so many things he wanted to do if he ever opened his own place he couldn't even sleep. "I was constantly putting my ideas on napkins," he says. One day, over coffee, Redzepi offered, "Just like that!" to let him use Noma as a practice run for his planned first restaurant opening while the older chef was away in Australia opening a pop-up restaurant. One thing led to another, and their partnership led to the creation of 108.

Located in a former industrial warehouse, 108 has its fair share of Noma DNA, but with Baumann's particular vision: "It's the kind of place with an à la carte menu seven days a week, where you can get drinks and share small plates with friends on a Friday night and enjoy a tasting menu with your girlfriend another night," he says. Dishes such as raw lamb with last year's pickles and seaweed sorbet with caviar earned 108 a Michelin star eight months after it opened.

Simplicity is Baumann's MO at home. His kitchen is small and sunlit. The wooden counters are filled with potted plants, cacti, and serving platters heaped with chili peppers and fava beans from his parents' garden, not showy appliances. He insists that the biggest inspiration and essential driving force behind his creativity and success has always been his beloved Copenhagen and his Danish family and friends, but Korea is never far away. That's why the shelves of his refrigerator are stocked with everything from handmade miso and soy sauce, smoked herring and fermented pastes, to condiments from half a world away as well as more garden-grown vegetables. All are tastes of home.

1. **PERILLA OIL**—"I got this as a gift in Korea and it can be added to chicken of the woods soup."

2. **SOY SAUCE,** a gift from Korea

3. **BLUEBERRY AND BLACK CURRANT VINEGARS**—"I use them at home with vegetables. I especially like to sauté romaine lettuce leaves in butter. Once they are juicy and warm, I splash a little vinegar and spoon over more butter."

4. **UMEBOSHI PASTE**—"A gift from good friends. I use it often on fish."

5. **CILANTRO FLOWERS,** from his sister's garden

6. **EGGS,** from his parents' hens—"The hens eat lots of herbs from the garden and my parents' leftovers. The yolks are bright yellow, which for me, is a good sign."

7. **GOD MORGON ORGANIC ORANGE JUICE**—"I start my day with juice along with a mug of hot water and lemon. Once I'm at the restaurant I drink a lot of coffee and tea."

8. **NATURLI ORGANIC SOY DRINK**—"I have a slight lactose intolerance so I drink soy quite often."

9. **SOY SAUCE,** another gift from Korea

10. **ARLA ØKO SKYR**—"My girlfriend likes skyr the best."

11. **HONEY-PRESERVED PINE CONES**

12. **SOYBEAN PASTE,** from the Mangkyengsansa temple

SMOKED BUTTER—Baumann uses his signature smoked butter for grilling meat, fish, or vegetables. The recipe is on page 41.

13. **SOYBEAN PASTE,** bought in Seoul

14. **CHICKEN OF THE WOODS MUSHROOMS**

15. **SWISS CHARD,** from his sister's garden

16. **AGED COW'S MILK CHEESE, SMOKED BUTTER, PARMESAN CHEESE, JUTLAND-STYLE CHEESES**—"My mother gave me these."

Q & A

What have you always got in your fridge? We always have miso, milk, eggs from my parents' house, Parmigiano, and whatever might be in season, especially from my sister's garden: apples, cabbage, Swiss chard, cilantro, chilies, potatoes, parsley.

You have a lot of unlabeled mysterious containers and jars—what are they? Well, friends and colleagues from around the world bring me all sorts of stuff. I have Korean soy sauce and wild sesame oil from a chef friend. The most interesting thing I have is honey-preserved pine cones from a couple of Russian chefs I cooked with last year. I always have soybean paste—I use it in sauces and soups, for fish, in dishes I cook for friends and family. It adds layers to the cooking. *Umami.*

It looks like something is growing on the bottom of the refrigerator! What is it? It's a chicken of the woods mushroom. I was out foraging with my girlfriend looking for puffball mushrooms and she found this gigantic chicken! It was so big I had to freeze it. I'm going to chop half of it up and cook it with vegetables and a miso sauce and make her a nice dinner.

Are there any foods you've banned from the fridge? Salmon, you'll never find salmon. When I was an apprentice chef, for the first three years, I was working in a salmon area, so I was just surrounded by it all the time. I wouldn't say I hate it, though—I just dislike it.

Does that plastic container in the bottom drawer say "smoked butter"? Sounds very restauranty—what is it? Yes, it's something we make in the restaurant, but easy enough to do at home, if you're motivated. (See how in the recipe opposite.) We use it for whatever we grill— meat, fish, or vegetable. It's a great asset and brings a lot of flavor to the product. The fat dripping onto the charcoal gives off an amazing aroma as well!

You were in Korea recently. Did you bring back anything interesting? I've got a bunch of stuff from temples, and each temple has something different. Some make a soybean paste called doenjang, or gochujang, a red chili paste; others make their own kimchi or miso sauce. It varies so much from region to region, and echoes their individual heritages. The tastiest thing I have I think is the homemade perilla oil, made from ground-up perilla seeds and given to us by the temple nuns.

The temple is called Mangkyengsansa, and it's a few hours northeast of Seoul. You get a real glimpse of the past there. It's just seven nuns living up there happily, cooking, farming, and meditating on the mountaintop. They also use their knowledge to enable the local famers to know what to grow and hook them up with chefs who will buy their produce.

Do you cook at home or does your girlfriend? We both do. If I'm cooking for Taya, it's normally some sort of fish, like monkfish sautéed in butter. But if she's cooking, and she is a fantastic cook, it will be a home-style Thai dish, my favorite thing to eat after a long day. I love *larb hed*, a minced mushroom salad flavored with fish sauce, lime juice, ground rice, and fresh herbs, or a cold noodle salad served with whatever condiment I feel like digging out of the fridge.

Where do you shop for food? Most of the time I eat in the restaurant, but if I do shop, it's mostly at small greengrocers or in the organic aisle of supermarket shops.

What do you feed your cat? My cat's name is Steak and we used to feed him store-bought cat food all the time, but one day we started making him special food. He loved it and his coat is healthier and his eyes are clearer. The dish I make for him is puréed chicken and corn. He just loves corn.

Sautéed Monkfish with Juniper-Smoked Butter and Champagne Sauce

I picked up this cold-smoking technique when I worked at Noma. I love using it, as the juniper imparts a light, lingering flavor. I usually bring this butter home from the restaurant but it's a technique that can all be done in a home oven as long as you do it carefully. The ice in the middle rack prevents the butter from melting.

For the monkfish:

1½ cups smoked butter (recipe follows)

One 2-pound monkfish tail (trimmed and cleaned, on the bone)

⅓ cup chopped garlic

½ cup fresh lemon thyme leaves

For the Champagne sauce:

3 tablespoons vegetable oil

2 cups sliced shallots

¾ cup Champagne

12 tablespoons unsalted butter, cubed

Salt, to taste

Heat half of the smoked butter in a pan over medium heat. Add the monkfish and sear on each side until golden, 1 to 2 minutes. Add half of the garlic and lemon thyme and continue basting.

Remove the butter (as it will have browned) and refresh the pan with the rest of the smoked butter, garlic, and lemon thyme. Continue basting until the center of the fish reaches 135°F on an instant-read thermometer or until the tip of a knife, once poked through to the bone, comes out very hot. Let the fish rest for 20 minutes in the pan before serving.

While the fish is resting, heat the oil in a saucepan. Add the shallots and sauté for 3 to 4 minutes over low heat. Add the Champagne, simmer, and reduce the liquid by one third, about 20 minutes. Strain. Add the butter cubes one by one while whisking constantly. Season with salt. Carefully remove the fish from the bone, divide among four plates, and serve with the Champagne sauce.

SERVES 4

Juniper-Smoked Butter

¾ pound unsalted butter

1 juniper branch (12 inches long, with fresh needles)

Cut the butter into cubes and place them in a roasting pan. Set the pan on the highest oven rack. Fill a second roasting pan with ice cubes. Place it on the middle oven rack.

Put the juniper branch in a third roasting pan. Light the branch on fire, then extinguish it after a minute by covering it completely with another pan, to avoid contact with the air. While the branch is still smoking, set the pan on the lowest oven rack. Close the oven door, but do not turn on the heat.

Relight the branch every 15 minutes for the following 3 hours so the oven remains full of white smoke.

Refrigerate the butter and throw out the juniper branch. You can make the butter up to 3 days in advance.

MAKES ¾ POUND

Wild Chicken of the Woods Mushroom Soup

I try to go foraging year-round when I have time. I find it very relaxing. A couple of cooks at my restaurant forage daily. The chicken flavor of these mushrooms and others too can be very meaty— it depends on the season. If you're not skilled at foraging mushrooms on your own, then feel free to use oyster, shiitake, or portobello mushrooms.

For the stock:

4 cups chicken of the woods mushrooms, chopped (or substitutes)

5 cups chicken stock

1 cup Korean fermented soybean paste (doenjang)

2 garlic cloves, minced

1 cup chopped carrots

1 cup chopped leeks

For the garnish:

3 cups sliced chicken of the woods mushrooms

⅓ cup sesame oil

1 tablespoon fresh chilies

1 cup long or green beans, chopped into 1-inch pieces

1 cup Swiss chard stems, chopped into 1-inch pieces

1 cup Swiss chard leaves, chopped into 1-inch pieces

Marigold flowers (optional)

Cilantro flowers (optional)

In a pot, bring all the stock ingredients to a boil. Reduce the heat and simmer for 2 hours, uncovered. Skim for impurities a few times, then strain, return to the stock pot, and cover. Keep the stock hot, but don't let it simmer. It will reduce too much.

Clean and slice the mushroom lengthwise just before using, to avoid discoloration. Sauté in sesame oil until lightly golden, about 8 minutes. Set aside. Slice the chilies and set aside.

Blanch the beans, Swiss chard stems and leaves in the hot stock for 1 to 2 minutes and set aside, reheating the stock if necessary.

Divide the mushrooms, beans, Swiss chard, and chilies among four bowls. Pour the hot stock over the vegetables. Garnish with the flowers if using.

SERVES 4

CURRENT HOMETOWN:
New York City

RESTAURANT THAT MADE HIS NAME: Daniel, New York City

SIGNATURE STYLE: Nouvelle French cuisine with a seasonal twist

BEST KNOWN FOR: His cookbook *My French Cuisine*; his mentorship of Team USA in the Bocuse d'Or competition; six James Beard Awards, including Outstanding Restaurateur and Outstanding Chef

FRIDGE: Samsung

DANIEL BOULUD

Being inspired by seasonal food may seem like a cliché in the culinary universe today, but it was the only reality that Daniel Boulud knew when he was growing up. Boulud, a fixture in Manhattan's culinary scene for almost four decades, comes from a family of farmers outside Lyon, France. "I remember so well the mushrooms picked right after the rain, sharing the *firsts* of every season, like strawberries, cherries, and peaches, new potatoes, or harvesting hazelnuts." He also helped his grandmother in the kitchen, learning to peel and cut vegetables that went into their ritual evening soup.

Although he loved the farm life, "the harvesting part was not for me!"—so he thought about getting a restaurant job. Thanks to a well-connected customer of his parents', he got his first apprenticeship at a local, two-Michelin-starred restaurant. From there he went on to train with some of the most highly venerated French chefs of his time, especially Roger Vergé, who schooled Boulud in the fine French classics, including bouillabaisse and *daube d'agneau*, a lamb stew. "My best time at Vergé was making seafood salads with melon, peach, and red currant, and original seafood terrines."

At twenty-five, he moved to Washington, D.C., to work as a chef to the European Commission. Although he hadn't planned on staying long in the United States, he ended up in a series of jobs in New York until he became the executive chef at Le Cirque, perhaps the most famous restaurant in the country at that time. There the owners gave him complete freedom, which

is what he'd craved, and he took advantage by focusing on presentation and updating the French menu with such new dishes as tuna tartare with curry sauce ("very cool in 1986," he says) and sea bass paupiette ("an instant classic!"), recipes that later became part of his repertoire. He describes his cooking mantra then and now as using classic French techniques and then reacting creatively to cultures and products to create new concepts.

After six years, he was tempted to go back to France, but instead opened his own place, Daniel. The rest is culinary history—Boulud became one of the best-known French chefs in the U.S., opening restaurants, publishing best-selling cookbooks, appearing on TV, and training a new generation of chefs.

He lives upstairs from his flagship restaurant, going back and forth between the two all day. You can tell he's serious about cooking from his kitchen, which is decked out in sleek marble and tiled in gray-and-silver tones. He's got a gas oven, a built-in steamer, and a flat-topped burner. His meticulously polished and organized chef utensils line a wall next to the stacks of cookbooks, some of them by French masters like Pierre Bocuse and Auguste Escoffier, and some by fellow chefs like Greg Marchand and David McMillan.

Having his family so close by is a comfort. "I just have to run up the stairs if I want to see my children," he says. "And sometimes, I'll turn around in the restaurant, and catch my son Julien high-fiving the chefs on the line or stealing cheese off the cheese cart. What could be better?"

1. **PESTO**

2. **BABY BOTTLE**— "My daughter drinks almond milk because she is dairy-free."

3. **THOMAS KELLER CHOCOLATE**—"Armando Mani is my favorite."

4. **GREEN & BLACK'S CHOCOLATE,** his wife's favorite chocolate

5. **MADAGASCAR BOURBON VANILLA BEANS**

6. **VANILLA EXTRACT**— "We think it's better to flavor our yogurt ourselves."

7. **FEVER-TREE CLUB SODA**

8. **TONIC WATER,** for Campari and tonics

9. **ORVAL TRAPPIST BEER**

10. **REISSDORF KÖLSCH BEER**

11. **SIPPING TEQUILA**— "Every year for my birthday I receive a bottle of tequila from Casa Dragones. I usually serve it when I have a large gathering of friends."

12. **BALSAMIC VINEGAR FROM MASSIMO BOTTURA**—"I prefer when the vinegar is cold, which renders it a touch thicker. Massimo Bottura gave it to me when he came to do an event at Eataly."

13. **EVERYDAY CHAMPAGNE,** for when friends show up

14. **SAN PELLEGRINO,** his go-to water

15. **FRESH PARSLEY, THYME, CHIVES, AND ROSEMARY**

16. **PICKLES OF ALL KINDS**—"The kids like the sourness of the brine."

17. **TABASCO**—personalized bottle, a gift from the owner of the company

18. **CHOLULA HOT SAUCE**

19. **CAPERS**

20. **ANCHOVIES**— "I love cooking with anchovies because they have a cured funkiness and a unique saltiness that enhances just about everything."

21. **SALTED ANCHOVIES**— "For my evening tartine. But smoked eel is my favorite."

22. **LA BOÎTE À ÉPICE BOMBAY AND DALI SPICE BLENDS,** for one-pot meals

23. **PRUNES**—"I buy Dalfour prunes by the case. We pour either tea or boiled water over them and refrigerate to make prune juice to put in cereal. Also, one prune a day keeps you healthy—it's very good for the system."

24. **CRÈME FRAÎCHE**—"For the scrambled eggs I make on the weekends."

25. **CRANBERRY-BLACKBERRY JAM**

26. **DOM PÉRIGNON**—"You don't need a special occasion to open a bottle of Dom Pérignon, just the time to appreciate it. It could be during a great movie with my wife or at brunch with smoked salmon. Sometimes there is no occasion, just a thirst for the best. I always have a chilled bottle available."

27. **STRIP STEAK**

28. **VACHERIN CHEESE**

29. **EGGS**—"Martha Stewart always sends me eggs of different colors from her many different types of hens."

30. **SALMON**—"The Balik artisanal cut of my smoked salmon."

31. **BELUGA CAVIAR**—"It's from Belgium and I save it for the weekends when we eat scrambled eggs and salmon."

32. **GOAT BRIE,** a favorite of his wife's—"We really like the small batch from Woolwich Dairy in Canada."

33. **VERMONT CREAMERY BUTTER**—"We use this butter at Restaurant Daniel so it's good for my household too."

34. **COMTÉ CHEESE**—"My kids love all types of cheese, but Comté is something I always have in the house because it can last for months."

35. **MAGRET DE CANARD (DUCK BREAST)**

36. **HARISSA**

37. **SWEET HOT MUSTARD**

38. **DESERT PEPPER SALSA,** a gift from a friend in Santa Fe

39. **POWERADE**—"I drink it after I've gone to the gym."

40. **SAKE,** gifts from Japanese clients

41. **ROSÉ**

42. **OMMEGANG BEER,** one of his favorites

Q & A

What is your favorite food after coming home from a long day at work? I always enjoy a good piece of chocolate (Thomas Keller makes the best), a nice cheese, dry sausage, or avocado. When I come home starving after midnight, I'll make myself a little tartine with sardine or anchovy, a little balsamic and oil, and wash it down with a beer.

What do you always have in the fridge? The children eat lots of avocado, and we always have lots of cheese: burrata, Comté, local goat Brie. There is almond milk for my daughter, and always a bottle of Dom Pérignon for me. I love Balik smoked salmon, beluga caviar, prunes, Dave's sliced bread, and eggs from Martha Stewart's farm. I also like a Campari from time to time, and my wife drinks Lillet on the rocks.

What do you never have in the fridge? Cola, sodas, or pizza. Pizza is so good we never leave any leftovers!

What do you cook for your family? In the springtime, they enjoy when I cook a leg of lamb with vegetables I find at the farmers market next to my country home. If I'm cooking on the weekend I'll make scrambled eggs with caviar, smoked salmon, that sort of thing. I always have a lot of caviar for when friends come over. And tequila.

What does your wife cook? My wife, Katherine, who has chef training, makes us a wonderful and varied breakfast every day, an important meal we share as a family. At times it could be a berry-mango smoothie with chia seeds, pea protein, yogurt, and almond milk, or a brioche submarine with eggs and my own brand of smoked salmon.

What is your favorite junk food? Plain salted potato chips, gummy bears, and the Frito pie topped with chili at Giants Stadium.

What foods do you hate? I am not fond of bananas and sea cucumbers.

Who does the food shopping in your house and where do you shop? Katherine does the majority of the shopping at our home. On weekends we go to the farmers market in Katonah, New York. During the week, for rare products, we "shop" in the restaurant's kitchen.

Do you ever make meals from cookbooks? I like to try friends' cookbook recipes to see if they work or not! From the Gotham Bar and Grill book I cooked a recipe with my wife recently—we made a snapper.

Tell us what an easy weekend dinner looks like in your house. A one-pot meal. The last one was a pork chop, a porcelet from Canada. I usually have two pots going simultaneously. I start some vegetables and the meat. The seasoning is important. I use a Bombay or Dali spice mix from a chef who used to work for me—I keep it in the fridge so it stays fresher. It cooks for about 30 minutes. I add whatever I have in the fridge.

Where do you buy your cheese? Have you ever smuggled cheese from France in your luggage? I buy my cheese from Murray's here in the city. In the old days, I would smuggle the homemade goat cheese from my family farm, not to mention an entire ham and sausages!

Can you get whatever French products you want, anything you crave? Well, I do live above the restaurant, but I also need to rely on a friend from the Massif Central in France for *tripoux* in a jar, calf's tripe, that I can't get here.

What is in your freezer? The real food we cook for our children in large batches so that we have a multitude of healthy meal options for them. We prepare them in ice cube trays.

Sardine and Pickled Onion Tartine

Tartines are easy to make—just toast bread, spread great ingredients, and enjoy. My wife loves anchovy tartines. I like them with avocado, radish, or whatever vegetable and pair it with sardines or anchovies, balsamic vinegar, and olive oil. Another favorite of mine is to rub garlic on the toasted bread, spread with ricotta, add some crudités, drizzle a little olive oil, top with fresh herbs, and voilà!

For the pickled red onions:

1 cup white wine vinegar

1 cup water

½ cup sugar

2 tablespoons grenadine

1 teaspoon salt

½ teaspoon each mustard seed, black peppercorn, star anise, cilantro seed

1 red onion, sliced

For the tartine:

8 slices sourdough bread, toasted

¼ cup mayonnaise

8 sardines packed in olive oil, split in half

1 avocado, peeled, pitted, and sliced

1 Persian cucumber, thinly sliced

3 breakfast radishes, thinly sliced

1 bunch basil, leaves picked

1 lemon, zested and juiced

½ teaspoon Espelette pepper

Fleur de sel to taste

To make the pickled red onions, combine the vinegar, water, sugar, grenadine, salt, and spices in a small pot and bring to a boil.

Place the sliced red onions in a heat-proof container and strain the boiling liquid over them. Let the onions come to room temperature and then refrigerate overnight.

To make the tartines, smear the mayonnaise evenly across all 8 slices of bread and gently place 2 sardine halves per slice, then arrange 3 to 4 slices of avocado on top. Place 8 to 10 slices of cucumber and radish on each slice of bread. Drain the pickled red onions from their liquid and place a few pieces on each slice.

Garnish each tartine with basil leaves, lemon zest, lemon juice, Espelette pepper, and fleur de sel.

SERVES 4

SEAN BROCK

You wouldn't think a James Beard Award and a *Bon Appétit* magazine cover were in the cards for someone from a Virginia coal town who was primed to take over his father's trucking business and didn't eat in a restaurant until he was sixteen. But that's exactly what happened to Sean Brock.

He's now in Nashville, manning the kitchen of Audrey, his new Appalachian-focused restaurant, after years spent running the award-winning Husk in Charleston, South Carolina, as well as its various branches. His love for Southern cooking goes back to his childhood. "I always had amazing food as a kid," Brock says. One of his favorite dishes was a wilted garden salad called "killed lettuces." "My mom would go to the garden, dig up a couple of young onions and snap some lettuce leaves. She would bring them into the kitchen and put them directly on the plate. The 'killing' happens when hot fat is drizzled over the lettuces and onions. You use whatever fat you have, then eat right away."

After his dad died suddenly of a heart attack when he was eleven, Brock and his mother moved in with his grandmother. "Her kitchen garden was larger than what we classify as farms today," he recalls. His grandmother was a master of jarring, canning, and pickling, passing on techniques that had been handed down from her grandparents. Maybe that's why he is always finding a new way to reuse coffee grounds, say, or leftover foods:

"It's the way I was raised, and you got in trouble if you threw anything away."

A self-described workaholic, Brock is obsessed with seed varietals, guitars, and antique automobiles and, for a difficult period, vintage bourbons. His home kitchen often serves as a testing ground—a place for working through Noma's fermentation recipes or planning his next cookbook—and his refrigerator is a testament to that.

"My rule to live or cook by is he who dies with the biggest fridge or pantry wins," he remarks. Void of alcohol, the shelves of his fridge are crammed with regional heritage seeds, milled corns, even descendants from his grandmother's garden. "See these leather britches, they're green beans. The seeds on the bottom—they were my grandmother's. I have kept these alive for the past ten years since she passed. You drop these into a pressure cooker and braise them with potlikker and it tastes like meat. I call it hillbilly seaweed because it has so much glutamic acid," says Brock.

At home Brock is often the one cooking: "How do you think I got such a pretty girl?" he asks in reference to his wife and mother of his child. "The joke around the house is that when there is no food around, I usually end up cooking one of the best meals I have ever cooked. I like to create really flavorful sauces—sweet, salty, bitter, fat, as long as this formula is there, I can match that to whatever we are eating."

CURRENT HOMETOWN:
Nashville, Tennessee

RESTAURANT THAT MADE HIS NAME: Husk, Charleston, South Carolina

SIGNATURE STYLE:
Noma-inspired Southern Appalachian food

BEST KNOWN FOR: His deep, historical knowledge of Southern food; his best-selling cookbook, *Heritage*; and his James Beard Award and nominations

FRIDGE: Samsung

1. **WATERMELON MOLASSES** (reduced watermelon juice)

2. **CHASHU FAT** (the fat from braised pork belly)

3. **BACON LARD**—"I keep it in my fridge like every good Southerner."

4. **CAROLINA AFRICAN RUNNER PEANUTS**—"It's the very first peanut that came to America. We have been trying to grow them for fifteen years. Last year was the first we had enough to cook and make oil with."

5. **BOB'S RED MILL YELLOW GRITS**—"I use at least seventy-five varieties of corn for grits and cornmeal. The list is always growing as we discover once-forgotten varietals."

6. **CHILI SAUCE**—"Each year I make a chili sauce. I take different kinds of chilies and bury them in salt. I let that go for six months and then I add vinegar for six months. It ferments and then I puree it. Shelf life in the fridge is forever."

7. **SOUR MUSHROOMS** (a sauerkraut made from salt, water, and mushrooms)

8. **BENNE SEEDS**—"The original form of sesame seeds that came to the South via West Africa. I get them from a guy once a year. I also turn them into vinegar."

9. **BUTTER**

10. **PORK BRAISING LIQUID**

11. **BUCKWHEAT HONEY**—"This is my favorite honey because it's so floral and nutty! I eat a tablespoon every morning."

12. **CAJUN BOILED PEANUT MISO**—"I bought the peanuts from a roadside stand. We take the peanuts and make traditional miso."

13. **COUNTRY HAM LEES**—"We make 'fish sauce' with country ham."

14. **MATCHLESS COFFEE SODA**—"It's a local Nashville product that I'm addicted to."

15. **SEEDS AND GRAINS**—"I toss them in the fridge until they get filed away in the seed bank. I collect seeds, so people just mail them to me, and some I grow and save each year."

16. **ROW 7 SEEDS**, from Dan Barber

17. **RICE PEA SEEDS**

18. **PETITS POIS VERTS**—"They look like lentils but they're actually peas."

19. **HIS GRANDMOTHER'S GREASY-CUT SHORT BEANS**

20. **HEAVY CREAM**

21. **SHIRO DASHI**

22. **FRESH PORK RACK**

23. **MUSHROOMS: SHIITAKES, ROYAL TRUMPETS, MAITAKES** (hen of the woods)

24. **DANDELION, KALE, SWISS CHARD**—"I'm going to make a meatless green gumbo with all of those greens. It's a once-a-year tradition. It cooks for a couple hours in a dark roux with onions and garlic."

22

1. **BEEF STEW**

2. **PORK AND CHICKEN STOCKS**

3. **WILD BERRIES—** from last summer for smoothies

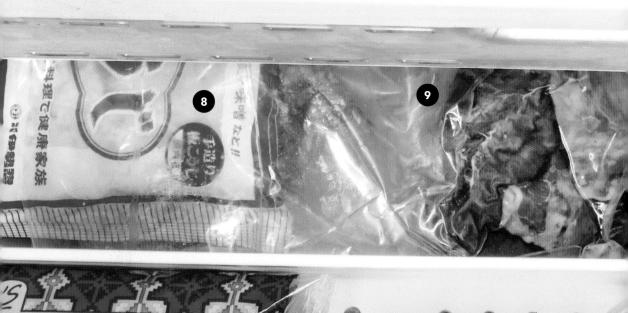

4. **CHOCOLATE CHIP COOKIES**

5. **KOJI RICE**

6. **PESTO**—from a friend who makes it once a year

7. **BRAISED PORK BELLY**—"I roast an entire belly, then portion it into little vacuum bags and throw them in the freezer for quick meals."

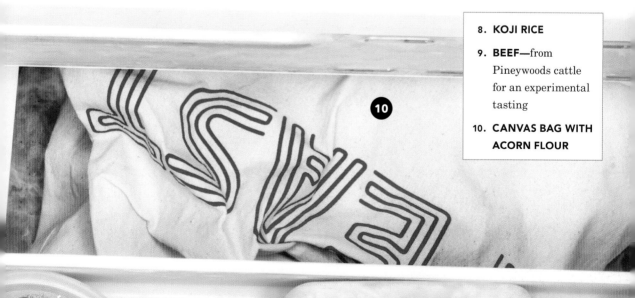

8. **KOJI RICE**

9. **BEEF**—from Pineywoods cattle for an experimental tasting

10. **CANVAS BAG WITH ACORN FLOUR**

Q & A

You keep your grits in the fridge? Yes, and in fact, when the corn is being ground I put it in liquid nitrogen and then grind, so that the heat of the stones doesn't dissipate the flavor of the grits.

What kind of grits do you use? My grits are Cherokee White Eagle variety. I'm obsessed with the terroir that corn carries. And it's a portion of my heritage—this is kind of crazy but my fifth-great-grandfather was Chief Red Bird [a half-Cherokee chief who lived in Tennessee and Kentucky in the eighteenth century] and his dad was Chief Great Eagle or something like that. The corn is not common in the South but it's available to grow. And it's a dent varietal—there is dent corn and flint corn. If it's smooth on the top and the dimples are on the side, like my flint corn tattoo, that's flint corn.

How do you cook your grits? Dent is usually used for grits and flint is usually used for polenta, because of the starch content. I have a theory with grits. I'm so obsessive: about the varietals, how they are stored, every aspect to keep as much of the flavor compounds together as possible. Most people would slow-cook in a pot—I don't love that because too much flavor escapes. It's also much easier to burn, scorch, or dry out. So I like to use pressure cookers or even a rice cooker. You literally keep it on warm and use three parts water, one part grits, and salt. I put it on the rice setting and leave it. You can't really overcook grits. I believe that steam is flavor and this traps it in. I'm also crazy about only using water, not stock or milk; I figure if we went to so much trouble to get this variety grown, I don't want to dump milk on it. I will sometimes put a little butter in there—depends what I am making.

Any other corn tattoos in the works? I plan to get my son Leo's name tattooed over my heart. So cheesy, I know. But it's a statement and a reminder.

You said you Noma-fied your redeye gravy? This is coffee shoyu—inspired from *The Noma Guide to Fermentation*. I've been making shoyus for about ten to twelve years. I drink a lot of coffee and have a lot of leftover grounds, so I was excited to see what would happen when I used them. You take leftover brewed coffee and as you cook country ham you deglaze the fat with coffee. I'm going to pour that over the grits I'm making. This couldn't be easier: you literally take three ingredients, dump them in a rice cooker, and turn it on. Then a month later you get soy sauce that tastes like coffee.

You keep garbage in your fridge? I took the waste of the restaurant in one day—the fish, meats, vegetables, egg whites, everything—and made garam with it. So basically no waste.

What is country ham fish sauce? It's a funky fermented country ham paste that we ground up and treated like fish sauce. You can add it to anything or everything to boost up flavor.

There's A1 sauce on that shelf—is that something you like? Yes, that stuff really lives in there. I'm crazy about it. It's for steaks. Here is the way I look at it—if I put it on a plate, beautifully plated in a restaurant setting, and told you it was tamarind fermented shit, you would say that is the most delicious thing you have ever had in your life.

That's a lot of cubed bread in the freezer. Anytime I have really great bread, I cut up the leftover bits and freeze them for making quick croutons to throw in salad. I also do the same for potatoes. These have been steamed and frozen. So for breakfast all I have to do is plop that into a pan and I have hash browns. My favorite thing to do is to panfry them really crispy and then douse them in crème fraîche, caviar, and chives.

Jimmy Red Grits with Greens, Egg, and Redeye Gravy

I like to serve this with braised pork. I make the pork and freeze individual portions so I can have them at the ready when-ever. My wife often adds them to this recipe when I'm not home.

For the grits:

One 1-liter bottle spring water

1 cup Jimmy Red Grits

1 fresh bay leaf

1 tablespoon kosher salt

½ teaspoon freshly ground white pepper

2 tablespoons unsalted butter

1 tablespoon fresh lemon juice

1½ teaspoons hot sauce

For the redeye gravy:

1 teaspoon canola oil

1 ounce fatty country ham scraps, cut into ⅛-inch pieces

2 tablespoons finely diced sweet onion

1 teaspoon minced garlic

1 tablespoon all-purpose flour

½ cup pork stock

½ cup day-old brewed coffee

1 tablespoon Noma coffee shoyu or soy sauce

1 teaspoon finely chopped sage

½ teaspoon dried thyme

½ teaspoon kosher salt

½ teaspoon freshly cracked Bourbon smoked black peppercorns

½ pound collard greens

4 eggs

To make the grits: Combine the water and grits in a container, cover, and refrigerate for at least 8 hours, or overnight. Use a fine-mesh sieve to skim off any hulls or chaff, being careful not to disturb the water too much so that the hulls don't sink back into the grits.

Transfer the grits and the soaking water to a pressure cooker, add the bay leaf, salt, and pepper, and stir to combine. Lock on the lid, bring the cooker up to high pressure, and cook for 15 minutes. Carefully release the steam from the pressure cooker. Remove the lid, stir in the butter, lemon juice, and hot sauce, and transfer to a serving bowl.

For the gravy, combine the oil and the ham in a small heavy-bottomed saucepan and cook over medium heat, stirring frequently, until the fat is rendered and the ham is crisp, about 4 minutes. Add the onion and garlic and cook them, stirring occasionally, until translucent, about 3 minutes. Add the flour and cook, stirring constantly, for 2 minutes to make a roux. Slowly stir in the pork stock and coffee and, stirring frequently, bring to a simmer, about 4 minutes.

Reduce the heat to low, stir in the shoyu or soy sauce, sage, thyme, salt, and cracked pepper, cover, and keep warm.

To serve, lightly wilt the collard greens in the same pan with the heat on as low as possible. Fry the eggs sunny side up. Spoon the greens over the grits and top with one egg per serving.

SERVES 4

CURRENT HOMETOWN:
New York City

RESTAURANT THAT MADE HER NAME: Dirt Candy, New York City

SIGNATURE STYLE:
Vegetarian haute cuisine

BEST KNOWN FOR: First vegetarian chef to compete on *Iron Chef*; her graphic novel–like cookbook, *Dirt Candy: A Cookbook*; and *Dispatches from Dirt Candy*, her column on Eater

FRIDGE: Ikea

AMANDA COHEN

By the time Amanda Cohen was born, her mother had taken what Cohen considered a well-deserved break from cooking; growing up in Canada, Cohen was essentially raised on "lots of pasta salad, that most 1980s of foods." Perhaps it was this emphasis on white food that led to Cohen's craving for vegetables in all their multihued varieties by the time she was a teenager.

A year in Hong Kong after her graduation from New York University really opened her eyes to the potential in produce. "The fact you could have a massive, delicious dim sum feast on Sunday that was entirely vegetarian blew my mind," she recalls. Vegetables were so inexpensive and there were so many types she had never tried before that every trip to the market became an adventure.

After living there, Cohen knew she wanted to cook—at the time though she thought it would be the career move that would give her the most freedom, especially to travel. She then went to culinary school in New York and began working in mostly vegetarian restaurants.

After years of working for others, Cohen realized that if she wanted to cook vegetables her own way, it would have to be in her own place. Dirt Candy opened in 2008 with nine tables—such a tight space!—in order to minimize any risk of failure. "What we weren't prepared for was that it would succeed," says Cohen. But how could it not? Dirt Candy's slogan is "Anyone can cook meat, leave the vegetables to the professionals," and she's

certainly a pro, whipping up such delectable dishes as roasted cucumber broth, rosemary cotton candy, and onion tartare. These whimsical plates were a hit.

Although Cohen has spent her most of her life in the United States, she is a familiar face on *Iron Chef Canada*. She was apprehensive about cooking on TV at first, but then realized the platform was too good to turn down. The first experience was "deeply, deeply stressful, especially because you can't look stressed. That camera sees right into your soul," she recalls.

Even though Cohen eventually lost that first season, the gain in notoriety was worth it, and in 2019 she came back as an Iron Chef. Prior to filming, she and her staff did "tight-knit team practices and drills." They were already a fine-tuned machine, but "we rehearsed to make sure we didn't panic and choke under the lights with the time limit and cameras bearing down on us," she says. "I took it very seriously, which made it even more fun."

Cohen doesn't cook much when she's at home—space is so tight in her spartan, galley-style kitchen that her oven and under-the-counter fridge face each other and cannot be opened simultaneously. Ditto for her dishwasher and freezer. When she does cook, she sticks to vegetarian meals. But often it's takeout on her days off, although she is not above sprucing up or rescuing leftover rice, which is what we ended up having for lunch on the day we met to talk about the contents of her tiny refrigerator, filled with the essentials picked up at a small spice shop downstairs.

1. **BEAN PASTE**

2. **PECORINO**

3. **HARISSA**

4. **TOFU**—"Dirt Candy is right on the border of Chinatown, so my husband usually picks up groceries on his way home. I get my tofu wherever I can, but there are more varieties in Chinatown."

5. **MISO**

6. **KALE**

7. **FOUR LOKO**—"I've never opened it and it's been in there forever."

8. **CHILI PEPPERS IN OIL**—"They're arbol chilis and it's an oil I made one Sunday when I was feeling particularly ambitious. It will probably live in our fridge for the rest of our lives."

9. **LEFTOVER RICE**—"We always order too much."

10. **LABNEH, BABA GHANOUSH, AND GIGANTE BEAN DIPS,** from Kalustyan's spice shop—"I buy as much as I can from them as often as I can. Part of the reason I can never move is I don't ever want to be too far away from them."

11. **MUSHROOMS,** from Chinatown

12. **HUMMUS**—"I end a lot of my nights squatting in front of the fridge dipping something—anything—in hummus because it's been a long service and I'm starved."

13. **OLIVES**

14. **COLD BREW COFFEE**—"The cold brew is my husband's. I live on coffee."

15. **VEUVE CLICQUOT CHAMPAGNE**—"I'm big on spicy food and nothing goes better with it than Champagne, or anything sparkling. I don't keep Champagne in my fridge to celebrate; I keep it in there for the next time I order Sichuan takeout."

16. **CHILI PASTE**

Q & A

What are those big green cubes in your freezer? I take whatever greens are about to go bad in the fridge. I blanch and puree them to always have something green on hand. It's a trick I brought home from the restaurant. We are always trying to figure out how to not throw things out if we have too much. I think the basis for this started with a spinach or green risotto. It totally works.

You have a small fridge for someone living in the U.S. Is it because you are Canadian? I have a small fridge because I live in a small apartment and I didn't want a big giant fridge blocking the tiny sliver of a view I have through my kitchen window.

What do you always have in your fridge? Wine. It goes with everything. Nothing to eat but that hard cheese rind? Have it with a glass of wine. Having takeout from that only slightly okay Chinese place on the corner because they're the only place open? Wine will smooth out all those rough edges. Nothing to eat in the house because you've been working late all week and haven't had time to go shopping? What do you care if you've got wine?

Do people ask you often if you are a vegetarian? I get asked all the time if I am vegetarian and I answer honestly that I am not. I'm too competitive. I want to taste what other chefs are cooking and most of them really only cook seafood or meat well. But tasting what they do is a good way to keep my technique sharp. I think all my customers expect from me is that I am a good chef.

Is cooking vegetables a much freer or more expressive way of cooking in comparison to meat? I don't know because I've never cooked meat!

Who is cooking at home? My husband cooks or we get takeaway nights when I'm not at work.

What foods do you hate? Or what foods would you never eat? I'm not sure a chef who hates any type of food has any place being a chef.

What is your favorite junk food? I love Canadian potato chips—All Dressed, Dill Pickle, Ketchup. Whenever I go back to Canada I come home with a suitcase full.

How is it food shopping in New York City? I don't do it.

Why do you refrigerate your tomatoes? My kitchen gets a lot of sunlight. I can't keep them on the counter. They are winter tomatoes. They have been in a cold room already, likely ripened there. It's perfectly fine to keep them in the fridge.

If you could move anywhere else just for the produce where would it be? South Africa. I was there recently for work and the quality of the produce blew me away. Where else can you get bananas, oranges, apples, butternut squash, and avocados all in season, all growing in the same places, all being sold at the same market?

Green Rice with Kale and Peas

This is a very flexible recipe because, depending what you have, you can substitute any grain for the rice. I don't make this at the restaurant; it's just a simple dish for home.

¼ cup extra virgin olive oil

¼ cup diced yellow onion

1 tablespoon minced garlic

4 cups leftover cooked rice

½ cup shelled peas

1 cup chopped kale

1 cup of green cubes or 2 large cubes (see Note)

2 tablespoons unsalted butter

½ cup grated Pecorino, plus more for garnish

Salt

2 tablespoons lemon juice

Zest of ½ lemon

Heat the oil in a medium pan on medium heat until it shimmers. Add the onion and garlic. Stir until cooked through. Once the onion turns translucent, add the rice and cook for 2 minutes. Add the peas, kale, and green cubes.

Once the cube has melted and the rice is hot again, add the butter and cheese. Stir a few times. Salt to taste.

Remove from the heat and add the lemon juice. Finish with the zest and any leftover cheese.

Note: To make a green cube, blanch any leafy greens or herbs. Shock them in cold water, strain, then puree and freeze in a large ice-cube tray.

SERVES 4

1. **GYOZA**

2. **COFFEE**

3. **CRANBERRIES**—"I have no idea how these got there or why."

4. **ORGANIC WINTER SQUASH**

5. **GREEN CUBES**—"I always have these on hand. I don't make orange cubes, only green."

6. **PEAS**

Butternut Squash Gnocchi
with Chickpeas, Harissa Butter, and Parsley

When I need a big bowl of pick-me-up comfort this is the dish that I crave. The richness of the dumplings and the bright spiciness of the harissa are the perfect combination on a dreary day, especially after a long hard week at work. Gnocchi's easy to cook and easy to eat—it's soft, it's pillowy, and it's filling—and for me that's the very definition of a comfort food.

1 to 2 large butternut squash (at least 3½ cups puréed)

1 cup plus 1 tablespoon cornstarch

3 tablespoons butter, unsalted

1 small can (7.75 ounces) chickpeas, rinsed and drained

1 tablespoon harissa

2 tablespoons parsley, minced

Salt

Pepper

To prepare the gnocchi, remove the peel, fibers, and seeds of the butternut squash. Cut into medium-size chunks. Place in a large pot and cover with water. Bring to a boil. Reduce to a simmer and cook the squash pieces until they are tender when pierced with a fork.

Drain the squash, let it cool, then puree until very smooth. If the mixture isn't completely smooth, push it through a strainer.

Measure out 3½ cups of butternut puree. Gently mix with the cornstarch. The mixture will look loose, but this is normal and it will firm up during the cooking.

Bring a large pot of water to a light simmer. Using a small scooper, scoop out batches of the purée and drop them into the pot. Do not crowd the pot; make sure each there is an inch in between each gnocchi. Gently cook each batch for 1 to 2 minutes until the gnocchi float to the top. Remove the gnocchi from the water with a strainer or slotted spoon and place on an oiled sheet pan. Let cool and refrigerate for at least 2 hours before use.

To serve, bring a large pot of water to a boil. Lower the temperature to a simmer. Drop the gnocchi in to reheat for about 30 seconds. In a large frying pan heat the butter, chickpeas, and harissa. Once the mixture becomes fragrant, add the gnocchi and sauté for 1 minute. Season with salt and pepper. Divide among four plates, sprinkle with parsley, and serve immediately.

SERVES 4

DOMINIQUE CRENN

Although Dominique Crenn knew she wanted to be a chef from age eight, her parents dissuaded her. But after getting degrees in economics and international business in Paris, she landed in San Francisco, where the first thing she did was seek out the best chef in town. That happened to be Jeremiah Tower, whose restaurant Stars was the most famous in the city at that time. Crenn, with no references or cooking qualifications, simply walked in the front door and asked for a job, and that evening she was manning the grill for a full house.

"Stars was such a formative experience," Crenn recalls. "Sometimes Jeremiah asked me to make up a new dish and execute something delicious on the spot. Creativity was expected, and there were no recipes, just guidelines. That requires a lot of trust."

Crenn's love for restaurants came while she was growing up in Versailles, France. Her father, a prominent French politician and a talented painter ("but a terrible cook"), used to take her to Michelin-starred restaurants, accompanied by his best friend, a restaurant critic. There she "fell in love with being surrounded by people taking care of me." Crenn's mother was an inspired cook at home, but she also had an adventurous palate, and went with her daughter to Indian, Vietnamese, and Japanese restaurants wherever and whenever they could. Crenn also accompanied her mother to the market. "I would always linger around the spices and come back with ginger and cilantro," she recalls. "I really liked the smells."

It's no wonder, then, that after Stars, Crenn went to Jakarta, where she worked as a chef at the InterContinental. She left only because Indonesia became engulfed in a civil war. She then spent the next twelve years working for other people. In 2011, she opened Atelier Crenn, which was dedicated to the memory of her father. She quickly earned a Michelin star, then a second, then, historically, a third—and opened several more restaurants.

Her meteoric rise, marked by her own personal drive, gumption, and just pure badassness (her word), has made her an inspiration to many women. As Crenn notes, "I want to push forward the next generations and inspire young girls to accomplish their dreams."

Although running four eateries is hectic, her kitchen at home that she shares with her wife is a respite. From her sink she can look out at the quiet Corte Madera Creek. Large serving plates for impromptu pupu platters dominate the tableware, and her counters and mini fridge are spare. Here, everything is about comfort food, with a little twist. After-work snacks are often grilled cheese sandwiches (hers are with aged Comté on a brioche). And there's always rosé. "I never drink Champagne, but I always have a bottle of rosé on hand," she says.

This marriage of food styles may have roots in Crenn's genes. Crenn, who was adopted when she was eighteen months old, recently took a DNA test, which led to an important discovery about her ancestry: "I found out that there's much more than French inside of me." There are ancestors from Southeast Asia to Siberia, from Africa and the Maghreb. "My style comes from always being open to looking at food in different ways, being inspired by others, and learning new things through connections and dialogue," she says. "Always evolving."

CURRENT HOMETOWN:
San Francisco, California

RESTAURANT THAT MADE HER NAME: Atelier Crenn, San Francisco

SIGNATURE STYLE: Coastal French with a focus on seafood and vegetables

BEST KNOWN FOR: The only female chef in the United States to receive three Michelin stars; James Beard Award for Best Chef in the West (2018)

FRIDGE: Sub-Zero

1. **PÂTÉ AND SAUCISSON**—"I'm French, I have to have pâté and saucisson. We made sandwiches for a hike the other day with saucisson, mustard, butter, and cornichons. It's all about the ingredients."

2. **EGGS,** from their chickens on the farm—"We had twenty-six but we lost two."

3. **CORNICHONS**—"These are from France and I can't live without them. I like the acidity. The American pickle is not that great."

4. **HOT PEPPERS,** for her wife

5. **GRAINY FRENCH MUSTARD**—"Of course I can't live without this."

6. **EDIBLE MARIJUANA**—"I don't smoke or eat it, but a friend sent me some samples. She is incorporating it into food."

7. **INNA JAM**—"We love jam and Inna is a local company. I really am into supporting local community business and farmers who have been here working their asses off. I want to be a part of it."

8. **MEYER LEMON**—"Another amazing Inna product."

9. **COCONUT WATER**—"I just drink it straight."

10. **SALMON**

11. **POMEGRANATE**—"We eat them for the antioxidants."

12. **ROMANESCO**—"My mom used to make this with a vinaigrette."

13. **LACTOSE-FREE COW AND SHEEP'S MILK YOGURT,** from the Sonoma Valley

14. **SHEEP BUTTER**

15. **POT DE CRÈME**—"I'm obsessed with petit pots de crème. They are organic French pudding, and these are caramel. I love the glass containers. In France, people make these at home in their yogurt makers. I make a chocolate version at Bar Crenn."

16. **CHEESE** (sheep's milk, Roquefort, and petit délice)

17. **RELAXATION HONEY TONIC**—"It's raw honey with apple cider vinegar. I drink this a lot."

18. **SPARKLING CIDER,** a leftover from Christmas

19. **KOMBUCHA**—"It's the only fizzy drink I like, I don't even like Champagne."

20. **FRESH JUICE,** from Good Earth Natural Foods store

21. **PATAGONIA MUSSELS**—"They remind me of French mussels."

22. **CRÈME FRAÎCHE**—"For me it's better than just cream and it adds a simple luxurious element. At the restaurant we make our own."

Q & A

This is the smallest refrigerator—it's just a drawer in the wall. How were you able to switch to such a small fridge? It helped me to be more conscious and thoughtful. What we had before was so big and often so empty. We realized it's a question of waste. When you are a chef you cook what arrives every day. I don't cook something that has been there for ten days and at the supermarket for already a month.

After all, what is the idea of a refrigerator? To keep things cold. But it became something where the bigger the fridge the cooler you are. In the supermarket you see now that they create double packs or triple packs, and it's all buy one, get two for free. . . . You can see that consumption is doubling and tripling. At Atelier Crenn we have a small kitchen and a small fridge. I think the new ideas for kitchen design are going to get more compact.

Did it take time to get used to pulling out a drawer instead of opening a door? Not really. It's only tricky when we want to cook large meals. When my wife's family of fourteen was in town for Christmas Eve we had to prepare the dinner at the restaurant and then bring all the food here.

Where do your eggs come from? From our biodynamic organic farm in Sonoma. We took it over two years ago. At the farm we have thirty varieties of vegetables, fruit trees like peaches, apples, pears, and persimmons, and walnuts as well as herbs. It's a no-kill farm.

What about the cheese. Is it French? Local cheese, it's a difficult subject. I use a lot of cheese from Vermont. In California, the cheese isn't up to the standard. The level at which they have to pasteurize the cheese often

takes away from the hard work they put into it. I always have a blue cheese, either Bleu d'Auvergne or Roquefort. I also have an unpasteurized sheep's milk cheese—it's a stinky one. And a really creamy one called *petit délice*—it's an organic triple cream cheese, also pasteurized.

Do you bring back food from France? I bring back cheese—but I've been caught at customs and they have taken everything away.

And the sheep's butter? Can you use it like regular butter from cows? It's absolutely delicious. For me it's so much better than the cow's milk. We live in a world where milk is not milk anymore. Cows being milked 24/7 is not natural. And the cattle industry in the U.S. is disgusting. I have found a couple of local yogurts though. And butter from Brittany is special; it's the best butter in the world.

Are the pâté and saucisson sec from France? No, they are from a local company. Food is energy and this is one I want to support. We need to care about our animals. I am not saying we need to be vegan but we need to balance everything.

How often do you go food shopping? We go to Good Earth Natural Foods store on the weekends and we bring things back from the farm. Larkspur, the town closest to us, also has a nice farmers market.

Any exceptions when it comes to food? I don't believe in junk food.

But your wife said something about nachos, right? They are for my wife. I eat them sometimes too, but without the spice.

Cured Salmon with Crème Fraîche and Lemon

This recipe is my go-to when unwinding on the weekend. A glass or two of rosé elevates an easy meal like this.

2 cups kosher salt

2 cups sugar

2 tablespoons minced fresh ginger

2 scallions, minced

2 garlic cloves, minced

2 tablespoons lime zest

1- to 2-pound salmon fillet, skin on

30 pita crackers (recipe follows)

1 cup crème fraîche

15 chives, minced

Zest of 2 lemons

Mix the salt, sugar, ginger, scallions, garlic, and lime zest together. Place the salmon on an oven tray and cover with the mixture. Cover with plastic wrap and store in the refrigerator for 24 hours.

Rinse the salmon. Pat it dry. Remove the skin and slice the fish thinly, beginning with the tail end, so that the knife is visible as you cut through.

Layer the salmon by placing a sheet of parchment paper in between each new layer. The salmon will keep in the fridge for up to 3 days.

Place a slice of salmon on each pita cracker, followed by dollops of crème fraîche, and sprinklings of chives and lemon zest. Serve immediately.

SERVES 4 TO 6

....

Pita Crackers

3½ cups bread flour

1 cup durum flour

⅛ teaspoon instant yeast

2 egg yolks

1½ cups plus 2 tablespoons water

2 teaspoons olive oil

2 teaspoons sea salt

Combine all of the ingredients in a large bowl. Mix with a wooden spoon or rubber spatula until you form a shaggy dough. Place the dough onto a clean work surface and knead it by hand for 8 to 11 minutes, until smooth. Place the dough into a clean bowl and allow it to rise for 3 hours at room temperature. It will double in volume.

Place the dough on a floured work surface. Divide it into ping-pong-size balls. Cover with plastic wrap or a kitchen towel and let rise for 1 hour. Roll out or flatten and stretch each ball by hand to approximately 6 inches in diameter. Let the rolled pitas rest for 15 minutes on a floured surface.

Place a large cast-iron skillet or heavy sauté pan over medium-high heat and begin to cook the pitas, about 2 minutes per side. Once you flip them over after the first 2 minutes, both sides will separate and puff into one pita. Set aside finished pitas in a clean kitchen towel to ensure softness.

To make crackers, preheat the oven to 350°F. Separate the sides of the pita and then tear apart each side to form 4-inch crackers. Toast in the oven for 5 to 7 minutes, until golden.

MAKES APPROXIMATELY 30 CRACKERS

CURRENT HOMETOWN:
New York City

RESTAURANT THAT MADE HIS NAME: 71 Clinton Fresh Food, New York City

SIGNATURE STYLE: Boundary-pushing interpretations of classic dishes

BEST KNOWN FOR: His pickled beef tongue with fried mayonnaise at wd~50; his love of molecular gastronomy; ten James Beard Award nominations and an award for Best Chef: New York City (2013); and his upscale doughnut shop, Du's Donuts and Coffee

FRIDGE: True Refrigeration

WYLIE DUFRESNE

Wylie Dufresne grew up in the restaurant business—his father owned a successful sandwich shop in Providence, Rhode Island—but dreamed of becoming a pro baseball player. A summer job at Al Forno, a fine dining mecca in Providence, convinced him that kitchen life was for him, and he enrolled in the French Culinary Institute after getting a degree in philosophy from Colby College.

His dad also played another instrumental role in his career. After Dufresne had spent six years with Jean-Georges Vongerichten at his flagship restaurant JoJo and as head chef at the glitzy Las Vegas steakhouse Prime, the senior Dufresne told his son he'd bought a dilapidated shop front on Clinton Street on the Lower East Side, and would he be interested in creating the menu? Dufresne immediately quit his job and they together opened what would become a Lower East Side destination: 71 Clinton Fresh Food.

From his tiny kitchen, Dufresne served up high-end dishes like freshly warmed mascarpone-stuffed figs and red snapper with Asian pear and sunchokes for such low-end prices that diners quickly caught on to what a great place this was. Rave reviews, including one from the *New York Times*'s restaurant critic Ruth Reichl, followed and the thirty-seater dining room was soon packed every night, despite the still rough neighborhood.

In 2003, he opened wd~50 right across the street. The new restaurant was even more ambitious, with Dufresne serving up dishes like pastrami on rye pasta. In an ironic final act, wd~50 became a victim of its own success; it was forced to close in 2014 when the landlord sold the building to make way for condos. Fellow chef David Chang famously said, "He should get royalties for every building that has gone up since he opened his restaurant."

Dufresne's next move surprised everyone, but it actually made sense for him. He'd always dreamed of owning a doughnut shop—his great-grandfather ran a diner in Rhode Island and introduced Dufresne to New England–style cake doughnuts when he was a kid—so he opened Du's Donuts and Coffee in a small boutique hotel in Brooklyn. His uniquely flavored doughnuts—from Creamsicle to yuzu–peanut butter—have again brought him fame and pushed the envelope. "I thought our approach to cooking would translate well to the blank canvas that is a doughnut," he explains. Even his two children get in on the act, happy to come up with flavors and put in orders.

So what does the man who invented deep-fried mayonnaise do when he gets home from a long day at work? Drink cocktails, apparently. Cooking duties are shared between him and his wife, Maile (a trained chef and the editor in chief of *Food Network Magazine*), in a kitchen that's full of light, counter space, and stockpots. Breakfast is one of their favorite meals (see the recipe on page 78). "It's a big part of my family's routine. My wife makes the pancakes, and I usually handle the French toast," he says.

After more than two decades cooking, Dufresne is happy to have found a certain balance. Besides, he likes being away, at least temporarily, from running a big-city restaurant. "It was time for a change," he says.

1. **APPLE CIDER,** from the farmers market

2. **SODASTREAM WATER,** waiting to be carbonated

3. **PREMADE GUACAMOLE,** for the kids' lunches

4. **CHICKEN THIGHS**

5. **LEFTOVERS,** from dinner the other night: cornbread stuffing, mashed potatoes, and chicken thighs

6. **CHICKEN STOCK**—"I used it for the chicken soup recipe I made with my daughter and it's also good for making sauces whenever we want."

7. **MY WIFE'S CHICKEN SALAD**

8. **DILL PICKLES,** from The Pickle Guys on the Lower East Side

9. **COLD PASTA,** for the children's lunch

10. **REMNANTS OF LAST NIGHT'S DINNER: RAVIOLI WITH PORK AND STEAMED BROCCOLI**

11. **CREAM CHEESE**—"It's the secret weapon to my scrambled eggs."

12. **PUMPKIN RAVIOLI**—"From the good people at TJ's."

13. **GROUND BEEF**

14. **YOGURT SNACKS**—"We have three different kinds for my youngest to snack on."

15. **JUICE BOXES**

16. **JORDAN SALCITO RAMONA SPARKLING WINE**

17. **CRACKER BARREL GINGER BEER**

18. **FEVER-TREE TONIC WATER**

19. **EGGS**

Everything Bagel Scrambled Eggs

Everything bagels, lox, eggs—they are all favorite breakfast dishes. Combining those flavors here is really about taking what everyone loves and approaching it differently. I like to use a high-sided pot to make the eggs. The nice thing about this is that you can scramble the eggs in the time it takes to make the toast.

8 large eggs

Kosher salt

4 tablespoons unsalted butter

6 tablespoons cream cheese

1 tablespoon furikake (or to taste)

3 tablespoons everything bagel seasoning

Whisk the eggs in a small bowl. Season with salt. Heat the butter in a medium high-sided saucepan over medium heat. As soon as the butter begins to foam, add the eggs. Cook, whisking constantly, until they have set in small curds and are beginning to look dry, about 1 minute. Immediately remove them from the heat and whisk in the cream cheese, furikake, and everything bagel seasoning.

Serve in small bowls with toast.

SERVES 4

Q & A

Do you have any childhood food memories? I have a fond memory of my grandmother teaching me how to make scrambled eggs. They were super loose and soft, scrambled in a pan with a fork. It was my first cooking experience.

How did you get interested in cooking? I've been working in restaurants since I was eleven. My first duty was peeling potatoes.

Describe your cooking style. Hot food that tastes good.

What is your favorite food when coming home from a long day at work? A cocktail—preferably a Manhattan.

What do you cook for your family? What are their favorite dishes? I love making breakfast for and with the kids. My wife prefers my scrambled eggs. But she cooks a lot and I often say she's a better cook than I am.

Did you change careers to give you more time at home? It certainly has better hours. I take my kids to school in the morning and then head to the doughnut shop. At night we used to eat separately, with the kids eating first, and now we eat together, and we are trying to not make two meals, which means everybody compromises. We light candles, and tell stories of the day.

How many fridges do you have, Wylie? There are a couple here. . . . In our last apartment we had four fridges. We had four because we were testing recipes at home. Here we have one, but we also have an ice maker, made by True. And I bought my wife a dorm fridge so she could always have a cold soda.

What about those Cracker Barrel sodas? I had never been to Cracker Barrel in my life, and they had all these sodas that reminded me of what I had when I was a kid. Just a bunch of old-fashioned sodas, like cream soda.

What do you always have in your fridge? Sparkling water, American cheese, and yogurt.

What would we never find in your fridge? Tomatoes.

What foods do you hate or never would eat? Tomatoes, and I'm not a big fan of oysters.

Any food vices you try to keep out of your refrigerator? No, I like to keep the vices in the fridge.

What is your favorite junk food? Ice cream is definitely my weakness.

Who does the food shopping in your house and where do you shop? It's a shared duty between my wife and me. We split it up between places like Fresh Direct, local supermarkets, and greenmarkets. We live in Union Square, a stone's throw from the farmers market. We are particularly fond of fall produce, like apples and root vegetables.

What is in your freezer? My freezer is packed! Lots of large ice cubes for cocktails, and a whole shelf for ice cream. A lot of food for the kids. An entire shelf of assorted nuts, like hazelnuts and pine nuts. Many a frozen novelty, and the macarons from Trader Joe's are surprisingly good.

There are tons of Traders Joe's products in your fridge! Do you have stock in it? No, but I should!

What's your favorite dish that your wife makes? Her chocolate chip cookies, and she won't give me her secret!

KRISTEN ESSIG AND MICHAEL STOLTZFUS

Pigs brought Michael Stoltzfus and Kristen Essig together. When Stoltzfus opened Coquette, his New Orleans eatery, a little more than ten years ago, he was lucky to have good purveyors. One of them, a truck driver for his pig farmer, set him up with Essig, a fellow chef and then manager of the Crescent City Farmers Market. The two got along well and soon moved in together around the corner from the restaurant. They drove to work together, cooked together, and soon Essig became co-chef and co-owner. The James Beard Foundation and *Food & Wine* nominations followed.

Essig grew up on the Gulf Coast of Florida, eating fried-grouper sandwiches with tartar sauce and her German grandmother's sauerbraten. She often spent weekends going crabbing with her grandparents, eating the boiled crabs on Sunday nights when her parents came to pick her up. Family dinners were a nightly occurrence, and usually the conversation turned to her parents' work. "Hearing them discuss how much of their work they didn't enjoy around the table every night inspired me to do something that I love, every day," she says.

While at Johnson & Wales culinary school in Charleston, South Carolina, Essig met Emeril Lagasse at a charity event. He was in the process of preparing a live TV show and asked her if she wanted a job. This was before celebrity cooking shows were so ubiquitous, so Essig had a hard time believing people would want to watch a chef cook on TV and figured her parents would be disappointed if she quit school. But after graduation she called Lagasse, and three days later she drove from Florida to New Orleans, where she began work at his namesake restaurant. Working there taught her how to be organized. "Walking into work every night was like walking into a battle. You had to find a way to center yourself, put your head down, and get your work done."

Stoltzfus also came from a shore culture—in his case, the Eastern Shore of Maryland, where his parents ran a dairy farm. "It was, as you'd imagine, lots of hard work, sweet corn, and cows," he says. Just before he was set to go to college his mother decided to open a bakery. She needed help and Stoltzfus set higher education aside to give her a hand. Although he barely had any basic cooking skills, he was a fast learner. He began picking up cookbooks and gave himself a crash course as he cooked his way through *The Culinary Institute of America Cookbook*.

After a few restaurant jobs in Maryland, he moved to New Orleans to work at the restaurant August and picked up some European-style techniques, including how to prep a *tête de veau*. "We had to burn and shave all the hair off a cow's head. Perhaps not my favorite task, but it was something I had never done before." Stoltzfus knew quite early that he wanted to open his own place and be his own boss. He opened Coquette in 2008.

Over the years, Coquette has become an anchor in the Garden District of New Orleans, the kind of place where its former chefs open restaurants just down the road. In 2019 Essig

CURRENT HOMETOWN:
New Orleans, Louisiana

RESTAURANT THAT MADE THEIR NAMES:
Coquette, New Orleans

SIGNATURE STYLE:
Louisiana ingredients with international inspiration

BEST KNOWN FOR:
Their fried chicken brunches, and becoming James Beard Award finalists four years in a row

FRIDGE: Kenmore

and Stoltzfus decided to open a second place, Thalia, which also serves as a place for community meetings. That sits well with Essig, who's an advocate for Shift Change, a local organization working to eliminate harassment in local restaurants.

When at home in a kitchen that is a tenth the size of the one at Coquette, Essig and Stoltzfus take turns cooking and cleaning up. "If not, we run into each other," says Essig. "We just do the best we can, it's not a musical."

Space is so tight they're unable to open the refrigerator door all the way, thanks to a large painting on the wall, and their table doubles as a countertop and home office. They do have a great view onto their small garden, though.

Their refrigerator is always stocked with Champagne and usually has at least a few boxes of leftover Vietnamese takeout and the occasional cut flower—a little aesthetic trick Essig picked up from her godmother, a florist who always kept blooms in her fridge.

1. **ASSORTED OYSTER AND CHESTNUT MUSHROOMS**

2. **CHEDDAR, GRUYÈRE, AND PARMESAN,** for easy meals on the restaurant's ciabatta

3. **YEAST**—"It's one of those things that we keep so that when the mood strikes and the recipe requires yeast, we have it on hand."

4. **GOLDEN TURMERIC JUICE**—"We use the turmeric juice at the restaurant for making pasta; at home we add it to salad dressings, cocktails, soups, and juices. It's concentrated, so we use it in small amounts right at the end so that the flavor is pronounced but not overwhelming."

5. **KIMCHI**

6. **FRESH ANCHOVIES**—"We like them on the restaurant's ciabatta with butter and sliced tomatoes when they're in season."

7. **JASMINE**—"I change the flower whenever I have time or find something pretty."

8. **CHAMPAGNE**—"At least two bottles at all times!"

9. **YARD EGGS, FROM GREENER PASTURES FARM**—"We like their motto—bugs, not drugs. They're called yard eggs because the chickens are free roaming."

10. **PRESERVED LOUISIANA MEYER LEMONS**

11. **COQUETTE BREAD-AND-BUTTER PICKLES**— "We call them B&B's, and we keep them in our $600 jar, which was given to us full of granola after we'd eaten an overpriced dinner in New York City."

12. **SIGGI'S VANILLA YOGURT**

13. **RANDOM FOODS IN TAKEOUT CONTAINERS: RICE, NOODLES, PEANUT SAUCE, AND HOISIN**

14. **LEFTOVERS FROM PHO TAKEOUT: BEAN SHOOTS, THAI BASIL, SLICES OF JALAPEÑO, AND LIME WEDGES, IDEAL FOR TOSSING WITH RICE**

15. **COFFEE BEANS**

16. **LEFTOVER TAKEOUT PHO BROTH**

17. **GOLDEN TURMERIC JUICE**

18. **MISSISSIPPI RED RICE**

19. **WINE BOTTLES, FROM THE RESTAURANT**—"At the end of the night we bring home the just opened bottles that were used for pouring individual glasses."

20. **MEYER LEMONS, BLOOD ORANGES, WHITE AND RED GRAPEFRUITS, LOUISIANA SWEET AND NAVEL ORANGES**—"We love citrus: we eat it, juice it, and mix it into cocktails. And when it's in season, it's all from Louisiana."

21. "Known as where all of our produce goes to die!"

22. **MORE CHAMPAGNE, RANDOM BOTTLES OF WATER**

Q & A

What's the story with that little dish of coffee beans in your fridge? Kristen Essig: Whenever we have something in our fridge that is kind of smelly, I leave a little bowl of coffee beans. They will pull odors in.

Tap water or bottled water? KE: I drink tap water and Michael doesn't. Although sometimes I refill the bottles with tap—don't tell Michael!

What is Southern-style cooking to you? KE: Southern-style cooking is so many things, but most important, it's a commitment to using ingredients that are regionally grown, to honor the people and cultures that grew, foraged, or created classic recipes, and making sure that we honor those traditions by educating our staff with their origins so that we can inspire and encourage young cooks to carry these recipes into the future. There is no way to say what Southern cooking is without looking back to the lives of the people who created it.

What is your favorite food when coming home from a long day at work? KE: Popcorn. Michael Stoltzfus: Egg sandwich.

What do you cook for each other? KE: Michael is great at making delicious "brothy" soups for us to enjoy throughout the week.

What do you always have in your fridge? MS: Eggs, kimchi, leftovers, orange juice, sparkling water, and Champagne.

How about cheese? KE: Our favorites are Harbison, Mt Tam, and Gruyère.

Who does the food shopping in your house? MS: We both shop as needed, but we do a lot of "shopping" from the restaurant. We like to bring home whatever produce looks especially beautiful, fresh eggs, or braised short ribs. And the housemade ciabatta. Meals at home are really centered on lots of rice and eggs with whatever extras we bring home from the restaurant.

What is in your freezer? KE: Almost always Martin's potato rolls, frozen steamed buns for quick sandwiches, and ice, lots of ice. We really don't keep much food in the freezer. It's mostly just ice storage.

Did you make those preserved lemons? KE: Yes, they are my favorite things right now. They are great to keep on hand for marinades, vinaigrettes, or chopped up to mix into salads and rice. They are super easy to make too: just mix together quartered lemons with three parts salt and one part sugar, a fresh bay leaf, crushed pink peppercorns, and a cinnamon stick. Then pack them tightly into a jar and cover with lemon juice and let them sit for at least a week in the fridge.

Charred Vegetables and Pho Rice

This is our "use everything we have in the fridge" recipe. It's also a great way to finish off all the small amounts of leftover broths and sauces, and you can pull it together in a flash once you have your rice cooked.

For the rice:

1½ cups pho broth (or any type of broth or water if you don't have pho)

1 cup long-grain red rice

1 bay leaf

Salt

Pepper

For the vegetables:

2 avocados

Juice of ½ lime

Flake salt and pepper to taste

Olive oil

4 cups assorted vegetables (broccoli, cabbage, bean sprouts, mushrooms, onions)

1 lime, quartered

Garnishes of choice: leftover takeout or peanut sauce, hoisin, purple basil, a fried or poached egg, kimchi, sauerkraut, or any other type of pickled vegetable.

Combine all the ingredients for the rice and follow the cooking instructions on the package or for your rice cooker.

Mash the avocados. Season with the lime juice, salt, and pepper, and set aside.

Preheat a large sauté pan over medium-high heat. Add a thin layer of olive oil once the pan is hot to just coat the bottom of the pan. Sear the vegetables, cooking in batches by individual type, until they are charred on one side. Remove to a plate on the side.

Season with salt and pepper. Divide the rice among four bowls. Serve the vegetables on top of the rice. Garnish with lime wedges and any other garnishes you like.

SERVES 4

PIERRE GAGNAIRE

In France, Pierre Gagnaire has the reputation of a mad culinary genius, risk taker, and poet. He's a creator who often changes his recipes in the middle of the dinner service. His frenetic energy in the kitchen is legendary, although, after nearly five decades in the service of French gastronomy, he seems to have calmed down a bit.

Gagnaire, who comes from a family of restaurateurs, was brought up in Saint-Étienne, just outside of Lyon. His father, also a chef, owned a Michelin-starred restaurant called Le Clos Fleuri, and, as the oldest child, Gagnaire was expected to follow in his footsteps—and so he started his apprenticeship as a pastry chef when he was fourteen, and then spent a summer at Paul Bocuse's restaurant in Lyon.

At eighteen, Gagnaire served his compulsory military service as a chef in the French navy. He loved it: "On a boat everyone is important, even the cooks—the food is very important. This life on the sea gave me the spirit that I have never experienced elsewhere," he recalls.

It might have also given him a taste of adventure. He stayed long enough in Paris to work at the InterContinental hotel and meet his first wife. Then the couple went to the United States, spending two years hitchhiking from Quebec to Acapulco before ending up in San Francisco, where Gagnaire intended to put down roots. His family had other plans, though. After a few months of constant cajoling under the pretext that his father was sick, his mother convinced him to come back to Saint-Étienne to take over the family restaurant in 1976.

That had its challenges, including friction with family members and a near constant state of fatigue from being the head chef. Still, Gagnaire began to attract attention. In 1978, an excellent review from a local critic (he went gaga over a lightly poached Saint Pierre fish with mild peppers) made him realize that cooking could be a way of expressing himself artistically and give meaning to his life, something he had never considered. Before this, he'd seen cooking as a way to escape his family.

To the consternation of his parents, he struck out on his own in 1981. He left the family business with no money and two kids. "It was a painful moment—my parents had invested so much in me. It was a loss, I felt very guilty, but it was clearly my liberation. I had to confront my family, and cooking helped me open a door onto something new," he says now.

In his typical take-no-prisoners style, he put everything of himself into his new restaurant, restoring a 1930s villa at great expense and filling it with contemporary art. Gagnaire took the guests' orders in the dining room, cooked, and then served them, often forgetting the original order in the process. His spontaneous cooking style led to the publication of his first cookbook, *Immediate Cuisine*, and three Michelin stars for his restaurant.

Success came to an end in 1996. Because of a slowing economy and a lack of high-end clientele, Gagnaire was forced to close his restaurant. He was ten million francs in debt, so he sold off all his beloved artwork and his magnificent wine cellar, and contemplated his future.

Luckily, help arrived from friends of friends, and he found a space in Paris at the Hôtel Balzac, whose proprietors were looking to replace their ailing Italian restaurant. The rent was

CURRENT HOMETOWN:
Paris, France

RESTAURANT THAT MADE
HIS NAME: Pierre Gagnaire,
Saint-Étienne, France

SIGNATURE STYLE: French
fusion—combining
unexpected flavors,
textures, and ingredients

BEST KNOWN FOR: Best
Chef in the World by *Le
Chef* magazine (2015), and
his many Michelin-starred
restaurants all over the
world, including Pierre
Gagnaire in Paris

FRIDGE: DeDietrich

affordable, the address perfectly positioned in a neighborhood close to well-to-do locals and tourists, and Gagnaire finally found his artistic home. Within two years, the virtuoso reclaimed his three Michelin stars.

The chef, who lives in the tony 16th arrondissement with writer Sylvie Le Bihan, his wife of fifteen years, and his extended family, spends most of his day at work. "My career takes up ninety percent of my time," he explains. "To be serious, you have to be in your kitchen." For instance, he hardly eats at home, and, for one of the most inventive chefs in the world, his simple kitchen and the contents of his refrigerator are surprisingly normal. There is cheese and charcuterie, cornichon pickles, and a comforting roast chicken. A lonely bottle

of sriracha and some nuoc mam are the only things remotely exotic.

That simplicity is deceptive, though. The chef is a master, able to whip up an inspired lunch in no time. For the meal he made during our interview, he began with sole fillets, which he quickly breaded in the bottom of a loaf pan since he couldn't find a better container. Suddenly, he noticed there were leftover vegetables in the pan, so he stood up and whipped up a creamy side dish with the extra bitter greens. He then rummaged through the fridge for more inspiration until he came upon a bottle of sweet chili sauce—and in went a spoon of that. *Et voilà!* He sat back down with a satisfied smile and a playful look in his eye as he proceeded to explain the contents of his refrigerator.

1. **SWEET CHILI SAUCE, SPRING ROLL SAUCE, SRIRACHA, NUOC MAM**

2. **YOGURT**

3. **BUTTER**

4. **PRESERVED LEMONS—**"They are made at my restaurant. I might use them in a fish recipe, with some of the charcuterie and grilled mushrooms."

5. **SOLE**

6. **LEFTOVER MANGO**

7. **BLACK TRUFFLES**

8. **EGGS—**"My wife buys these at the supermarket. She goes every eight days or so, depending on her mood."

9. **CHERRY TOMATOES**

10. **BABY SPINACH**

11. **APPLESAUCE**

12. **GROUND BEEF PATTIES**

13. **ROAST CHICKEN—**"My wife cooked this the day before for dinner. Cooking bores her."

14. **CARROT SALAD,** from the vegetable market

15. **RADICCHIO**

16. **POTATO AU GRATIN**

17. **PUNTARELLE—**"My wife shops for vegetables at a nearby market that has a great vegetable selection."

18. **RIBEYE STEAK**

19. **APPLESAUCE**

20. **HEINEKEN—**"These belong to my wife's son. If I drink beer I don't drink this one. I prefer better ones like Belgian beers."

21. **CUCUMBER, SPINACH, CARROTS**

Q & A

Your home seems quite busy this morning. Yes, we just moved here. We wanted a smaller place, as some of the kids have moved out. My wife, Sylvie, has three children, who were living with us before, and I have two children and four grandchildren. Today there is my wife's daughter and her son, who is home with a sore throat. When I met my wife, she was living in London. I fell madly in love and I brought us all together under one roof in Paris. We are a reconstituted family that works really well. I travel a lot, so she was able to take care of her kids as she wanted.

Your fridge looks like it serves a lot of people. We also have a garde-manger on the windowsill. We keep cheese in there.

Who cooks at home? Sylvie. She isn't a foodie and I think that's good. I wouldn't be able to be with someone else who was hysterical about food.

When do you cook for the family? I cook when we are on vacation. And my wife is happy about that. I have a house in Belle-Île-en-Mer, and there I cook quite often.

Your Paris kitchen seems quite spartan as well for a three-starred Michelin chef with restaurants all over the world. Our life isn't modest—I won't exaggerate. But we have a modest kitchen. It's not a Bulthaup [a German kitchen manufacturer]; it's not sponsored. It's actually an Ikea kitchen. I am lucky to be independent. I am a free man—it's very important to me.

What do you eat at home? I always eat at the restaurant. I eat dinner by myself after the last service. It's often the moment when I reflect. Then after, I often speak with the cooks or maybe with a client. I travel a lot so when I am in Paris I want to be at the restaurant. Of course I would like to go home, more than before actually. But I am a professional. I enjoy what I do but it's a career.

Any late-night snacks? Never charcuterie. That is the quickest way to put on weight. If I let myself have a little something after dinner, it is most often a cigar.

What do you eat for breakfast? It's very simple—lots of coffee followed by lots of tea.

Pan-fried Sole with Cauliflower and Bitter Greens

This is the kind of dish I like to make while on vacation—I like to cook for my friends and family, but I don't like to be in the kitchen for a long time. Everyone likes sole, especially when we are away for the weekend at Belle-Île. I add in the puntarella because I appreciate bitterness and I go to the market on the island for the fish or I buy directly from a fisherman.

For the vegetables:

⅓ cup olive oil

2 cups small cauliflower florets

3 tablespoons butter

¼ cup water

1 teaspoon black peppercorns

¼ puntarella or chicory, leaves separated and sliced in 2-inch pieces

2 cups sliced radicchio leaves (2-inch pieces)

For the fish:

½ pound sole fillets (4 to 8 fillets, depending on size)

3 eggs

1 cup flour

⅓ cup olive oil

½ lemon

Sea salt

To serve:

3 ounces Camembert

Sea salt

Preheat the oven to 300°F. Heat half of the olive oil in a nonstick skillet over high heat. Add in the cauliflower, and sauté for 1 minute. Add the butter and water and sauté for another 2 minutes, stirring often.

Remove the cauliflower. Add the peppercorns to the pan with the rest of the cooking oil and the remaining juices. Cook over medium-high heat with the puntarella and the radicchio for 2 minutes.

To cook the fish, cut it into 2-inch segments. Beat the eggs in a mixing bowl. Add the fish and coat with the egg. Pour the flour into a separate mixing bowl. Dredge each piece of fish in the flour.

Heat the oil in a large nonstick skillet or saucepan over medium-high heat. Cook the fish pieces for 3 minutes, turning once. Squeeze lemon juice over the fish and sprinkle with sea salt.

To serve, reheat the cauliflower and bitter greens in the oven for 3 minutes if necessary. Divide the Camembert among four plates. Place the fish and vegetables over the cheese and sprinkle lightly with sea salt.

SERVES 4

CARLA HALL

A self-proclaimed elevator talker, Carla Hall is at ease anywhere—whether delivering homemade sandwiches to barbershops, cooking on *Good Morning America*, or explaining why you can never have enough chowchow pickle while peeling shrimp in her kitchen. Raised in Nashville, Hall grew up watching her grandmothers, both excellent cooks, in the kitchen. She still remembers her Nashville grandmother's good-for-you soul food (green bean salad with pickled red onions, tomato pie with garlic bread crust) and the Sunday lunches at the home of her other grandmother, who lived in New York City. "It's funny, but she would never make the corn bread until she saw the whites of our eyes and we were inside the door," she recalls. So cooking was obviously in her genes, but it took Hall a while to realize it.

Instead, her dreams were more focused on the theater than making meals. It wasn't until she was modeling in Paris that she became more interested in the foods of her childhood. One day over brunch with a fellow Tennessean, the conversation turned to mac 'n' cheese and Hall realized that she "had no idea how her mother made her mac 'n' cheese." Then she made her first chicken potpie, a gift to friends who were letting her sleep on their sofa, following a recipe (except for the part where she swapped celery in for leeks) from a cookbook by the Culinary Institute of America. Even though it took her what felt like three days to make, her friends went crazy over it. She had made "something that everybody wanted," Hall remembers. And she understood what she wanted to do next.

She landed in Washington, D.C., without a job, spent two hundred dollars on a mail-delivery truck, and while working from her sister's home, began selling sandwiches and soups to local businesses. Her success gave her the confidence to go further. "There was a certain power I felt when people were waiting to see me arrive at their door with smoked turkey on biscuits, soups, or cakes," she says. Cooking school in D.C. and a catering business followed.

It wasn't until she began cooking on TV that Hall fully embraced her grandmothers' legacy and began putting her own version of soul food on the table. And while she never won those *Top Chef* competitions (though she was voted a fan favorite), she remembered her grandmother's advice at a key moment in the competition: "It's your job to be happy, not rich. If you do that, then everything else will follow."

Hall is deservedly very proud of making soul food—just using seasonal ingredients and making lighter fare than her grandmothers did. "My grandmothers would make large pieces of collard greens cooked in pork and cook them for a long time. I cook them with smoked paprika and olive oil. I cut them into thin ribbons to speed up the cooking time while keeping them tender."

She divides her time between New York City, where she films *Strahan and Sara*, and Washington, D.C. The kitchen of her apartment in New York is on the small side. There's a huge battery of pots and pans, since Hall uses it often for recipe testing. She does get homesick, though. "The things that I make up here are greens, corn bread, and beans. I make the things that make me feel good, those homey things."

CURRENT HOMETOWN:
Washington, D.C.

SHOW THAT MADE HER NAME: *Top Chef*

SIGNATURE STYLE: Cooking with love—and her Southern-influenced food

BEST KNOWN FOR: Cooking on *Strahan and Sara*; her cohosting days on ABC's *The Chew*; and her cookbooks, including *Carla Hall's Soul Food: Everyday and Celebration*

FRIDGE: Liebherr

1. **KOMBUCHA**—"My husband, Matthew, drinks this."

2. **WATER**

3. **BEER**—"We don't drink beer but I do cook with it. I had this one for making a beer bread. I also use beer in my chili recipe."

4. **WILLIAMS FAMILY KITCHEN NONO SAUCE**

5. **MAYONNAISE**—"I picked up the generic brand when I was on a quick run to the store. So I bought Hellman's the next time they had it at the store."

6. **TRUFFLE KETCHUP**—"A swag bag gift."

7. **CHOWCHOW PICKLE**—"I keep the jarred ones for gifting and the others in plastic I will use for events."

8. **APPLE CARDAMOM SHRUB**—"I use this as a mocktail mixer."

9. **DANIEL BREAKER'S HOMEMADE HOT SAUCE**—"Daniel and his son make a batch every year and give them out at their annual Christmas party."

10. **SRIRACHA**

11. **GREEN OLIVES**—"I snack on these and use them in Greek salads. I also like them with a chicken and cooked tomatoes dish."

12. **GREEK YOGURT**

13. **SAUERKRAUT**— "I made it myself once, but generally I buy it."

14. **HOMEMADE TOMATO SAUCE,** from a friend

15. **SHRIMP**

16. **WORCESTERSHIRE SAUCE**

17. **DIJON MUSTARD**

18. **WOLFERMAN'S TRIPLE BERRY PRESERVES**

19. **HOMEMADE SIMPLE SYRUP,** for stirring into tea or cocktails

20. **CHILI SAUCE**

21. **HABANERO TEA SYRUP,** for making sweet tea soda

22. **EDUARDO GARCIA'S MONTANA MEX SWEET AND SPICY HABANERO SAUCE**

23. **ALMOND BUTTER**—"Sometimes you feel like almonds and sometimes you feel like peanuts. I use almond butter in smoothies."

24. **PEANUT BUTTER**—"If I'm going to have nut butter with jam, I then use peanut butter."

25. **MINT**

26. **SWEET POTATOES**— "I'm not here a lot so I keep these in the fridge so they don't go bad."

27. **FETA CHEESE**— "I usually keep this up top, but there was a space issue, so I put it in the veggie drawer."

Q & A

You seem to do a lot of batch cooking.
For our Thanksgiving and Christmas, we always have collard greens and chowchow, which is a pickle relish. I grew up eating chowchow. The first time I had to make chowchow was for an event. So I thought if I'm making it for them, then I'm making it for myself as well. I must have made thirty pounds of chowchow when I only needed ten pounds for the event. So I gave lots of it away. Since it's a pickle, it doesn't go bad—it only gets better.

How do you eat your chowchow?
I eat the chowchow on everything—on eggs for breakfast, hot dogs, tortilla chips, on everything. I like chowchow so much I basically use the other food like a spoon. I love sour. I love pickles.

Something we'd never find in your fridge?
Honestly even if I had canned cranberry sauce in there, if I want it and I'm buying it, it's okay. I can't be food-shamed.

Where do you go food shopping in New York? Trader Joe's around the corner, Fairway, the farmers market on Wednesdays at Union Square. One thing I have never done is order my groceries online. Another thing I don't do here is order delivery. When you are not from that mindset it is strange. I do a little carryout, but I can count the number of times I have done it here. In D.C., I shop at Whole Foods, as it's close to my house, and a daily farmers market. I like shopping there because I can taste. I can get onesies—just one of something.

What is next to your refrigerator? A standing pot rack? I have to do a lot of recipe testing, so I need a variety of pots and pans and I got this pot tree to make it easier.

Now when I'm cooking for myself I use them more often too.

Any clever uses for leftovers? For me if I cook a soup, I will eat it every single day until it's done. I have no problem with leftovers. Sometimes if I make a pureed soup I will later use it for a sauce.

Any New York City food memories?
The first time that I came to New York, I went to see *Bubbling Brown Sugar* and that changed my world—it was after seeing it that I imagined I wanted to be an actress. After the play, my other grandmother, Thelma, made fried chicken at my uncle's apartment in Harlem. Because he didn't have anything in his fridge, she went out and got flour, salt, and pepper. It was the best fried chicken I ever had.

What were your biggest crowd-pleasers during your catering years? I would say curry chicken salad on croissants and also biscuits with smoked turkey. I still make the same biscuits.

Guilty pleasure? Chocolate sauce over ice cream. Although I don't have any right now.

You said you really like oatmeal. Do you prefer steel-cut or quick oats? I don't like quick oats. I love toasted steel-cut oats. I make the oats with half fruit juice and half water. I also love savory oats with spinach and kefir—yes! There is a store here called OatMeals. I eat a lot of oatmeal and I can talk to people for days about oats.

What are your favorite things to snack on while you cook? I usually eat the ends of the vegetables I am cutting. I snack on nuts and grapes too.

Shrimp Wedge Salad

I like this dish, inspired by Laura Prepon, because everything cooks in a packet (which basically poaches the shrimp in its juices), the pan stays clean, it's ready in eight minutes, and your place won't smell like fish. The lemon slices are the secret to not overcooking the shrimp.

For the shrimp:

1 vine-ripened tomato

1 pound extra-large shrimp, peeled and deveined

2 scallions, sliced on the bias

2 garlic cloves, thinly sliced

1 teaspoon lemon zest

1 tablespoon lemon juice

¼ teaspoon salt

⅛ teaspoon chili flakes

2 lemons, sliced

For the salad:

1 head romaine lettuce

2 tablespoons crumbled feta

2 tablespoons chopped Spanish olives

¼ cup minced flat-leaf parsley

1 tablespoon minced chives

For the shrimp: Cut the tomato in half. Squeeze the juice from one half in a bowl. Reserve the other half for the salad. Add the shrimp and all ingredients through chili flakes to the bowl. Mix well.

Prepare a parchment packet: Cut two 15-inch squares of parchment paper and one of aluminum foil. Lay the parchment paper on top of the aluminum foil and then line it with the lemon slices. Place the shrimp mixture on top of the parchment paper. Fold all the ends together firmly to make a tightly sealed packet.

Heat a skillet over medium heat. Place the packet in the skillet. Cook over medium heat for 8 to 10 minutes.

For the salad, slice the romaine vertically into four wedges. Divide the wedges among four plates.

Stir 1 tablespoon of the feta into the shrimp. Spoon the shrimp over the romaine wedges. Sprinkle with Spanish olives, the remaining feta, minced parsley, and chives. Dice the other tomato half and sprinkle over the wedges.

SERVES 4

CURRENT HOMETOWN:
New Orleans, Louisiana

RESTAURANT THAT
MADE HIS NAME:
Turkey and the Wolf,
New Orleans

SIGNATURE STYLE:
Gas-station comfort
food

BEST KNOWN FOR:
Being named a James
Beard Award finalist
(2019); making *Bon
Appétit*'s Ten Best
New Restaurants 2017
list; and his potato
chip layer sandwiches

FRIDGE: Frigidaire

MASON HEREFORD

Hailing from White Hall, Virginia (population 700), the heavily tattooed, mustachioed chef Mason Hereford looks more like an overgrown stoner cartoon character than a chef who, in the space of a few years, has been revolutionizing American casual fine dining. It's true that his childhood palate was highly informed by the processed food that could be had on the shelves of the country stores between his house and school. But his parents also thought he was a sophisticated eater, since he ate grown-up and spicy foods whenever he could.

This love of gas station and convenience store food continued into his teens, culminating in his culinary holy grail: a sandwich called the Jefferson from the Market, a food shop at an Exxon gas station in Charlottesville, Virginia—an under-seven-dollar dream of a meal made with turkey, sharp cheddar, cranberry relish, and herb mayo on French bread. He ate this sandwich at least twice a week for eleven years and remembered it always.

After college, Mason followed a friend to New Orleans, first working in a Mardi Gras–themed sports bar called Fat Harry's, where he alternated nights working the door and flipping burgers, and then on to Coquette, the well-known local fine dining establishment owned by Kristen Essig and Michael Stoltzfus (see page 80). When he heard they were hiring, he went in and asked for a *stage* in the kitchen. "I didn't know much when I started," he recalls. He worked his way up to head chef in a few years, and more importantly, got the taste for "higher end stuff," and creative cooking.

"Other than all the cooking skills I developed at Coquette, the few years of creative freedom on the menu was my biggest takeaway. It's an incredible experience to get to learn guests' reactions to your food before you take the plunge into opening your own restaurant," he explains. "That got me ready to open my spot after helping some buddies open their own places around the city."

Turkey and the Wolf is inspired as much by other cutting-edge sandwich shops like Charleston's Butcher & Bee, as by the dearth of any non–po' boy sandwich shops in town. Served on vintage McDonald's plates bought by his mom on eBay, his dishes include a version of the above-mentioned Jefferson ("We make ours with ham and arugula rather than turkey and romaine, and I still eat it at least once a week," Hereford remarks) and fried bologna slathered with hot English mustard, "shrettuce" (what he calls shredded lettuce), mayo, and American cheese on white bread. Patrons sometimes wait hours to discover his fresh take on America's favorite standby.

For Hereford, the team that works the kitchen is as important as what they make: "If you compare the pride I feel from attracting and keeping wonderful people to work at Turkey and the Wolf, and the big write-ups we've gotten, the write-ups ain't shit. Yeah, they have been incredibly helpful in sustaining a profitable business, which we needed, but it's the group of people that I work with that would have made it happen either way. It's all about a delicious good time, fun, and friendships."

1. **SLICED BOLOGNA**—"This is the best size for the sandwich. Thicker would be too much bologna flavor and thinner would be not enough."

2. **SAUERKRAUT**—"I put it on potatoes or eat it out of the can with a fork."

3. **SPICY OLIVE MIX**—"I often add these to sandwiches. I find cream cheese to be a good vehicle. I've messed around with tomato cream cheese, white truffle cream cheese, chimichurri cream cheese, Chicago hot dog garnish cream cheese, etc."

4. **SPICY PICKLED CHERRY PEPPERS**

5. **CRUNCHY DILL PICKLES**

6. **DUKE'S MAYONNAISE**—"Duke's tastes the best. I've never made a mayo I like more than Duke's. Also, it comes from Virginia and so do I."

7. **AMERICAN CHEESE SLICES**

8. **BOLOGNA**

9. **ORANGES**

10. **EGGS**

11. **SPAM**—"I eat Spam by searing it off in a pan on both sides and throwing it on a breakfast sandwich. Often on a biscuit. It's fast and delicious and doesn't get enough love."

12. **CHORIZO**

13. **HANDMADE TORTILLAS**—"Made at work by our kitchen mom, Migdalia Pabon. I keep them in a bowl with a towel so they don't dry out."

14. **LOCAL KUMQUATS**—"I will throw them in a salad. But you can candy them into a jam or marmalade or throw them in a chutney and they're great."

15. **LABNEH**—"I dress it up with salt, good olive oil, and lemon and we dip bread in it."

16. **BANANA PEPPERS**

17. **HAM AND CHEDDAR LUNCHABLES**—"Because I never grew up and I like shit from the nineties, and this is my favorite kind."

18. **LEFTOVER SAUCES** from taco night

19. **COLLARD GREENS**

20. **JALAPEÑOS,** the thing he eats the most of

21. **A GIANT VIRGINIA HAM**—"My mom ships one down to New Orleans once a year. To cook it you soak it in water overnight and roast it in the oven in a pan with white beans covered in shallow water."

22. **BLUE KOOL-AID**—"Although I admit, purple is my favorite flavor. I drink it in cocktails or with my Lunchables."

23. **JIMMY DEAN SAUSAGE**

24. **SMIRNOFF ICE**—"If you mix Smirnoff with Mountain Dew it's very refreshing and delightfully trashy."

25. **TOPO CHICO**—"We have it at the restaurant so I just steal it since we like fizzy water."

Q & A

Describe your cooking style. Not without humor. Bigger on flavor than technique. Playful. Use the best ingredients you can, but don't be afraid to use the corner store as your pantry. People often describe my cooking as nostalgic, lemony, spicy.

Would you consider your cooking high-end stoner food? Even scientific research has shown that THC can make you smell and taste food more acutely. What's really interesting for me though is to try to cook food that tastes as good as it would if you were stoned, even when you're not or don't smoke weed: big and aggressive flavor combinations, lots of textures, lots of herbs, borderline too much of some ingredients—that kind of stuff.

What do you like to eat when you come home from a long day at work? I love dips: queso, guacamole, pimento cheese, hummus, baba ghanoush, labneh, peanut butter, salsa macha, whatever. I dig cheese and pickles—as stolen directly from the eating habits of my girlfriend, Lauren Agudo. I love anything Lauren makes. Tacos.

Do you cook much at home? Honestly, Lauren does 99 percent of the cooking at home. I mean, I could do Thanksgiving for like fifty people every year. Thanksgiving stuff is my favorite to cook. Gravy, mashed potatoes, stuffing, sweet potatoes, and collard greens. Soul food type of stuff. I make lobster pasta and a seafood feast on Christmas Day for Lauren and my old man. I like making avocado tacos and big-ass salads. Spicy stuff like pozole [a traditional Mexican hominy stew] and dope black beans. But it gets serious mostly on holidays.

What do you always have in your fridge? Pickles, cheese, wine, dips, hot sauce, Duke's mayo, leftovers, herbs, and jalapeños.

What would we never find in your fridge? Miracle Whip. It's fucking gross. And Hunt's ketchup as well. I only have Heinz. Also, Diet Coke, which is disgusting, but my mom drinks it—it's a horrible habit.

Do you really love mall food-court Chinese? What is your favorite junk food? Hell yeah! When I first moved to New Orleans I was heading outside of town to hit the mall just for the Chinese food. I love that shit! Best part of flying too. I also like beef jerky. Hot Cheetos and hot Funyuns. Purple Doritos. Pringles—barbecue and salt and vinegar. Those little pretzels with the peanut butter inside. Ritz crackers. Club crackers. Both need stuff to put on top. Can you tell I like junk food? I love Cheez-Its on top of Blue Bell Cookies 'n Cream ice cream.

Ice cream with Cheez-Its on top?! Yes! My mom used to eat ice cream with peanuts on top. I inherited that love, and found that the best peanuts to put on top were the saltiest: Planters dry roasted peanuts. From there, with a little help from my friends, drugs, and alcohol, I tried other snack foods on my ice cream. Now, I rarely eat ice cream at home without putting Cheez-Its on top. And I eat a lot of ice cream.

You do love those Lunchables, don't you? They're great. It's a perfect-size snack that is nostalgic and delightfully lacking in quality. It's also the most substantial snack you can get at certain late-night gas stations. I love to buy semi-prepared foods and doctor them up.

What's a typical 3:00 a.m. snack? Freezer dumplings from the Asian grocer, and probably jalapeños at that hour. Or popcorn with any kind of spice blend.

Collard Greens and Grits with Peanut Salsa

I love peanut salsa. This dish is basically inspired by my love for Daniela Soto-Innes's salsa macha, which she serves at Cosme.

For the collard greens:

4 tablespoons unsalted butter

6 to 8 garlic cloves, finely chopped

¼ cup red wine vinegar

¼ cup rice wine vinegar

⅓ cup sugar

2 teaspoons Zatarain's Creole Seasoning

1 teaspoon kosher salt, plus more to taste

1 teaspoon freshly ground black pepper

2 teaspoons Korean chili flakes

4 bunches collard greens, stems removed and leaves chopped (10 cups chopped)

½ cup water

For the grits:

1 cup milk

1 cup water

1 teaspoon salt, plus more to taste

½ cup good stone-ground grits

2 tablespoons unsalted butter

⅓ cup cream cheese

1½ teaspoons Tabasco Green Pepper Sauce

½ teaspoon freshly ground black pepper

2½ tablespoons sour cream

For the peanut salsa:

1 cup grapeseed or other neutral oil

5 cloves garlic, peeled

8 or 9 dry pasilla peppers, seeds and stems removed

12 arbol chilies, seeds and stems removed

2 packed cups cilantro, stems included

1 cup natural chunky peanut butter (creamy works, but I prefer the texture of crunchy here)

2 teaspoons kosher salt

For the presentation:

½ cup roasted and salted peanuts, chopped

¼ white onion, thinly sliced

1 bunch cilantro, chopped

1 lime, cut into wedges

To cook the greens, heat and melt the butter in a large, heavy-bottomed pot over medium heat. Add and cook the minced garlic until fragrant and cooked through.

Add the remaining ingredients except the collards and water. Cook for 10 minutes, allowing the flavors to develop.

Now add the collard greens and water. Depending on the size of your cooking pot, you may need do this in batches, waiting a few minutes for the collard greens to begin to break down before adding more. Cover and cook over low to medium heat for 2½ to 3 hours.

Cool the collard greens in their potlikker, which should be quite reduced and just coating the greens. Set aside.

For the grits: Bring the milk and water and 1 teaspoon of salt to a boil in a medium pot. Whisk in the grits, stirring constantly until they simmer, about 2 minutes. Simmer over low heat for 30 to 40 minutes. Add all the remaining ingredients. Whisk everything together, making sure the butter and cream cheese are fully incorporated.

To make the peanut salsa: Heat the grapeseed oil in a small heavy-bottomed pot. Fry the garlic at medium-high heat for about 5 minutes, until golden brown. Using a slotted spoon, remove the garlic and set aside.

Cook the pasilla chilies in the hot oil (about 300°F). Using tongs, submerge each chili for 5 to 10 seconds in the hot oil. Remove it once the chili has darkened in color and has a bubbly texture. (Be careful not to burn the chilies—you'll know by the smell and overly dark color—which will make the salsa taste bitter.) Fry the arbol chilies in the same fashion. Let the oil cool down.

Pulse the two chilies, the cooking oil, and the garlic in a food processor for 20 seconds. Add the cilantro, natural peanut butter, and salt, and pulse again for 20 seconds.

To serve, divide the grits and collard greens among four bowls. Garnish with peanut salsa, roasted peanuts, sliced onion, cilantro, and a generous squeeze of lime.

SERVES 4

Love Letter to a Muffuletta Sandwich

I love white bread. Always have. My mom used to serve it on a plate covered in pulled turkey and gravy. These days I've grown quite fond of thick buttery white bread toast. Putting olives, provolone, and cold cuts on a sandwich was inspired by the muffuletta, a famous New Orleans sandwich— my favorite can be found at Central Grocery & Deli on Decatur Street. I eat there a few times a year and this is the only thing I ever order. Adding fun stuff to cream cheese is a move we do a lot at the restaurant. The cream cheese is the coolest part of the sandwich—and this recipe makes more than you need.

For the cream cheese:

1 cup spicy olives, pitted

2/3 cup spicy pickled cherry peppers from a jar, stems removed

2/3 cup capers

1 pound cream cheese

2/3 cup crumbled feta

Kosher salt to taste

For the sandwich:

½ cup butter, room temperature

8 thick slices white bread

4 tablespoons Duke's Mayo

8 thin slices mortadella

8 slices provolone cheese

20 thin slices soppressata

2 cups arugula

½ red onion, thinly sliced

½ cup pickled banana peppers

For the cream cheese: In a food processor, pulse the spicy olives, cherry peppers, and capers until everything is finely chopped, but not pureed. Transfer the ingredients to a fine-mesh strainer and push them until you squeeze out any excess liquid.

Pulse the cream cheese, feta, and a pinch of salt until smooth, about 1 minute. Add the rest of the ingredients back into the food processor with the feta cream cheese and pulse until fully incorporated. Muffuletta cream cheese can be made up to 2 weeks ahead of time and stored in the refrigerator. Leave out at room temperature around 30 minutes before using so it spreads more easily on sandwiches and bagels.

For the sandwiches: Heat a nonstick or seasoned cast-iron pan over medium heat. Spread butter on both sides of the white bread slices. Toast them in the pan until golden brown on both sides. Set aside for 1 minute so they're firm.

Spread the mayonnaise evenly across the four bottom slices of bread. Add the mortadella, provolone, and soppressata slices, divided equally, onto the bottom bread slices. Pile on the arugula, red onions, and pickled banana peppers. Spread a liberal layer of muffuletta cream cheese on the top slices of bread and stack the slices on tops of the rest of the sandwiches. Don't be afraid to go wild—the cream cheese is the key ingredient! Cut the sandwiches in half and serve.

MAKES 4 SANDWICHES

JORDAN KAHN

Although Jordan Kahn may be one of the least understood chefs in America, there is no doubt that he is one of the most creative—a result perhaps of his grandmother's influence. Originally from Savannah, Georgia, Kahn began helping his Cuban grandmother when he was five years old, spending hours watching her cook. "*Ropa vieja*, black beans, *platanos maduros*, and yucca are the flavors of my childhood. It's like she was grooming me," he recalls. "Although I think that my grandmother, like most Latin grandmothers, had a cultural responsibility to make sure the children are plump and chubby!"

When he was thirteen, his mother bought him Thomas Keller's *The French Laundry Cookbook*, and he read it cover to cover before the night was over. "I didn't quite know what I was reading exactly, nor that it would change the course of my life forever," he recalls. He took the book everywhere with him, and had soon memorized all of the recipes, anxiously dreaming of the day that he could start his cooking career.

Three years later he graduated high school early to attend Johnson & Wales University in Charleston, South Carolina, finishing the two-year course in just eight months. Shortly afterward he wrote a lengthy letter to Chef Keller begging for a job. Keller responded by offering a three-month apprenticeship at the French Laundry restaurant near Napa, California. "I was very, very lucky," Kahn says. "Someone, out of nowhere, gave me the chance to touch the sky." After three months, Kahn stayed on, learning to be attentive to little details from his newly found mentor, pastry chef Sebastien

Rouxel, and gaining enough confidence and skill to eventually open Keller's new venture, Per Se, in New York City as a pastry chef de partie.

He followed that job with several more before becoming head pastry chef at Varietal. Although the place closed some months later, diners and critics alike were impressed with Kahn's unique desserts—unlikely items such as mushroom caramels and eggplant puree tarts with fish sauce and Thai chilies. "I was exploring various tastes and experimenting with boundaries," he says now.

Kahn moved to Los Angeles, where he eventually opened Red Medicine, inspired by late-night visits to Chinatown with colleagues. Red Medicine was a game changer, offering delicate fusiony Nordic/Vietnamese cuisine paired with high-ticket Alsatian wines and an ear-splitting rock soundtrack. To Kahn, the pairing was obvious: "Our ingredients were from California, our abundant use of herbs was inspired by Vietnamese cooking, and our aesthetic was inspired by the new Nordic cuisine movement." He immediately got rave reviews for dishes such as Japanese-style heirloom rice and spot prawns cooked tableside on hot stones. A couple years later, after the rent became too high, Kahn opened Destroyer, a futuristic-looking breakfast and lunch spot that serves comfort food with a twist—beef tartare with grains, say, or smoked egg cream and germinated radish.

But it's his latest restaurant, just across the street from Destroyer, that's attracting buzz now. Kahn calls Vespertine "the most important thing I will ever do, with the exception of perhaps children. It is what I will be remembered for."

CURRENT HOMETOWN:
Los Angeles, California

RESTAURANT THAT
MADE HIS NAME: Red
Medicine, Los Angeles

SIGNATURE STYLE:
Food as art

BEST KNOWN FOR:
Vespertine; his job at
French Laundry at age
seventeen; and his
rock star haircut

FRIDGE: Frigidaire

Housed inside an undulating corrugated metal tower known as the Waffle, the restaurant offers a degustation menu that disregards current fads. "At Vespertine everything is connected and is part of the whole," says Kahn. Specially made black clay pots influence the presentation of his cuisine; customers are encouraged to lift leaves or search the bottom of the bowl for trout roe, white asparagus, or bougainvillea and other flowers that come from his garden.

But while his food at Vespertine may be complex, eating at home is simpler, and his kitchen reflects that. His countertops are pristinely barren; the walls are white, and his refrigerator is almost empty. Under the counter is a small collection of cookbooks, with a well-worn copy of *The French Laundry Cookbook* placed in a prominent position.

"I usually get home after work at about four a.m., so I eat an avocado with some salted yogurt or nuts, or ice cream," says Kahn. Meals for friends also tend to be vegetarian. "Everything depends on the occasion, but cooking vegetables over a fire at my friend's farm with lots of herbs, citrus, and fruit from the trees with large amounts of butter and olive oil is amazing."

Kahn, ever reflective, remains philosophical about what he has achieved thus far: "Everything is the result of those who have had the greatest impact on my life: not only chefs but artists, musicians, painters, filmmakers, and photographers. I am the individual result of the art that has inspired me. Being thoughtful in your choices and rigorous in your methods can have a lasting impact on those around you, leaving beautiful memories."

1. **CBW MUNICH PURE MALT EXTRACT**—"What is neat about this is that it's a little sweet. I will put it on top of ice cream or put it in a banana smoothie. It doesn't need to be refrigerated but the cold makes it easy to scoop."

2. **CREAM CHEESE**

3. **BURNED ONIONS**—"I use them for making a savory version of the Icelandic rye bread porridge."

4. **MARIONBERRY JAM**

5. **BROWN BUTTER**

6. **BARREL-AGED SOY SAUCE**

7. **LA CROIX**—"I like most of the flavors except for the coconut. I hate that one."

8. **ICELANDIC RYE BREAD**—"I always have this in my fridge. One slice will allow me to go an entire day without eating anything else."

9. **RED BOAT FISH SAUCE**

10. **ZINFANDEL VINEGAR**

11. **BEER,** for rye bread porridge (see page 113)

12. **SESAME OIL**

13. **SHIRO DASHI**

Q & A

What do you always have in your fridge? I always have heirloom grits in my freezer. I'm originally from the South and grits are hard to find here on the West Coast, so I always buy large amounts when I can, and vacuum-seal them in small quantities.

What would we never find in your refrigerator? Alcohol, as I don't drink. On rare occasions, though, I do use alcohol for cooking. I also don't like frozen vegetables and microwavable "meals"—only ice cream.

What foods do you hate? Or never eat? I hate beef liver. I hate cooked salmon. I don't eat raw garlic. After eating it, your body acts as a human reed diffuser, and you smell like garlic for days sometimes.

What is your favorite junk food? I have an unhealthy relationship with candy of all forms.

Who does the food shopping in your house? I do, and it usually consists of many flavors of La Croix sparkling water, ice cream, and yogurt. I usually shop at three a.m. or later, so it is usually a twenty-four-hour grocery store.

What is in your freezer? Ice cream, fruit pops, Mexican-style coconut pops called *paletas*—I have a mild addiction to sugar and heirloom grits.

Your favorite ice cream flavor? I don't discriminate much with things that have sugar. My most recent discovery is Ben & Jerry's Oat of This Swirled. It's essentially oatmeal cookie ice cream but with no raisins.

Tell us about something really special you have on hand. I have some Zinfandel vinegar made by my good friend Stefan Hagopian. He is a biodynamic farmer/doctor of osteopathic medicine, and his produce plays a big part in Vespertine. The vinegar is made from his 2016 harvest, and is the most incredible wine vinegar I've ever tasted.

How did you discover malt? Why do you like to use it? I happened to find malt while I was shopping for sorbets and ganaches. When my pastry supplier is out of stock and I need something on the fly, I go to the brew supply store—it's a good source for things like dextrose, glucose, sorbitol, et cetera. Malt is essentially an inverted sugar like glucose, but rather than being neutral, it carries the flavor of the malted barley. It is a type of sugar with very little sweetness, making it ideal for adding to savory dishes.

You don't seem to have much fresh produce in your fridge—why is that? I live right near Vespertine so it's easier for me to get produce from our walk-in refrigerator.

Icelandic Rye Bread

This Icelandic rye bread has a bit of a personal story to it. The year before I opened Destroyer, I took a trip to Iceland. I arrived at the airport at six a.m., got the rental car, and was in Reykjavík an hour later. The entire city was still asleep. I was pretty tired from the flight, so I decided to pull over on the side of a random street and take a nap in the car. About an hour later, I was woken up by some noises outside. There was a line forming on the sidewalk next to the car. It turns out I'd accidentally parked in front of the best bakery in Iceland, Brauð & Co. I went in and ordered one of everything. I noticed the super-dense seeded rye breads that are typically some of my favorite things to eat in Scandinavia, so I ordered a few loaves to sustain me for the entire week. The owner/head baker has a friend who lives in Los Angeles and he gave her a bottle of natural starter from his rye doughs to bring to me as a gift. The rye starter that he gave to us is still the same starter that we use in our Icelandic rye today—just be aware that the starter takes about two weeks to ferment.

---

1 cup plus 3 tablespoons warm water

3 cups rye starter (recipe follows)

3¼ cups rye flour

1 rye kit (recipe follows)

3 tablespoons salt

For the rye starter:

2 cups rye flour

2 cups warm water

For the rye kit:

4 cups rye berries

1 cup sunflower seeds

¼ cup pumpkin seeds

⅓ cup dark-roasted malt powder

5 cups water

For the rye starter: Mix the rye flour and water together and let sit at room temperature for 7 to 10 days until you notice it bubbling and smell a sour, lactic acid scent. Throw away 80 percent of the mixture and replace it with the same amount, equal parts water and rye flour. Repeat this process for at least 5 days in a row until the starter is ready to be used.

For the rye kit: Soak all the ingredients in the water for 24 hours.

For the bread: Mix together the water and the starter until dissolved. Mix in the flour and work with your hands until it is fully incorporated. Add the rye kit with all its liquid. Add the salt and mix again by hand.

Portion the dough into three loaf pans that have been sprayed with cooking oil. Cover with plastic wrap and leave overnight in the fridge.

Remove from the fridge and let the bread proof for 2 hours.

Make a vertical incision along the top of each loaf with a wet knife. Bake at 400°F for 45 minutes. Reduce the heat to 300°F and bake for another 15 minutes. Check for doneness—the internal temperature should reach 205°F.

MAKES 3 LOAVES

Rye Bread Porridge with Hazelnuts and Herbs

We were making some adjustments to the rye bread recipe at Destroyer, so I had a half loaf in my fridge. One night after getting home, I wanted something warm and comforting but had only goat butter, rye bread, and some marionberry jam in my fridge. I crumbled the rye bread into a pot with some foaming brown butter and cooked it for a few minutes until it became toasted. Then I added some water, milk, and a beer I had in my cupboard leftover from a dinner party I had years ago, and cooked it down like a risotto. I finished it with goat butter and some dried thyme. I ate it with a spoonful of the marionberry jam and a dollop of goat butter on top. It was better than any porridge I've ever had because of the complexity of the bread's flavor.

1/3 cup hazelnuts

4 tablespoons unsalted butter

Icelandic rye bread, torn into small pieces (2 cups) (see recipe on page 111)

1 cup beer

2 cups organic whole milk

1 teaspoon sea salt

1 tablespoon cream cheese, at room temperature

2 tablespoons brown butter (see Note)

2 tablespoons fresh herbs

Preheat the oven to 350°F. Place the hazelnuts on an oven pan. Toast them for 6 minutes. Let cool and then chop coarsely.

Melt half of the unsalted butter in a large wide pot over medium heat until foamy and light brown. Add the bread and stir for 3 to 4 minutes over low heat until toasted. Add the beer and stir until incorporated. Add the milk and stir until incorporated.

Simmer over low heat, stirring often, until the porridge is creamy and loose but not wet, like the consistency of risotto. Add the salt, then vigorously stir in the remaining unsalted butter, cream cheese, and brown butter.

Divide the porridge among four bowls and serve warm with the hazelnuts and fresh herbs, or whatever sweet or savory topping you choose, such as marmalade, syrup, bacon, a fried egg, aged cheese, roasted mushrooms, or grilled onions.

SERVES 4

Note: To make brown butter, place 1/2 pound of unsalted butter in a medium pot over medium heat. Once the butter is completely melted and begins to boil, use a whisk to stir it constantly. After several minutes, the liquid evaporates, and the remaining butterfat toasts and becomes fragrant. When the butter begins to foam and increase in volume, take it off the stove and allow it to cool to room temperature.

CURRENT HOMETOWN:
Edinburgh, Scotland

RESTAURANT THAT MADE HIS NAME: The Kitchin, Edinburgh

SIGNATURE STYLE: Scottish products with French technique

BEST KNOWN FOR: The Michelin star (for The Kitchin) he got at age twenty-nine; TV appearances on the BBC's *MasterChef*; his cookbook *From Nature to Plate*

FRIDGE: Electrolux

TOM KITCHIN

Tom Kitchin started his kitchen career at the bottom, cleaning pots at a local pub near where he grew up in the Loch Leven countryside. But he's been climbing the ladder ever since then, working with legendary chefs in the U.K. and France. Kitchin credits Pierre Koffmann in London with teaching him the foundations of cooking—using seasonal produce and every part of an animal or fish. He also learned the art of butchering and filleting, skills that he is now passionate about passing on to the chefs who work for him.

Although trained in classic French cuisine at Guy Savoy in Paris and Alain Ducasse in Monte Carlo, Kitchin has always been guided by Scottish tastes, one reason he chose to return to Edinburgh, where he was born, to start his own restaurant, The Kitchin. "I am fanatical about working with the seasons and only use the best of Scotland's produce," he says, which these days includes sea kale and root vegetables.

That's why cullen skink—the traditional Scottish chowder of smoked haddock, potatoes, and leek that Kitchin first tasted at age twelve and got hooked on—is on the menu at The Scran and Scallie, the pub he owns that is close to his family home, and where he often drops by on weekends with his sons for lunch and a beer.

And while Kitchin still cooks at his namesake restaurant, he stops by his other four restaurants around Edinburgh daily. When he comes home late or has been traveling for work, his favorite meal is a smoked salmon lasagna, made by his wife, Michaela, who is also his business partner and mother of their four sons. The two created Kitchin's first restaurant together.

His kitchen at home is a gorgeous open space with Nordic-inspired pastel hues and light-colored wood. "It was a poky little area, but we changed it five years ago to connect the dining and kitchen area. Michaela, my wife, is Swedish so she likes the open living," explains Kitchin. There's also a wall of back-to-back serious-chef appliances—steam oven, wine fridge, a full-size freezer, and, of course, the refrigerator.

On its shelves are testaments to the couple's backgrounds: Swedish fish pastes and herrings—lots of them—share space with local meats and Marmite. Even though Kitchin is steadfastly locavore, he does admit, with a chuckle, that some of his shelves hold Swedish specialty goods from Ikea. Plus, he loves the Swedish Christmas traditions and songs followed by schnapps, "although, after all these years I still don't know all the words to the songs in Swedish!" he says.

1. **LOCAL EGGS**—"These are from a program in which kids buy eggs from farmers and then they sell them door to door."

2. **HERRING IN HONEY MUSTARD SAUCE**

3. **SWEDISH JAM**

4. **HP SAUCE,** for Sunday breakfast bacon sandwiches

5. **MARMITE**—"I generally eat it on toast."

6. **SOFT GOAT CHEESE AND BRITISH STILTON**—"The fridge changes as we get towards the weekend, when I'm off. These cheeses are what we might eat on a Sunday night if we are a bit peckish."

7. **CHAMPAGNE**—"If we have a special occasion coming up, we'll always make sure we have one chilled and ready!"

8. **WHITE WINE**

9. **OLIVES**

10. **CAPERS**—"I like to add capers to a dish at the last moment or make caper butter."

11. **WILD HALIBUT**—"I vacuum-pack these at the restaurant and bring them home. I always have takeaway stuff from the restaurant."

12. **SMOKED WILD SALMON**

13. **ANCHOVIES**—"This is for a dish the Swedes like to do. It's like a French potato gratin, but with chopped anchovies added in. It's a very December kind of dish."

14. **COLMAN'S ENGLISH MUSTARD**—"It's a lot stronger than a Dijon. It's great added to a béchamel or on a ham and cheese."

15. **PRESERVED LEMONS**—"I add the skin to pasta or fish."

16. **CHORIZO**—"A great ingredient for a midweek meal. I love to mix it with fish or artichokes."

17. **HOMEMADE SAUSAGES,** from his pub

1. **SWEDISH FISH PASTES**

2. **SUPERGLUE**

3. **KETCHUP FOR BARBECUES**

4. **TIN OF SNUS**—"That's Swedish tobacco and it's like the equivalent of a cheeky cigarette."

5. **OYSTERS**—"A particular favorite of mine is oysters with steamed sea bass and leeks. It's a great dish to make for a romantic meal."

18. **ARTICHOKES**

19. **LOCAL HONEY**

20. **LOCAL YOGURT**—"We like to have it in the morning, sometimes with cereal or added to porridge. Porridge is a good start to the day even if it sometimes involves a bit of negotiating with the kids."

Q & A

What do you cook for your family?
We have four boys—Kasper, Axel, Lachlan, and Logan. Fortunately, they eat mostly everything. There are a few moans here and there but that's just kids for you! Five nights a week, I'm working at The Kitchin so Michaela cooks. The two nights I'm not in the kitchen, I love to cook, and more often than not, it's a nice Sunday roast, either chicken or beef—the kids love this!

Why Sunday? Sunday is a family day and the Sunday roast works with our schedule. The boys have football matches at nine and ten, and then they have little things to do here and there. Sometimes we go to the pub we own not far from here. We will go have lunch and a beer and meet another family. So come five p.m. we will come back here for the big meal.

So is that Sunday's roast chicken in your fridge? Yes, it's from St. Brides. It's hard in the U.K. to get a proper chicken. It's important that the kids see the head, its whole format, where it comes from. The birds from St. Brides are a cut above the rest—they're free to roam around all day in the grass at the family-run farm, and are raised for a lot longer than the average bird, which is reflected in the fantastic flavor.

Where do you do your food shopping?
One of my favorite things to do at the weekend is to go to the farmers market in Stockbridge with Michaela and our boys. It offers fantastic fresh produce from around here. We like to work our way around the market and get some great bread, delicious cheese, and cured meats from Peelham Farm, a little family-run farm located close to the Berwickshire coast. Welch Fishmongers, in the Newhaven area of the city, is also a personal favorite if you're looking for really great fresh seafood.

Do you like most Swedish food? I like all Swedish food aside from this stuff, Kalles. I call it cat food.

Does your wife like Marmite? Marmite, it's love or hate. I'm on the love side and my wife is on the strawberry jam side. My wife has been converted to brown sauce and that's a big thing. Something changed with children and pregnancies. Now she is partial to a bacon sandwich now and again.

What foods would you never eat? I don't particularly hate any food—I'm up for trying anything as long as it's cooked properly—however, I do try to steer away from processed foods.

Do you have any favorite kitchen utensils? My favorite kitchen utensil has to be the Microplane. I first started to use them when I was working for Alain Ducasse in Monte Carlo. That would have been about 2003. I think maybe I'd seen them before, but I'd never seen the range you could have—all the different sizes. The restaurant was right on the border of Italy, and they used to do a lot of risottos. As a young chef, you got all the great jobs. I remember Microplaning blocks and blocks of Parmesan fresh every day for risotto. A really tedious job but the Microplane made it a lot easier!

What is the story with the superglue in your fridge? I don't know why but we always keep it here—maybe it's to keep it out of the way from the twins. They get into quite a lot of mischief.

What do you use the HP Sauce for? For our Sunday breakfast. It's the only day we do a cooked breakfast, although we do have porridge during the week.

Is your freezer well organized? We had things labeled—I don't know if anyone does that anymore. It has an eclectic mix of everything from special vacuum-packed chicken jus from the restaurant, to pizzas, ice cream, and wild berries, which we use for crumbles—and, of course, backup bread!

Pot-Roasted Sunday Chicken

Who doesn't like a roast chicken? This chicken recipe is always a safe bet when entertaining; absolutely everyone who tries it asks me to share the recipe with them afterwards. "Pot-roasted" just means you cook everything together in one pot, which maximizes all those lovely flavors. The secret is to keep a good eye on everything, and insert a small knife into the vegetables periodically to test when they are all cooked through because they cook at different times. I love how the vegetables take on the lovely chicken and garlic flavors.

---

1 free-range chicken, about 1½ pounds

Olive oil

Sea salt

Black pepper, freshly cracked

¼ pound pancetta or bacon, in one piece

16 to 20 small new potatoes, scrubbed

6 small red onions or shallots, peeled but whole

4 carrots, peeled

4 thyme sprigs

3 bay leaves

Cloves from 2 heads garlic, peeled and halved

¼ cup brandy

¼ cup dry vermouth

1¼ cups chicken stock

1 tablespoon butter

Preheat the oven to 400°F.

Place the chicken on a chopping board and use a small sharp knife to remove the wishbone, then tie the legs together with kitchen string for even cooking. Smear the chicken all over with olive oil and season well with salt and pepper.

Heat a cast-iron pot or roasting pan over medium-high heat, then add a splash of oil. When it is hot, add the pancetta and color on both sides—this gives extra flavor. Remove the pancetta and set aside.

Add the chicken to the pot and brown on all sides, turning it over with a roasting fork. Remove it from the pot and set aside.

Turn the heat down to medium. Add the new potatoes, red onions, carrots, thyme, bay leaves, and garlic. Return the pancetta to the pot. Season well with salt and pepper, then stir everything together. Use a wooden spoon or spatula to push the vegetables to the sides of the pot, and return the chicken in the center.

Put the lid on the pot or cover with foil and place it in the oven for 60 minutes. The vegetables and garlic might be tender before the chicken is cooked, depending on their size. Check the vegetables after 15 minutes—the onions will probably be done first. To check, slide the tip of a small knife into the vegetables and if there's no resistance, they're ready. Baste the chicken with all the lovely juices. As each vegetable is done, remove it and wrap it in foil to keep hot until you're ready to serve.

When the chicken is cooked through (the juices run clear when you pierce a thigh), remove it and any remaining vegetables from the pot and set aside in a bowl (to collect the juices) for 5 minutes, covered with foil. Add in the previously removed vegetables.

Pour the collected cooking juices back into the pot along with the brandy and vermouth. Stir to deglaze the pot and boil until the liquid reduces by half. Add the chicken stock and continue boiling until it reduces by one third. Whisk in the butter and adjust the seasoning with salt and pepper.

Serve with the chicken and vegetables straight from the bowl.

SERVES 4

JESSICA KOSLOW

Raised on sprouts and healthy fare from California farmers markets, Jessica Koslow would seem an unlikely candidate for a career in the sweet side of the food business. But Koslow had a yen for sugar from a young age and couldn't get enough of the Rice Krispies treats she and her dad would make together—much to the chagrin of her health-conscious mom. So maybe it's no surprise that she's ended up helming a restaurant known for its luscious and unusual jams.

While she was a pastry chef in Atlanta, Georgia, making preserves was part of her everyday routine. When she moved back home to Los Angeles, she remembered thinking how much produce was taken for granted. "I was determined to take what I had learned and apply it to the farmers market," she says.

In 2011, Koslow opened Sqirl as a preserves company, using unsold berries from the farmers market that she jarred and squirreled away. The exotic jams, made from local fruits and herbs, with such evocative names as Seascape Strawberry and Rose Geranium, flew off the shelves. A year later, Sqirl was serving breakfast and lunch—or anytime food, as Koslow describes it—with dishes like sorrel pesto rice, "kabbouleh," and chopped breakfast salads that mesmerize customers.

Now she's branching out with her newest gig, Onda, a collaboration with Mexican chef Gabriela Cámara of Contramar in Mexico City, and is excited by the thought of running a full-scale restaurant. Cooking with others has often been important to her—whether inviting guest chefs, such as Magnus Nilsson, to her kitchen or cooking pop-ups at the Frieze art fair.

Although she spends much of her day at Sqirl, Koslow is enthusiastic about cooking at home, which is a mere seven minutes away from the restaurant. "If given the chance to cook, I'll take it," she says, though she often does takeout too. Her meals at home are a mix of high- and lowbrow, along the lines of "Georges Laval Champagne and a samosa in a takeout box. Or I'll make a hot dog with French's mustard and artisanal kraut from Brassica and Brine—show me the range life has to offer," she says.

When she does cook, she includes lots of vegetables. "It's likely you'll find a small but delicately cooked protein, a grain, and at least two veggies," she says. Occasionally, she'll stumble across a combination that later appears on customers' plates. "One example is a version of a chicken and rice porridge that was so delicious that I decided it needed to be on the menu at Sqirl—and that's how the Long-Cooked Chicken and Rice Porridge with Cardamom Ghee became a dish there."

Her navy blue, quintessentially California kitchen—with citrus fruits scattered on the marble countertops—is also ground zero for testing out jams. With jam there is "always a new combination to play around with. And failures lead to successes," she notes. Once while making a jam of kumquat and rhubarb, she got the ratios wrong and the jam was more kumquat than rhubarb. "It was bitter and the color was a muted gray. I could have stopped," she recalls. Instead, I reversed the ratios and what do you know, it's a vibrant pink color and absolutely one of my favorite jams that we make!" One thing's for sure—Koslow is never in a rut.

CURRENT HOMETOWN: Los Angeles, California

RESTAURANT THAT MADE HER NAME: Sqirl, Los Angeles

SIGNATURE STYLE: Next generation California cuisine

BEST KNOWN FOR: Her ricotta toast and jams, and her cookbook, *Everything I Want to Eat*

FRIDGE: Sub-Zero

1. **GEORGES LAVAL CHAMPAGNE**—"He's absolutely one of my favorite Champagne producers. The vines have been farmed organically for well over thirty years, the wine is fermented in neutral oak barrels with indigenous yeast—I could go on."

2. **DOMAINE DES MARNES BLANCHES CÔTES DU JURA SAVAGNIN**

3. **SESAME GINGER SALAD DRESSING**

4. **JUS DE RAISIN DU MAS DE GOURGONNIER GRAPE JUICE**—"My husband and I picked up this grape juice in Provence. I enjoy picking up food that I've never seen nor will ever see at home."

5. **STIEGL GOLD AUSTRIAN BEER**

6. **RAW WHOLE MILK**—"It's friendlier for me to digest than regular milk."

7. **RADISHES**—"We eat them with dip at breakfast."

8. **ORGANIC DATES**

9. **HOT SAUCE**—"My friend makes his own lacto-fermented sauce and we always have it on the table."

10. **BRASSICA AND BRINE SAUERKRAUT**

11. **TAKEOUT INDIAN BASMATI RICE AND DINNER** from last night

12. **EGGS FROM CHINO VALLEY RANCHERS,** delivered twice a week

13. **GREEN PROVENÇAL OLIVES**

14. **SQIRL WILD BLACKBERRY AND MEYER LEMON JAM**—"Jars that have dented lids or don't seal correctly end up at home or at a staff or friends' homes."

15. **ORGANIC SEASONAL MISO**

16. **HONEY ROSEMARY APPLE BUTTER (LEFT) AND RANGPUR MANDARIN WITH SEGMENTS MARMALADE (RIGHT)**—"I'm testing all these jams for the Sqirl cookbook. The flavors include kumquat and chamomile, Rangpur lime with mandarin segments (a marmalade), mango passion fruit, blackberry-apple butter, and apple-pomegranate jelly. I loved making apple jelly with passion fruit—making a jelly set from natural pectin is very challenging and then the seeds are just so beautiful."

17. **TAKEOUT SAMOSAS**

18. **HUMMUS**

19. **MARINATED ANCHOVIES, SALAMI, SMOKED TROUT**—"These are all for SNACKS! I like to eat these with little crackers or bread."

Black Razz Jam

Be sure to keep some saucers or little plates in your freezer for testing the jam. I prefer the plate to be ceramic or porcelain but any will work.

2¼ pounds blackberries

2¼ pounds raspberries

6 cups sugar

⅛ cup plus 1 tablespoon lemon juice

Place the blackberries and raspberries in a food processor and pulse until they are chopped but still a little chunky. Alternatively, put the berries in a large bowl and crush them with your hands. Or, for a mix of textures, puree half in the food processor and squeeze the other half with your hands.

Transfer the berries to a large bowl and stir in the sugar and lemon juice. Let sit for at least a few minutes, or up to 30 minutes.

Pour the mixture into a stainless-steel jam pot. Put a few saucers in the freezer for a plate test.

Cook over high heat, stirring and scraping the bottom of the pot so the sugars don't burn. Use a fine-mesh skimmer to skim off any scum. Take the temperature with a candy thermometer. Cook until the temperature reaches 217°F, about 10 to 12 minutes.

If the jam is bubbling more than you can manage, turn off the heat, skim, then turn the heat back on. As the jam cooks, the solids will separate from the liquids and then rejoin. The surface will look matte at the beginning and then suddenly look shiny and glossy. Sometimes with blackberry jam, the surface will form what look like dry patches. This indicates that the jam is nearly done.

Prepare the plate test. Spoon a little bit of jam onto your frozen saucer. Put the plate back in the freezer for 1 minute. Take the plate out and slide a finger through the jam. It's done when it parts and you see a strip of clean saucer. If it doesn't, return the pot to the heat, stir frequently, and test after another minute.

Let cool and pour into sterilized jars. Always follow USDA guidelines for home canning.

MAKES EIGHT 8-OUNCE JARS

Q & A

What was the last meal you prepared at home? Well, my husband and I just watched the Oscars, so I brined and cooked off a chicken, cooked rice we brought back from Hokkaido, married it with frozen summer corn and Aleppo pepper (I'm a fan of frozen peas and corn!), and served it with roasted carrots from Windrose in Paso Robles, tossed in nigella and garam masala. We plopped our friend's lacto-fermented hot sauce on the table and had an award-winning night.

Your restaurant has been compared to a daytime *Cheers*. How do you manage between regulars and tourists? The regulars should feel like they are integral to the heartbeat of the restaurant. And visitors need to feel a sense of wonder when they enter the doors. The requirement of our staff is to understand this and to be the bearer of energy.

Sorry to ask since you probably get this a lot—how did the crispy rice come about? I'm obsessed with the Thai crispy rice salad. Every day, we had leftover rice at Sqirl that was cooked off, and we didn't want to waste it. So we started putting it on sheet trays in the walk-in and then frying it the next day. When we found out how delicious that was and how well it worked, then we played around with adding our pork sausage and our lacto-fermented hot sauce to it. By playing around, we came upon this recipe.

You are part of Edible Schoolyard and other chef-driven community initiatives. Tell us about your role. I sit on the board of MAD [Make a Difference]. The organization started in Denmark, with the goal being to bring chefs from all around the world to talk about issues that we all face. I'd say the biggest issues we talk about are around wellness. How can we find time for us while being there

for others? How can we develop a healthy kitchen culture and what does that look like? How do we mentor future leaders, and what does mentorship look like?

What is your favorite takeout food? The takeout food in the fridge is Indian. My husband, Ryan, and I tend to get vegetarian for two meals and it lasts us three meals!

Does your husband cook at home? And if so, what? Ryan is a huge fan of Cajun food. He's a "follow the recipe" kind of guy, and his bible is Donald Link's *Real Cajun* cookbook. I love when he cooks for me because I know it takes him a whole day of planning and cooking. It can be scary to cook for a chef, but know that we just appreciate being cooked for!

Where do you shop for groceries? At a wonderful store in Echo Park called Cookbook—it's small, but mighty. Robert Stelzner and Marta Teegan opened this store in 2010 and it's one of those places I'd just love to leave my credit card on file! They are at the farmers market with the best chefs picking up the finest produce for their shelves. It's one of those "trust me" places—every item in the store has a reason for being there. My favorites are Andante cheeses from the cheesemaker, locally smoked trout, Marin Sun Farms beef/protein, and French hot chocolate mix.

Favorite naughty snack? My desert-island food is ice cream.

Do you often check out the jam competition? Yes, my friend told me how delicious this yuzu marmalade is and she's right—this yuzu marmalade is legit! I like to taste other jams—to consider texture, sugar/acid/pectin content. It's important to taste what's out there.

LUDO LEFEBVRE

Ludo Lefebvre has come a long way from Auxerre, the town in rural France where he was born and raised. Now the proprietor of various restaurants and a TV show host, he was a high school delinquent whose cooking career started thanks to his father. "My dad gave me three choices: hairdresser, mechanic, or cook. I loved to eat, so I chose to cook." He dismisses the notion that there were any other influences: "I wasn't following my grandmother around the kitchen when I was a child, getting inspired and all," he says.

Lefebvre got his first chance when his mentor, Marc Meneau, who oversaw his kitchen training in France, convinced him to go to America and make money. Meneau helped him with contacts, but despite offers from Daniel Boulud and Charlie Trotter, Lefebvre chose to work at L'Orangerie in L.A., because, of all things, he was a *Baywatch* fan: "The lifestyle seemed so amazing, so I thought, why not?"

But he became frustrated with the fine-dining world and began to cook on his days off in a baker friend's kitchen, virtually inventing the L.A. pop-up concept in the process with a series of online-booking-only surprise dinners. Stellar reviews in the *New York Times* and especially by Jonathan Gold in the *Los Angeles Times* brought things to a fever pitch. Soon investors came knocking, resulting in a series of successful brick-and-mortar establishments such as Trois Mec, Petit Trois, Trois Familia, and, Lefebvre's dream, a fried-chicken franchise.

Running a small empire can have its downsides. "I typically don't eat when I get home unless my wife and kids leave me a box of cold pizza sitting in the fridge," he says.

But then again, he's not complaining about being at the center of the California culinary scene: "It was like lightning in a bottle, and I found out the kitchen is my happy place."

CURRENT HOMETOWN:
Los Angeles, California

RESTAURANT THAT MADE HIS NAME: LudoBites, his pop-up concept, Los Angeles

SIGNATURE STYLE: Gallic comfort food

BEST KNOWN FOR: His pop-ups; his award-winning restaurant Trois Mec; his many TV appearances and awards; and his cookbooks, including *LudoBites*

FRIDGE: Fisher and Paykel

1. **TRADER JOE'S ORGANIC SRIRACHA AND ROASTED GARLIC BBQ SAUCE—** "My wife does most of the shopping. TJ's has really good 'staples' and always fun twists on products."

2. **BONNE MAMAN GOLDEN PLUM JAM—**"The whole family eats jams. My daughter loves to put strawberry jam in yogurt. One of the best things for breakfast is a French baguette, butter, and a Bonne Maman jam."

3. **VIOLET MUSTARD—**"I love mustard, it's my favorite condiment. I'm also from Burgundy where it's a staple."

4. **MOUTARDE ROYALE AU COGNAC POMMERY MUSTARD**

5. **MAILLE DIJON MUSTARD**

6. **PURE LAVENDER HONEY—**"My wife and Luca are big honey eaters. Luca just loves to eat honey straight out of the jar."

7. **BOURSIN CHEESE SPREAD—**"I like to call Boursin the 'French Velveeta.' In France, everybody has it in their refrigerator at all times. It definitely brings back lots of memories from my childhood."

8. **BORDIER BUTTER**

9. **HOMEMADE VADOUVAN—**"I first used vadouvan in the 1990s when working in Saint-Étienne with Chef Pierre Gagnaire. I love the flavor—it's not better than regular curry, just quite different. As it has gotten expensive to import, I now make my own."

10. **FRESH BEANS**

11. **WHISKEY SALAMI AND ASSORTED CHEESES**

12. **BLACK RUSSIAN TOMATOES—**"The best is to eat them sliced with a little olive oil, salt and pepper, basil, and mozzarella. They are so flavorful."

Q & A

Any childhood food memories? It may sound strange to Americans, but one of my favorite things to eat as a kid was escargots. I used to eat them like they were M&M's. I've eaten over a hundred in a day!

What about dishes your mother made for you? I used to love when she made me *hachis parmentier* [shepherd's pie] and ratatouille, and my favorite was when she made her special chocolate cake.

Do you cook often for your family at home? Family mealtime is important, but because of my obligations to my restaurants, I can't always be at home at night, so we have breakfast together every day. Sometimes it's toast, sometimes baguettes, sometimes we all have cereal; but we all eat together in the morning as a family.

What do you like to cook when you do have time? Because we live in California, we do a lot of barbecuing outside, fresh-grilled meats and vegetables. Nothing complicated, just fresh. We also have crepe nights. I just cook up a bunch of crepes, both savory and sweet, and everyone gets to make their own dinner and dessert.

Do you ever miss the food of France? California is the best in the world for fresh produce. But I will always take the cheese and butter of France over any other!

There seems to be a lot of cheese in your refrigerator! I am French. I wouldn't believe any person who says they are French and doesn't buy a large selection of cheese. Cheese is a big part of the everyday. We use Havarti and white cheddar on sandwiches for the kids [his twins, Luca and Rêve] and string cheese and Babybel as snacks for lunch boxes. My wife, Kris, seems to have a plate of cheese, salami, and crackers on her desk almost every day. Many times when I come home from work late at night or midafternoon on a day off I am guilty of eating a few pieces of string cheese or Babybel just plain. I justify it as a good source of protein.

What is your favorite junk food? I am torn between Pringles and Kit Kats or Twix.

Duck-Fat-Fried Chicken with Piquillos Ketchup

Fried chicken is all about the crunch. I love it, it's so versatile. The inspiration for this piquillos hot sauce comes from a well-known dish in the southwest of France called *poulet basquaise*. It's a little bit sweet and sour, which makes it pair nicely with the chicken.

For the chicken marinade:

1 chicken (around 3 pounds)

3 cups light soy sauce

1 cup sesame oil

½ cup chili oil (without seeds)

3 tablespoons chopped fresh ginger

2 tablespoons chopped fresh garlic

For the piquillos ketchup:

1 cup piquillo peppers, drained

2 cups raspberry vinegar

4 cups water, plus more as needed

½ cup sugar

Kosher salt

White pepper, ground

1 tablespoon Tabasco

For the fried chicken:

6 cups duck fat

¼ cup herbes de Provence

1 pound cornstarch

Salt

Pepper

Marinate the chicken: Combine the soy sauce, sesame oil, chili oil, chopped ginger, and chopped garlic in a bowl. Mix with a whisk, set aside. Clean the chicken, leaving the skin on. Cut chicken breast and legs into pieces. Place all the chicken pieces in a large bowl. Add the marinade and coat. Cover with plastic wrap and keep in the fridge overnight.

Make the ketchup: Combine the piquillos with the raspberry vinegar, water, sugar, salt, and pepper to taste in large saucepan. Bring the mix to a boil, then reduce to a low simmer. Cover and cook for 1 hour, stirring every 10 minutes. The liquids will reduce to a syrupy consistency. Carefully blend the piquillo mix in a blender until it is completely smooth, adding water as necessary. Once the mix is completely pureed, add the Tabasco and stir it in gently. Set aside in the refrigerator.

To fry the chicken: In a saucepan, slowly heat the duck fat over medium heat to 320°F. Place the chicken legs in a bowl, and lightly toss with half the cornstarch. Carefully lower the coated chicken leg into the duck fat, and fry for approximately 12 minutes (check the temperature of the meat with a meat thermometer to ensure the center is cooked to 160°F). Remove the chicken legs from the duck fat, place on paper towels to drain the excess fat, and season with herbs de Provence, salt, and pepper. Place the chicken breasts in the bowl, and lightly toss with the remaining cornstarch. Carefully lower the chicken breasts into the duck fat and cook for 8 minutes. Remove from the duck fat, place on paper towels to drain the excess fat, and season with herbes de Provence, salt, and pepper.

Serve the chicken while hot with the piquillos ketchup for dipping.

SERVES 4

BARBARA LYNCH

As a child growing up in South Boston, Barbara Lynch got an unconventional education in taste and initiative by shoplifting her first jar of pesto and crank-calling Julia Child. This self-taught chef, who on the first day of her first job had to cook for 150 people on a Nantucket dinner boat, began experimenting with food early on. Her mother was baffled by her daughter's direction. "When I started learning more about food, my mother would say, 'Where did you come from?' I think that she was surprised at, and I hope proud of, my new interest," recalls Lynch.

In high school, Lynch spent more time cutting classes than attending them—until she took a home economics class. There she tasted food "that I had never been introduced to in Southie." Soon after, Lynch was trying out recipes from her mother's *Good Housekeeping* magazines and wowing her family with twenty-ingredient recipes.

Lynch lied her way into jobs at restaurants, learning about Italian and French cuisine by reading cookbooks by Alain Ducasse. She ended up working under the acclaimed Boston chef Todd English, first at Michela's and later at Olives. He had a hot temper and his kitchen was challenging and brutal. But English taught her to embrace big powerful flavors, and, more important, "I also learned a lot about how I wanted (or didn't want) to run

my own kitchen one day," she says. In addition, Lynch, who has ADD, found focus among the clatter and stress: "In the kitchen, I can do anything and have a million projects working at once."

After a few formative trips to Italy, Lynch hit it big when she was named one of *Food & Wine*'s Best New Chefs in America for her cooking at the Galleria Italiana. That's when she knew it was the right moment to open her own place—No. 9 Park; twenty years later, it still defines fine dining in Boston. Not one to take her time, she quickly opened eight other restaurants, including several in her old neighborhood in the South End.

Lynch now divides her time between a loft next to her Fort Point restaurants and a quiet house in Gloucester, where she lives with her husband and daughter. In her home kitchens Lynch is the perennial innovator—testing dried foods and experimenting with marijuana-based recipes. The long marble-and-granite countertop in the kitchen of her spacious loft is the kind of place you want to hang out with a glass of wine in your hand, sampling from the little bowls of olives, bits of poached lobster, and dried oranges. The refrigerator is a study in towering stacks of leftovers, basics like sliced bread and milk, and some local lobster ready to be tossed in a salad or nibbled on with a glass of wine.

CURRENT HOMETOWN: Boston, Massachusetts

RESTAURANT THAT MADE HER NAME: No. 9 Park, Boston

SIGNATURE STYLE: Simple Italian and French-inspired dishes

BEST KNOWN FOR: Her memoir, *Out of Line: A Life Playing with Fire*; several James Beard Awards, including for Outstanding Restaurateur (2014); and her many restaurants, especially Menton

FRIDGE: Samsung

1. **CORNICHONS**

2. **COLD-BREWED GREEN TEA**

3. **2015, YVES LECCIA BLANC**

4. **SILK SOYMILK**

5. **DEHYDRATED ORANGE SLICES**—"I use them to add flavor or texture to a dish. They're also a healthy snack for travel."

6. **ASSORTED CHARCUTERIE**—(coppa, summer sausage) for snacking and last-minute entertaining

7. **LEFTOVER CHICKPEA PENNE WITH EVOO**

8. **WHOLE ROASTED CHICKEN**—"This was left over from earlier in the week. I like to pick at it during the week if I want something but don't feel like cooking."

9. **UNSWEETENED ORGANIC SHREDDED COCONUT**—"I use this on chia puddings for breakfast."

10. **VERMONT CREAMERY CRÈME FRAÎCHE**

11. **PEPPERIDGE FARM SOFT 100% WHOLE WHEAT BREAD**

12. **HOMEMADE MARINARA SAUCE**—"I always have some on hand."

13. **CHIA SEED PUDDING**—"I prepare this ahead of time for breakfast."

14. **365 ORGANIC COCONUT OIL,** for cooking and blending in smoothies

15. **MUG OF BEEF STEW**

16. **CAMPBELL'S OVEN SAUCES CHICKEN POTPIE**—"This is one of my favorite comfort foods. The Campbell's oven sauces remind me of growing up."

17. **WILD RICE SALAD WITH ASPARAGUS AND HALIBUT**—"This is another leftover. I like to cook with light ingredients at home."

18. **DOMAINE DU BAGNOL CASSIS BLANC**

19. **MARINATED MIXED OLIVES**

20. **NEOCELL BEAUTY BURSTS COLLAGEN SOFT CHEWS**—"They help keep my skin, hair, and nails healthy."

21. **PICKED AND CLEANED LOBSTER MEAT**

22. **LIVE LOBSTERS**

Q & A

You were raised by your mom, right?
South Boston was very working-class Irish when I was growing up in the seventies. My father died before I was born, so my mother raised me and my five brothers and sisters. She worked several jobs to support our family, so we never really had much parental supervision. I grew up in a housing project, and became resourceful and self-sufficient at a young age.

Your first job was cooking at the age of thirteen for a local priest. Did you know you wanted to be a chef at this young age? I've been interested in food since I was young, and even though I wasn't cooking particularly fancy food, it still sparked something in me. That job led to another at an ice cream and sub shop, where I waitressed and made subs. It wasn't until my high school home ec class, though, that I realized a future in food could mean more than casual joints. My teacher, Susan Logozzo, deserves a lot of credit for channeling my energy to cooking (and for keeping me in school). I was also inspired by Chef Mario Bonello of the St. Botolph Club, who showed me the magic of fine dining.

Did your mom cook for you? Although my mother didn't cook fancy food at home, I loved her tuna fish sandwiches (the secret is pickles!), her meatballs made with crumbled Saltine crackers, and her stuffing, which I still make every Thanksgiving. She worked such long hours, though, that she mostly left us to fend for ourselves.

Apparently you were quite the entrepreneur in high school, even though you weren't very good at studying. Any stories you can share? I have a ton of stories, including stealing an MBTA bus when I was thirteen (my feet didn't even reach the pedals!). My friends knew me as our high school bookie, placing bets for my teachers . . . or at least collecting the money. One of my favorite stories from that time isn't actually from school itself, but from working at the St. Botolph Club, a private club in Boston's Back Bay. During my first week as a waitress, there was one crazy busy night. I was instructed to send plates of salad upstairs from the kitchen in an old dumbwaiter, one tray at a time, for a party on the second floor. I figured I could game the system and save time by sending up two trays at a time, each one overloaded with plates. The dumbwaiter started up before I heard the crash . . . and all of the brand-new fine china plates went flying down to the basement! Chef Mario was fuming and fired me on the spot. Luckily, after a few days of cooling off, he hired me back. I learned the hard way that some rules aren't meant to be broken.

How would you describe your cooking style? I love to cook simple things at home. When you start with good ingredients, you don't need to add a million components to each dish. My home cooking is typically rustic Italian, though I love to rely on classic French technique.

What is your favorite food when coming home from a long day at work? I usually reach for whatever is easy and relatively healthy. If there are leftovers, I'll usually dig into those (I try to have greens and grains on hand at all times), but I've also been known to whip up a PB&J or tuna fish sandwich late at night.

What do you cook for your family? What are their favorite dishes? I love to make one-pot meals for my daughter, who's fourteen— beef or seafood stew, chicken potpie, pasta with beans. My daughter loves pasta—as do I!

What do you always have in your fridge? I always have eggs, a variety of dairy (lots of cheese, different types of milks, and crème fraîche), as well as lots of fresh produce and herbs.

What would we never find in your fridge? I don't love fermented foods—so I would never have kimchi or sauerkraut in my fridge. I'm also not a huge hot sauce fan.

Are those gummy bears in your freezer? Yes, well almost. It's a mix for gummy candy. Since legalization in Massachusetts, I've been experimenting with pot gummy recipes at home. I just got some Lego molds that I LOVE! My friends come over to taste them.

What foods would you never eat? I wouldn't say "never eat"—especially not in the hands of a great chef—but I'm not really a fan of broccoli. Broccoli rabe, however, is a different story!

What is your favorite junk food? I LOVE Cheez-its.

Who shops for food at your house and where do you go? I typically do all the food shopping, unless it's for a big dinner party and I need help! I love Formaggio Kitchen, run by my friends Ihsan and Valerie Gurdal. They now have three locations around Boston and they carry the best condiments, cheeses, wine, prepared foods, and extras you never knew you needed. When I'm in Boston, I often shop at Foodie's Markets in Southie; when I'm in Gloucester, I love Common Crow. I try to support independently owned grocery stores as much as I can. I also love picking up produce from my friends Ana Sortun and Chris Kurth's farm stand, Siena Farms, in the South End—it's right next to three of my restaurants and full of seasonal produce from their farm just outside of Boston.

What is in your freezer? Blanched French fries ready to be fried, Brigham's vanilla ice cream (I worked at Brigham's when I was a kid and have a soft spot for their vanilla), hash browns, frozen pizzas (my daughter and I love Half Baked's pies, made in Vermont), and some spoons to depuff my eyes when I wake up in the morning!

You seem to recipe-test a lot at home. I do! I love to think of new ways to use my favorite ingredients so I end up experimenting a lot at home. I actually have a line of dehydrated foods called MADE that I created to preserve fruits and vegetables that didn't sell from my old produce shop. I found that I could use them to make super-nutritious meals at home really quickly and without much effort. Dehydrating can also intensify the flavor of an ingredient. I always keep dehydrated olives in my pantry, which add rich flavor and interesting texture to make a dish really sing.

What is your home cooking mantra? If you use beautiful ingredients and prepare them simply with great technique, you don't need all of the other bells and whistles. You can never go wrong.

Lobster Salad with Winter Citrus and Fennel

This recipe is inspired by a dish I enjoyed years ago at Lulu Rousseau's wonderful Parisian bistro, L'Assiette. Lulu was a master at cooking simple food perfectly, something I deeply admire and preach to my staff regularly! The whole truly is greater than the sum of its parts here—just a few simple but pristine ingredients combine to make an elegant and delicious dish. I especially like to make this in the winter, with beautiful winter citrus that complements the sweetness of the lobster.

3 citrus fruits (blood orange or Cara Cara oranges, if available)

1 tablespoon unsalted butter

Meat from 2½-pound cooked lobster (or ¾ pound picked lobster meat)

1 medium fennel bulb, thinly sliced

1 tablespoon fresh tarragon

2 teaspoons chopped dehydrated olives (see Note)

1 teaspoon plus 1 tablespoon crème fraîche

Sea salt

Pepper

2 radishes, thinly sliced

Remove the peel and pith from the citrus fruits. Segment the peeled fruit over a bowl; reserve the juice as well as the citrus segments.

Melt the butter in a medium saucepan. Add the picked lobster meat to the melted butter just to warm through.

Place the fennel in a large bowl, add the reserved citrus juice, citrus segments, tarragon (reserve a few pieces for garnish), dehydrated olive pieces, and 1 teaspoon of the crème fraîche. Mix well to combine. Season to taste with salt and pepper.

Spread 1 tablespoon of crème fraîche on the bottom of the serving plate. Spoon the fennel mixture on the plate, then top with the warmed lobster. Garnish with sliced radishes and the reserved tarragon, and sprinkle with sea salt.

SERVES 4

Note: I dehydrate Taggiasca olives at home and store them in an airtight container in the pantry. To make them, spread olives evenly on a baking sheet and bake in a 150°F oven for 1 hour, or until they've lost their moisture. They're pretty shelf-stable when dried, and can last for a few years. If you don't have time to make dehydrated olives, you can substitute marinated Taggiasca olives.

GREGORY MARCHAND

In 2009, Gregory Marchand created a revolution on the rue du Nil, a tiny street in a forgotten part of Paris's garment district. With very little means, he opened Frenchie, a tiny gourmet bistro that offered a limited number of high-quality dishes at reasonable prices. Frenchie became a true neighborhood bistro, but with an international flavor, the culmination of Marchand's journeys and a reflection of his personality.

Marchand, who was a picky eater as a child, spent his formative years in an orphanage in the town of Nantes on the west coast of France. His grandmother was an excellent cook, as was an aunt who was a chef, and although the two wanted to adopt the boy after his mother died, social workers stepped in and nixed that idea. "They thought it would be too much change for me," Marchand says. "But I definitely think I got something from that side of the family."

When the orphanage chef was around during the week, Marchand would sometimes help him with a bit of the cooking. "He did stuff like salmon with beurre blanc sauce," he recalls. On weekends when he was off, Marchand would occasionally take over and make brunch for everyone. That experience made him realize that cooking was a way he could fend for himself once he left the orphanage. "It was about survival," he says. "I have no regrets. Even if I was a plumber, I would have done the best I could." So cooking became his singular mission, and at seventeen, he went to culinary school. Even though he admits he wasn't the best student, he was determined to gain as much experience as possible.

Marchand left France at eighteen, traveling and working in London, Hong Kong, and New York. He met his wife, Marie, in London while working for Jamie Oliver. Marie then followed him to New York. After two years working at the Gramercy Tavern, the couple returned to France when Marie was seven months pregnant, almost too far along to fly. With no job and a family to think of, it was a now-or-never moment—and Frenchie was born.

Now, a decade and a Michelin star later, the street has become home to the Frenchie mini empire, including a wine shop; FTG (Frenchie to Go), a deli and takeout; and Frenchie Bar à Vins, a wine bar. Marchand's purveyors have followed him here too, opening stores that supply both his restaurant and home fridges. "We never go to the supermarket." He laughs. "It's all here."

For someone who grew up with few family members, spending time with his is obviously a priority. On the weekends, Marchand cooks bourgeoisie style: one dish, cheese, and a dessert. In the refrigerator, there is Philly cream cheese for his daughter's toast at breakfast, and organic Heinz and HP Sauce for her dad. There are also preprepared provisions in the freezer for the kids. "We have lots of frozen organic vegetable soups for the nanny to heat up," explains Marchand.

Marchand, who shuttles often between his restaurants in London and Paris, is always satisfied with simple comforts. The first thing he picks up after a long journey home? "A roast chicken from the Montorgueil market," he says. "It's best with just a warm piece of bread and a good cheese."

CURRENT HOMETOWN:
Paris, France

RESTAURANT THAT MADE HIS NAME: Frenchie, Paris

SIGNATURE STYLE: French with an international influence

BEST KNOWN FOR: The pocket-sized kitchen at his Michelin-star restaurant, Frenchie; his London restaurant Frenchie Covent Garden; and his natural wine selection

FRIDGE: Miele

1. **ALMOND MILK—**"My wife makes a drink with it: almond milk, curcuma [turmeric], and dates."

2. **APPLE JUICE**

3. **RASPBERRY JAM—**"Our friends give us lots of jam, but I'm not a big jam guy and the kids eat mainly Nocciolata."

4. **SRIRACHA—**"I bought it in East Hampton when I visited some friends."

5. **ANCHOVIES**

6. **MOZZARELLA**

7. **BUTTER—**"Always salted. I am from Brittany."

8. **SHREDDED CHEESE**

9. **SAVORA MUSTARD**

10. **ORGANIC YOGURT,** for his wife and children

11. **CHESTNUTS**

12. **MONT D'OR CHEESE—**"This is for a family meal later this week. I will put it in the oven with a dash of *vin jaune*, a clove of garlic, and wait until it's melted. Then we eat it with potatoes, pickles, and charcuterie."

13. **MONOPRIX ORGANIC MUSTARD—**"I use this for making a French vinaigrette."

14. **FRENCH GRAINED MUSTARD—**"This I love serving next to the Morteau sausage, a smoked sausage from the Jura region of France."

15. **PHILADELPHIA CREAM CHEESE—**"My daughter likes this for breakfast on toast."

16. **KIRI CHEESE SPREAD—**"Sometimes when I come home at night at one a.m., I have Kiri and ham. And then my wife gives me shit about where all the ham went."

17. **PICKLED GUINDILLA CHILI PEPPERS**

18. **SRIRACHA BOTTLES—**"I know, two more bottles. I really like to eat spicy food."

19. **BIGORRE PORK RILLETTES, MADE WITH BLACK BIGORRE PORK** from the Basque country—"You eat it with cornichons and some pickled guindilla peppers."

20. **BLACK TRUFFLE OIL**

21. *COLATURA DI ALICI—*"It's a juice of pressed, salted anchovies, kind of like Italian nuoc mam. I love this."

22. **APRICOT JAM,** from a friend

23. **BLACK TRUFFLE—**"For my son's birthday tomorrow, I'll make a truffle risotto. I also like to take the scrapings from the restaurant on Friday night to do a scrambled eggs on Sunday."

24. **CAPERS,** from the restaurant

25. **RED WINE**

26. **APPLE JUICE**

27. **MILK**

28. **HAM**

29. **MAPLE SYRUP**

Sausage and Lentil Stew with Chestnuts

This is one of my wife's favorites—sometimes I make it ahead of time for her and the kids when I'm not home for dinner. This is an example of very simple bourgeois cooking that I do at home—I do one big main dish.

---

3 onions, chopped

3 cloves garlic, minced

Olive oil

1½ cups dried green lentils (preferably verte du Puy)

4 carrots, diced

1½ cups chestnuts, cooked and peeled

4 sprigs thyme

3 bay leaves

10 cups vegetable broth

1½ pounds French Morteau sausage (or smoked Polish or farmer's sausage)

2 tablespoons crème fraîche

Salt

Pepper

2 tablespoons red wine vinegar

2 tablespoons stone-ground mustard

Sauté the onions and garlic in the olive oil in a medium-size pot over low heat until translucent. Add the lentils, carrots, chestnuts, thyme sprigs, bay leaves, and broth. Simmer for 5 minutes. Add the sausage (whole) and simmer for another 40 minutes, or until the sausage and lentils are cooked.

Remove the sausage and let it rest. Remove and puree one third of the lentils. Add the pureed lentils back into the stew with the crème fraîche. Season with salt, pepper, red wine vinegar, and stone-ground mustard.

To serve: Slice the sausage, add it to the lentil stew, and divide among four deep plates or bowls with additional mustard on the side.

SERVES 4

Q & A

How important is your fridge to you?
The fridge doesn't matter that much, as we buy fresh every day. Besides, we are moving apartments soon and I'll just take the refrigerator that comes with the place.

What do you have for breakfast?
In the morning I always try to have a yogurt with different ground seeds, which are better for digestion, and nuts. Then I add some seasonal fruit and banana. My son likes it too. It's the kind of breakfast that takes me through to the end of lunch service. Then I eat around five p.m. I try to only have two meals a day.

Why all the mascarpone? Tomorrow is my son's birthday and he asked his mom to make a tiramisu and he asked me to make pasta with truffles. At school he tells everyone that his dad's truffle pasta is his favorite dish—so chic.

What do you have in your fridge in London? I'm not even sure. Probably what friends leave when they come by.

Of all the cities you have lived in, which has the best food? Often I describe Paris as a fine dining city. London and New York are the fun dining ones. My cuisine today is a reflection of my experience—rooted in France but open on the world and different cultures.

Do you food-shop at the restaurant?
Not at the restaurant. I love the action of going to the market. I have a basket, I like picking things out. I like the ambiance of shopping on the rue du Nil. I could easily do a shopping list for my sous-chefs, but I actually like doing food shopping. I go quite a lot.

Do you ever go to big supermarkets?
We buy every day at the market. When my wife leaves work she goes to the butcher or fishmonger on the way home. We don't need to stock too much at home. I think this is a kind of Paris thing. We have small shops; here you don't need to go to big stores like Whole Foods or Sainsbury's. Our basics we have delivered. I never go to the supermarket.

Never ever? One thing that makes my friends laugh on holidays is when we go to the supermarket. It's about the only time I ever go. And I'm amazed, I'm either like "This is cool! or "Look at all this crap and processed food!" They go every week. Going every week would be a burden. We live in a bubble.

Have you ever made a meal your family didn't like? This always happens with my seven-year-old daughter, she's a little picky. When I do a meal at home I always need to find or cook something else for her. For the lentil stew I'm making, I will keep lentils aside for her, because maybe she doesn't like the sausage or who knows—maybe she will! It should go away soon. Marie and my son, Tom, are my greatest fans, however. As a kid there were a lot of things I didn't like. I guess Lily is a little like me.

A few things you always have in your fridge? Eggs—you can do so many things with them. Butter—always salted. Good cheese. Apple juice—I blend it with spirulina in the morning.

Who cooks at home? I cook often on Sundays or when friends come over. Otherwise I'm usually at work. Marie cooks a lot at home. She's a great cook. We order in a lot too.

DAVID McMILLAN

For someone who prides himself on living out of Yeti coolers, who stores his non-alcoholic beer directly in the river's crevice and aspires to live off the grid completely in a solar-powered house, having a conventional refrigerator is purely an afterthought. But that's David McMillan—a renaissance man whose take on Quebec-style cooking is a sassy, tongue-in-cheek interpretation of French bourgeois cooking. His first restaurant, Joe Beef, landed on various best-restaurant lists, something McMillan and partner Fred Morin accept only begrudgingly. He hangs out at Joe Beef a little less these days now that the crowd has become less local and more fashionable. Yet it's still a restaurant that is comfortable serving lobster and foie gras next to cans of Molson beer.

McMillan divides his time between a bachelor's apartment—which feels more like an Airbnb crash pad and overlooks the alley garden with its cherry tree and trout pond that serve his restaurants—and two country homes, a rambling farm and a cabin he dis-covered while on a camping trip as a child. He spends more time on the farm with his three children and whoever drops by—friends, coworkers, or his ex-wife. McMillan has a self-deprecating humor (he claims his career "still hasn't taken off") and is unpretentious about his cooking; he isn't above smashing Pringles for simple potato pancakes, for instance.

His rough-and-tumble upbringing may explain that lack of pretention. He cooked with his grandmother and always appreciated her Saturday roast chicken. He didn't have a knack for schoolwork but liked eating in good restaurants—at least the ones he could afford with the money he made dealing drugs. David ended up in the kitchen more or less by chance—"I used to sell weed to a chef, and one night he asked me to help out," he recalls—but within three days on the job as a commis chef, he impressed Pierre Elliot Trudeau with his mussel soup. He was hooked and quickly got his first official post at Le Caveau in Montreal. "It was staffed by old French cooks from Lyon who had come to Canada for the Centennial Festival in 1967," he says. The restaurant taught him *la cuisine du marché*, or French market cooking, the type of cuisine featured at Joe Beef. "I still practice this form today as it's the most logical way of cooking."

McMillan's apartment, which is above his restaurants, is handy for making quick trips out to the smoker or to his sprawling ad hoc garden. There are no gadgets in sight on his counters, just a cutting board and an aloe vera plant. He towers above his standard-size refrigerator and has taken to storing most items on the highest shelves for easier access. His fridge has a certain "born again" edge to it. After his children were born, he decided to stop his excessive drinking, and now keeps only nonalcoholic beer and protein drinks from Costco. You can find those next to his pickled produce and the duck confit pinched from his restaurant downstairs. He's slightly overenthusiastic about nose-to-tail eating too, explaining "pigs ears—they are the calamari of the pig." In all, he's as adventurous as his clientele. "The dining population is very advanced here," he says.

CURRENT HOMETOWN:
Montreal, Canada

RESTAURANT THAT MADE HIS NAME: Joe Beef, Montreal

SIGNATURE STYLE: Seasonal French market cuisine

BEST KNOWN FOR: Serving lunch to Prime Minister Justin Trudeau and President Barack Obama; being on the World's 50 Best Restaurant List; and his cookbooks, *The Art of Living According to Joe Beef* (a James Beard Award nominee) and *Joe Beef: Surviving the Apocalypse*

FRIDGE: Frigidaire

1. **KROMBACHER NONALCOHOLIC WHEAT BEER**—"I talked about my favorite nonalcoholic beers on the radio and since then everyone is sending me some."

2. **PICKLED GREEN TOMATOES**

3. **JOE BEEF MARINARA SAUCE**—"This is from end-of-the-season tomatoes straight from my garden."

4. **HOMEMADE WINE,** a naturally effervescent wine from Ontario pinot noir grapes

5. **GINGERBERRY KOMBUCHA**

6. **BUTTER**—"I always use salted."

7. **SUNFLOWER SEED BUTTERS**—"I like to have a choice between smooth and chunky. I'm allergic to peanuts."

8. **PICKLES**

9. **CHERRIES**—"We made about sixty jars this year from the cherry tree in the alley."

10. **ORANGE JUICE**

11. **GREEN TEA**

12. **GOOSE HAM,** from cured, smoked goose breast

13. **DUCK LEG CONFIT**

14. **PIG'S EAR**

15. **ENDS FROM THE CHEESE BOARDS AT THE RESTAURANTS**—"I bring whatever is left on Saturday night here or to the farm. It could also be the end of a roast or a last duck leg. I've never sat down to eat in my restaurant in my life. It's bad luck. I was brought up in the French system where you don't do that."

16. **CANNED PEACHES**—"I love cold peaches. I eat them straight out of the can or with ice cream, whipped cream, or condensed milk. If you are out of maple syrup you can also pour the peach syrup over crepes with salted butter."

17. **KOMBUCHA**

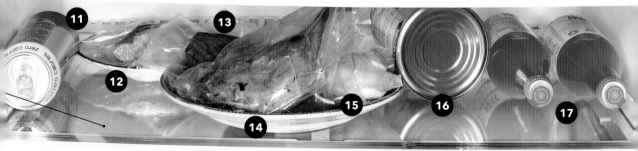

BEAR MEAT

Q & A

Describe your farmhouse refrigerator.
I have an 1840s farmhouse with a mini fridge and a Yeti cooler. The basement stores potatoes, carrots, onions, sausages, ham, and honey. I eat that stuff, to be honest. If I need anything there is a pig farm and a chicken farm across the road. I can also live on bread and cheese and sunflower seed butter.

That sounds very back to basics. I have another place where I go in the summer up north, a cabin that is only accessible by boat. Generally I live off the coolers. There is a river on the property with a pit. I put the beverages down into a crevice. In the summer when it's blazing hot, the beer is literally one degree Celsius. The old-timers have a technique in the winter: they leave their wine and booze in a crate at the bottom of a local lake. As it's so deep, it doesn't freeze.

Something you can't live without when at your cabin? I can't live without Darjeeling tea, in the winter or summer.

You mention using a cooler. Does it work well for you? I fill up the cooler at the frozen section of the grocery store. I might just get two frozen ducks, and then I put cold beverages next to the frozen ducks. Then I'll put fruit and vegetables on top of the frozen ducks. Then I put eggs and dairy at the top. I build my Yeti from the bottom up, with the frozen stuff at the bottom and the fragile stuff at the top. I can leave it on the porch, and it'll still be frozen for seven days. If you put a frozen turkey in a hard Yeti cooler, it will stay cold for two weeks.

You've got a lot of drinks in your refrigerator here. I drink Heineken 0.0—it's nonalcoholic. Nonalcoholic beer is a bigger thing now with weed being legal. I think the weed people want to drink beer, but they can't deal with the alcohol plus the weed. I really like kombuchas too. Some kombuchas are close to weird natural wines. There is middle ground between strange natural wines, kombucha, and artisanal beer.

Are those olives or cherries? They are cherries. They come from a tree in the alley. Even if it's a parking alley, we plant a lot of food back there. Generally no one steals anything. People are respectful.

Do you travel to the USA much? I'm often bummed when I travel—there is no kidney, no duck. I like the eclectic range of protein here. I don't really love steak.

Does everyone eat sweetbreads, liver, kidneys, and the like? Amazingly, yes— my kids and my customers.

How do you get your children to be adventurous eaters? I put what I make on the table. There is always fruit, like apples, and cheese, and there is also liver or beef. They choose.

Do you have any food vices? I eat a lot of milk chocolate and Pringles, especially off-brand Pringles. They are actually healthier.

What do you keep in your freezer?
I have bear meat in the freezer. I can't keep bear downstairs in the restaurant as it's wild game.

Do you hunt? It's from my neighbor. I mainly trap—mainly hares. Wild turkeys aren't so good. They are dry, and they taste like poop.

Duck Confit with Cherries, Apples, and Chickpeas

When I'm thinking up with a dish, I always stick to a simple rule: "Would the animal I'm cooking eat the ingredients I'm preparing it with or live near the ingredients?" So this combination works. Any well-made and delicious store-bought confit will do here. Who wants to make confit at home anyway!

1 apple

2 to 3 small shallots

2 pieces duck leg confit

⅓ cup pig ears confit or bacon (optional)

2 tablespoons cooking oil or duck fat

Fleur de sel

1 sprig thyme

One 15.5-ounce can chickpeas or navy beans

Olive oil

2 cups borage or sunflower sprouts

Black pepper

10 to 12 sour cherries

Preheat the oven to 350°F. Cut the apple in quarters and remove the core. Peel the shallots and cut in half. Julienne the pig ears or bacon (if using).

Heat a large oven-safe pan (ideally around 12 inches long) over medium heat with a small amount of oil or duck fat until it starts to shimmer, but not so hot that it smokes. Place the duck legs, skin side down, in the pan, pressing lightly to get as much contact as possible with the hot surface. Add the pig ears and shallots (cut side down), and salt lightly.

Place the pan in the oven. Add the apples and thyme sprig after 10 or 15 minutes, and keep cooking for another 10 to 15 minutes, until the duck skin is crisp and the shallots are cooked through.

Rinse and drain the chickpeas. Toss them with a bit of olive oil and salt.

When the duck, shallots, and apples are ready, carefully remove them from the pan and drain the excess oil. Cut the duck legs in two across the joint.

Put a generous handful of borage on each plate. Divide the duck legs, shallots, and apples evenly among the plates. Top with the chickpeas and pig ears (if using). Salt and pepper to taste. Finish with a few sour cherries on each plate.

SERVES 4

153

ENRIQUE OLVERA

If he hadn't had a flair for romance, Enrique Olvera might never have become a chef. Born in Mexico City, Olvera grew up in a household steeped in food. His paternal grandparents were bakers, and during summers he would work behind the shop counter and watch with fascination as the bakers kneaded the dough and transformed it into fresh bread. He would also spend hours roaming the Mercado San Cosme, known for the quality of its street food, which he ate with gusto.

But he didn't get serious about cooking until he fell in love and began to make romantic meals to impress his high-school sweetheart (and now wife), Allegra. Those meals turned into a series of weekend parties for friends, and then their friends' families, all of whom began to realize Olvera's cooking talent. Some even became future investors. Although his parents expressed doubts about a future as a chef—"Working in the kitchen in Mexico seemed more the kind of profession you are obliged to execute, not a choice," Olvera explains—Allegra encouraged him to continue, and Olvera became determined to show people that chefs could occupy a respectable place in society.

When Olvera told his parents that he wanted to study the culinary arts, his father, who had resisted taking over the family bakery himself to become an engineer, insisted that his son have at least a bachelor's degree. Eventually they decided to send him to the Culinary Institute of America (CIA) in upstate New York. Here Olvera learned European techniques, inspired by the chef heroes of the day, Jean-Georges Vongerichten and Thomas Keller, and entertained notions of working in a hotel or small restaurant.

One day at the beginning of his studies, his father was in New York City and invited him to lunch at a restaurant of his choice. They wound up eating at Le Bernardin, Eric Ripert's three-star Michelin restaurant in midtown Manhattan. "It was impressive, like when you listen to your favorite band playing your favorite song," Olvera recalls. One bite of the delicately cabbage-wrapped sole with foie gras he had ordered convinced Olvera that his future lay in fine dining. "I now knew exactly what I wanted to do."

With six months left on his visa after he graduated from the CIA, Olvera went to Chicago and found a job at one of the city's chicest French restaurants with the intention of learning everything he could. He was even able to stay in a small apartment owned by his dad, who went to Chicago often on business. "I was so lucky to be able to stay rent-free; otherwise I never could have made it work!" Olvera says now.

When Olvera first opened Pujol, the food seemed derivative of the haute cuisine techniques he'd learned in the United States. That's when the chef had his second epiphany, realizing that he needed to combine Mexican traditions and techniques to create high-end Mexican cuisine that didn't yet exist.

Take Olvera's *mole madre, mole nuevo*, which reinvented the traditional Mexican chocolate and chili pepper sauce. The mole madre has been aged for over a thousand days: "Several years ago the cooks at the restaurant realized that if we reheated the mole for a certain amount of

CURRENT HOMETOWN:
Mexico City, Mexico

RESTAURANT THAT
MADE HIS NAME: Pujol,
Mexico City

SIGNATURE STYLE:
High-end Mexican food

BEST KNOWN FOR: His
one-thousand-day-old
mole sauce at Pujol;
his best-restaurant
awards; his status as
an ambassador of
Mexican cuisine; and
his many restaurants,
including Cosme and
Atla in New York City

FRIDGE: Sub-Zero

days, the flavor was more complex. So we decided to keep a small amount of it and to feed it with new ingredients," he explains.

A few years ago, disappointed with the quality of Mexican cuisine in New York City, he opened another restaurant called Cosme (after his favorite childhood market) and Atla, an all-day café. His duck carnitas (cooked in Mexican Coca-Cola) and husk meringue and corn mousse dessert have become two of the most emblematic dishes on the menu at Cosme.

With seven people living at home, including his three children and two nannies, as well as thirteen animals, things can be as hectic as the restaurant kitchen. So food tends to be simple. "Our nanny is from Oaxaca and is a really amazing cook. But we basically eat tortillas and avocado three times a day," says Olvera. Other daily staples are breakfast smoothies with nopales (cactus), blueberries, and chia; food swiped from the restaurant walk-in or smuggled from abroad.

1. **WHITE WINE**

2. **WATER**—"It's very traditional here to put citrus and chia seeds in the water and we go through a carafe per day."

3. **NOPALES**—"I like them raw or just grilled, just with some key lime and salt."

4. **EGGS,** from the chickens in Olvera's backyard

5. **BUNA COFFEE**

6. **HOMEMADE SALSA**

7. **TORTILLAS** (blue, red, and yellow corn)

8. **FRUIT PÂTÉ**—"This is a sweet, hard paste made of fruit for my children, who eat it just as it is for dessert."

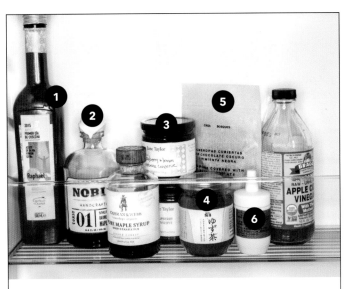

1. **CASTILLO DE CANENA EXTRA VIRGIN OLIVE OIL** from Spain

2. **NOBLE TONIC 01 MAPLE SYRUP**

3. **JUNE TAYLOR RASPBERRY AND LEMON VERBENA CONSERVE**

4. **YUZU JAM**

5. **CHOCOLATE ALMONDS** from Casa Bosques

6. **HONEY**

9. **BLACK BEANS**—"We always like to keep some in the fridge, and often use them for soups."

10. **PRICKLY PEAR**—"Allegra likes them with eggs."

11. **FRESH CHEESE**

12. **SALTED PLUMS,** for before-dinner snacks

13. **MORE TORTILLAS**

14. **CHAYOTE SQUASH**

15. **FRESH CHEESE**

Q & A

Are you always so healthy? We don't eat meat at home, only outside. So our home is pretty much vegetarian.

There's no ketchup. Why? Here we don't eat ketchup. Everything is salsa. I don't really know what we would put it in.

Is that a prickly pear? Yes, that's a chayote; we eat them either like that or boiled. We eat them with tacos. We eat everything with tacos. It's the way of eating more than a dish. We never plate tacos. Since I was a kid, we basically have tortillas like this—we'll have some sort of stew and serve it with tortillas.

What would people never find in your refrigerator? We would never have American cheese slices or leftover pizza. We don't have milk, though we do have cheese. No sodas.

What about tomatoes? It depends how long you are going to keep them in there. If you are using them that day it makes no sense. But if they are already a little ripe then it's better.

What is your family's favorite meal when you're the cook? Beef entomatadas.

You have lots of interesting things that don't look Mexican. Do you bring a lot back from your travels? We are big food smugglers. Yesterday we smuggled potatoes from Peru. We also brought back some corn. We smuggle lots of food. When we go to New York, we go to Whole Foods and drag it back here to our fridge.

Is Mexican customs cool if you bring things in? I tried once, saying I was a chef. And they wouldn't let me bring potatoes.

Do you have a couple of suggestions about cooking tortillas at home? You should never turn the tortillas more than three times over the flame. You can tell when the tortilla is cooked; it's when the edges are turned up. It should be quick on the first side, ten seconds. Then the second side the edges puff up. The last side is ultra-fast, and then you're done.

What were some of the first meals you cooked for your wife when you were a teenager? One of them was pasta, for sure, something simple, with vegetables since she was vegetarian at the moment.

Your guilty pleasure? Olives with a little Tabasco and lime as a snack before eating a meal—and ice cream while I'm watching a movie on Sundays.

Roasted Salsa de Molcajete

We eat this salsa with tortillas and avocado. To make it, I always prefer to use a molcajete—it is a large mortar and pestle made from volcanic stone and it gives a different texture and flavor. If you don't have one, though, you can always use a blender.

5 large very ripe tomatoes
¼ large white onion
2 fresh serrano chilies, or to taste
1 unpeeled garlic clove
½ cup chopped fresh cilantro
Salt

Place a cast-iron skillet or comal over high heat. Place the whole tomatoes, onion, chilies, and garlic on the hot skillet and completely char on all sides. Transfer the charred ingredients to a molcajete or blender, add the cilantro and salt to taste, and grind or blend until desired consistency. Serve with tortillas and avocado.

MAKES 3 CUPS

CURRENT HOMETOWN:
New York City

RESTAURANT THAT MADE HIS NAME: Ivan Ramen, New York City

SIGNATURE DISH: Ramen

BEST KNOWN FOR:
Being a New Yorker who opened two successful ramen shops in Tokyo; his mastery of ramen; and his cookbooks, *Ivan Ramen* and *The Gaijin Cookbook*

FRIDGE: Samsung

IVAN ORKIN

Ramen, dubbed the maverick cuisine of Japan, came as an epiphany and even a fluke of sorts for Ivan Orkin. While Orkin started off as a chef in New York, he eventually moved to Tokyo. There, on the brink of turning forty, he found his career coming full circle, all based on a simple idea: "With ramen I can do whatever the fuck I want." This realization led him not only to a mastery of Japanese cooking but also to success back home.

As a child, Orkin simply wanted food that was better than the TV dinners put on the table when his parents went into Manhattan to see the ballet. Although "my mom cooked competently, she wasn't interested in cooking. She told me she wished there was a pill she could take every morning so that she wouldn't have to eat." Dining out is a favorite childhood memory. "My warm feelings as a kid were very often related to food," he says.

At age fifteen, he snapped up a weekend job at Tsubo, a Japanese restaurant that gave him his first taste of authentic Japanese cuisine: "I had only eaten at one or two Japanese restaurants with my parents before working at Tsubo," explains Orkin. While in college he majored in Japanese and perfected his kitchen skills, cooking breakfast for his classmates in exchange for the work they did on his assignments. "I was a great student for the things that interested me, but not that many things did," he notes. He also doesn't look back very fondly to culinary school at the Culinary Institute of America—he credits it with teaching him how to fold in egg whites, and not much else. "I don't think I really cooked until I worked at Lutèce and Mesa Grill," he says now.

In 2006 Orkin opened his own restaurant in Tokyo. "It was all on me," he says. "Day in and day out, I was in the small kitchen of my two-hundred-square-foot, ten-seat restaurant." That gave him the discipline necessary for success. "When I opened, I was super serious—I didn't set off to invent a mac 'n' cheese ramen." Yes, there was a strong Western influence in his cooking, "but it was very Japanese focused." Instead of using premade or even fresh noodles, Orkin created his own recipe. But the raves came when he threw in some rye flour, in a nod to his hometown. His restaurant became so popular that Orkin opened another in Manhattan.

At home, just north of New York City, Orkin considers himself a homemaker in a fifty-fifty Japanese-American family. Here, where ketchup and Japanese Bull-Dog sauce have equal status, he is a little less brash, despite his three refrigerators. "I have three kids. I do a lot of cooking," he says. Unlike their father, his children don't enjoy going out to eat very much. "I guess it's because we eat really well at home," says Orkin ruefully.

The main refrigerator is spic and span. "For the Japanese, the end of the year is a cleansing time. So we start the New Year by emptying all our drawers. We throw away what we don't use. We organize our Tupperware and throw away those that don't have lids."

Orkin avoids cultural clichés, though. "Even now I don't call Ivan Ramen a Japanese restaurant, but I haven't fallen into the trap of the matzo ball ramen or anything like that," he says. In his opinion, that wouldn't benefit a bowl of ramen.

1. **SUSHI GINGER**

2. **PICKLED RED CHILIES**

3. **BLACK BEAN GARLIC SAUCE**

4. **TOMATO PASTE**

5. **KOREAN BARBECUE PASTE**

6. **TOASTED SESAME SALAD DRESSING**—"The bottled stuff is pretty darn good. I use it on a shabu-shabu salad: thinly sliced boiled pork belly served with lettuce, tomato, and cucumber. You can make this salad really fast and everyone likes it."

7. **CREAMY UMAMI SAUCE**

8. **FUNKY CHINESE CABBAGE PICKLES**— "I use them for yaki soba."

9. **CURED YOLKS,** from the restaurant

10. **VACUUM-PACKED OKRA AND SEAWEED**

11. **SWEET BLACK BEANS**— "I cook them in sugar and soy and they are good on vanilla ice cream."

12. **KATSUOBUSHI SOAKED IN SOY SAUCE**

13. **TOFU HAMBURGERS**— "We are obsessed with these. This is now comfort food for me. It goes well with potato salad, and you can serve it with Bull-Dog sauce."

14. **CELERY**—"For my son. He is not a huge vegetable eater, but he really likes celery sticks."

15. **WHIPPED CREAM,** left over from a family party—"I normally make my own, but my sister brought this over."

16. **CHOCOLATE MILK**

17. **BEER**

18. **CHAMPAGNE**

19. **BROCCOLI**— "The sure thing my ten-year-old will always eat."

20. **BROOKLYN-MADE SAKE,** served at the restaurant

21. **CHILI,** left over from a football game

22. **SALTED SALMON,** for nigiri

23. **JAPANESE PICKLES**

24. **JAPANESE PICKLED MOUNTAIN VEGETABLES**

25. **PICKLED PLUMS**

26. **PORK BELLY**

27. **PICKLED GINGER**

28. **LITTLE NUBS OF VEGETABLES,** to be used quickly (white radish, cucumber)

29. **LEFTOVERS FROM SUPERIORITY BURGER: BEETS AND RICE AND BEANS**

30. **PEANUT BUTTER**

31. **BLACK OLIVES**

32. **DIJONNAISE**

33. **MISO PASTE**

34. **SESAME OIL**

35. **TONKATSU SAUCE—**
"My liquid gold. It's great on a hamburger or bread-crumb-coated fried shrimp, chicken, or pork."

36. **BLUE CRUSHED ICE FLAVORING,** from Japan—
"It goes with our son's ice shredder. He likes to make snow cones."

37. **LEMON SOY SAUCE**

38. **MAYONNAISE**

39. **JAR OF MISCELLANEOUS TAKEOUT CONDIMENTS—**
"Sometimes I do a sauce where I blend all of my Asian condiments together and something good usually comes out of that."

40. **YAMAKI NOODLE SOUP SAUCE WITH DRIED BONITO**

41. **YUZU JUICE**

42. **SPICY CHILI SAUCE**

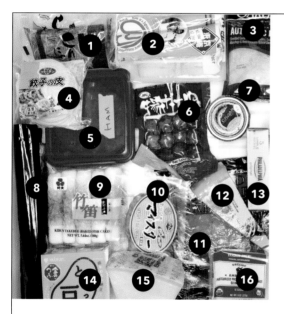

4. **GYOZA SKINS,** for making dumplings

5. **HAM**

6. **SEAFOOD MEATBALLS**

7. **SALMON EGGS—**"We love them and eat them all the time. They make everything better. A bowl of rice with a pile of salmon eggs and soy sauce is delightful."

8. **BACON**

9. **FISH CAKES**

10. **CHINESE SAUSAGES**

11. **SMOKED SALMON**

12. **JARLSBERG CHEESE**

13. **CREAM CHEESE**

14. **NATTO** (fermented soy beans)

15. **PARMESAN CHEESE**

16. **AMERICAN CHEESE**

1. **KONNYAKU** (yam jelly)

2. **SHIRATAKI NOODLES,** for hot pot

3. **MEXICAN CHEESE**

Q & A

Your wife is Japanese and you lived in Japan for a long time. Do you eat mainly Japanese at home? If push came to shove foodwise, this is definitely a Japanese house. We don't have bread all the time but we do always have rice.

Who cooks at home? Together with my wife we do a lot of planning. We do Sunday meal prep for the whole week: shopping, blanching, marinating. Then we have options for the week. Otherwise we find food goes in the garbage because it goes bad or you're starving and nothing is prepped and you end up having to go out or race around. We have had a lot of success thinking a few steps ahead.

Do you shop at stores like Costco for your meal prep? I often go to Trader Joe's and Costco. I'm not that Brooklyn guy who will only have food made by some hippie. It's not realistic. Once a month we will go to Costco or order a bunch of meat from the restaurant. I break it down, vacuum-seal it, then freeze and label it. So there are a bunch of protein options in the freezer. We are a family of five—my kids are all boys.

Luckily you've got a good-size fridge. But you have two others, right? I've got two downstairs and a wine fridge. I have lots of beer, Champagne. I like my Champagne really cold. My wine fridge doesn't keep it cold enough.

Wouldn't it just be easier to have one big refrigerator, like a professional walk-in? That would be awesome. I would have one in a fucking heartbeat. You can hang meat. If you have a walk-in you can cool things on a sheet tray. You can have tall bottles. It's about how you can store things.

Do you ever overstock? Any Japanese techniques for not overconsuming? Even a professional cook—sometimes you buy too much or something gets buried deep in. It's disappointing when you realize it isn't good anymore. If you haven't used something for a number of times you should consider getting rid of it. My wife, Mari Sawamura, was basically the Marie Kondo a generation before. She is an interior decorator. She would do TV shows like that, with a before and after.

A good organizational tip for the fridge? We keep a container on the bottom shelf in which we put all the leftover little nubs of vegetables that need to be used quickly.

Guilty pleasure food? I'm in my fifties so I like to be careful what I eat. I lost a lot of weight when I gave up sweets, but an ice cream sundae with hot fudge and nuts is one of the greatest things of all time. I don't get tired of that at all.

A quick fix for a sandwich? American cheese—it can tie together any sad sandwich and make it a good sandwich.

A rule to eat by? The rule in my life more than what I will and won't eat is that I try to not eat while I'm doing something. If I do eat while I watch TV, read the paper, or am on a conference call, I eat lettuce or an apple. If I eat an ice cream sundae I want to be in the moment, I want to enjoy every calorie and feel like I had a great experience.

Hiyashi Chuka (Cold Ramen Noodles)

This is the cold noodle standard in Japan. Literally translated to "chilled Chinese," it's mainly served during June and July, but you can eat it anytime you like. The beauty of this dish is that almost any array of veggies and protein work, and it's a great way to finish off leftover vegetables and meats. Cold ramen noodles are classically topped with cucumbers and tomatoes as well as slivers of omelet and finely julienned ham. The delicious "soup" that coats the dish resembles drinkable vinaigrette.

For the garlic oil:

4 garlic cloves

⅓ cup canola oil

For the "soup" base:

¾ cup sake

¾ cup mirin

2 cups soy sauce

⅔ cup honey

1¼ cups rice vinegar

¾ cup brown rice vinegar

¼ cup sesame oil

1 tablespoon salt

For the assembly:

4 portions fresh or dried ramen noodles (see Note)

½ pound smoked ham, cut into thin julienne strips

One 3-egg omelet, cooked, cooled to room temperature, and slivered

1 English cucumber, peeled, seeded, and cut into thin half moons

4 small tomatoes, cut into wedges

1 bunch scallions, sliced thinly

To make the oil, crush the garlic lightly. Combine the garlic and canola oil in a small saucepan. Cook over very low heat, to infuse the oil, until the garlic is soft, about 20 minutes. Strain and reserve the oil, and save the garlic for something else.

To make the base, combine the sake and mirin in a heavy-bottomed pot. Bring to a boil and simmer for 3 minutes to remove the alcohol flavor. Add soy and honey to the pot, stirring to dissolve the honey. Remove from the heat and allow the liquid to cool. Add the remaining ingredients, including the garlic oil. Cool and reserve.

To assemble, cook four portions of ramen noodles according to the package directions. Quickly chill them in a colander under cold running water. Divide between four bowls. Divide the soup base equally among the bowls. Top each bowl with small piles of the garnishes. Sprinkle with the scallions.

SERVES 4

Note: You can buy ramen noodles at Asian supermarkets or use instant noodles (just throw away the flavorings).

Yaki Udon (Fried Japanese Thick Noodles)

This is a perfect "clear out your fridge" recipe. I recommend you treat it more as a road map. You can buy meat and veggies specifically for this dish if you want, but the great thing is that you can use any leftover meats and nubs of produce that you don't know what to do with, and you're on your way to a quick, easy meal. Follow the basic knife cuts and amounts, but otherwise have at it! I like to use a wok to cook this meal, but any heavy-bottomed sauté pan works just as well, though it may take longer to cook.

For the sauce:

⅓ cup soy sauce

¼ cup mirin (Japanese sweet cooking wine)

½ cup sake

¼ cup oyster sauce

1 tablespoon sugar

1 tablespoon sesame oil

For the udon noodles:

Two 8-ounce blocks of frozen udon (see Note)

2 tablespoons vegetable oil

½ pound thinly sliced pork belly (available in Asian supermarkets; see Note)

1 onion, cut in ¼-inch slices

½ cup julienned carrot

1 red bell pepper, cored and cut in ¼-inch strips

⅓ medium head green cabbage, shredded thinly (about 2 cups)

Katsuobushi (Japanese dried bonito flakes)

Beni shoga (pickled ginger)

To make the sauce: Combine all the ingredients in a small saucepan over low heat and stir until the sugar is dissolved. Set aside.

To make the noodles: Remove the noodles from the packages and place in a bowl of warm water. Gently pull them apart and leave in the water as you sauté the vegetables. (Keep a strainer nearby to drain the noodles.)

Heat a wok or heavy-bottomed skillet over medium-high heat. Add 1 tablespoon of the oil and heat until barely smoking. Add the pork belly and stir until just barely cooked, about 1 minute. Remove from the pan and set aside.

Add the onions and cook until just softened, about 3 to 4 minutes. Add the carrots and peppers and cook until softened, another 3 to 4 minutes. Add the cabbage and cook until fully softened, about 5 minutes. Add back in the pork belly and combine. Remove everything from the pan and set aside.

Drain the noodles very well and pat dry with paper towels. Wipe out the pan, add the other tablespoon of oil, and heat until barely smoking. Add the udon, and cook, stirring occasionally, until lightly crisped, about 5 minutes.

Add the vegetables and meat back to the pan with the udon, mix well, and pour the sauce over everything. Combine well. Cook, stirring occasionally, until the sauce thickens, about 5 minutes.

Serve on individual plates and garnish with a big pinch of katsuobushi and about a teaspoon, or more to taste, of beni shoga.

SERVES 4

Note: You can find udon noodles in the freezer section of any Asian market and usually in packs of five blocks. If you can't find them, substitute approximately one (8 ounce) frozen block of any cooked and cooled Asian-style noodle. If you can't buy the sliced pork belly, half-freeze the pork until it is very firm but not rock hard, and then slice it as thinly as possible.

PACO PÉREZ

The tiny, isolated beachside town of Llançà, for all its charm, may seem an unusual place to find one of Spain's culinary masters. Virtually deserted during the off-tourist season, intrepid diners come here from the world over to taste the inventive *mar i muntanya* (surf and turf) cuisine of Paco Pérez. But it makes total sense to Pérez. "Even before people came to visit, the fishermen used to light fires on the beach and cook fish and drink and talk about life. I love this place—the light, the sea, and the skies. I have a connection, and I am meant to be here," he says.

Pérez grew up in Empordà, the Catalonian region in Spain known for its wine, and started working at his family's tapas bar when he was twelve. He did a bit of cleaning and serving, and found it an enriching experience. Always curious, he soon found himself in the kitchen, experimenting. "One day I heard about pizzas, and tried to cook one on hot stones outside under the sun. Of course, it was a disaster!" he recalls.

Cooking school was, unfortunately, out of the question—Barcelona was too far away and the costs of bus fare and culinary school kept Pérez at home. He continued working summers and weekends at local restaurants. Eventually he trained with Ferran Adrià at the legendary El Bulli in nearby Roses. Adrià had a huge impact on the young chef: "He taught me how to approach food with the senses: the smell, the feel, and taste." His final training was just across the French border with chef Michel Guérard, one of the founders of nouvelle cuisine, where he learned some French as well as respect for what he was doing.

After working with Guérard, Pérez did military service (compulsory in Spain when he was a teenager). "My task was to cook, and my superiors used to like what I made. Therefore, I could go to the market sometimes to buy what I needed, which was a respite," he says. After he was discharged, he heard about a family who needed help at a tiny beachside restaurant called Miramar. He decided to make a little extra cash one holiday weekend, and met Montse, the proprietors' daughter. They fell in love, married in 1984, and Pérez put down roots for the last time.

Montse's family were originally from Barcelona but had fled the city during the Spanish Civil War. They'd opened the restaurant in 1939, building the business up from a simple shack to a forty-five-room inn and restaurant. In the 1990s, when Catalonian creative cooking became better known, they decided to upgrade the family business.

Concentrating on seasonal items sourced from the nearby area, Pérez decided to use many of the more technical approaches that he had learned over the years, such as smoking, fermentation, and spherification, the process of turning liquids into shapes. His avant-garde approach let him celebrate the restaurant's Mediterranean roots in a modern way. "We weren't going to serve guests a tomato salad or a plate of pasta," he says. "People come to restaurants for a special experience." And so dishes such as griddled sea cucumbers (served under a glass dome filled with smoke from burning vines) and a "sea floor"—sea urchin and caviar with Hollandaise sauce served along with a 3D-printed coral design—came

CURRENT HOMETOWN:
Llançà, Spain

**RESTAURANT THAT MADE
HIS NAME:** Miramar,
Llançà, Spain

SIGNATURE STYLE:
Avant-garde Catalan

BEST KNOWN FOR:
His Michelin-starred
restaurants and his
passion for Catalonia

FRIDGE: Balay

to delight and surprise guests and earned the restaurant two Michelin stars.

Pérez and his family live just behind the restaurant, and there is little separation between work and home. "It's not difficult," he says. "You learn how to deal with all the responsibilities, and you just need to be happy and make others happy." Meals, which are often on the fly in his tiled, homey kitchen, tend to be quick and easy. "At home there's no Thermomix or anything—I cook like a normal person there!" says Pérez. "We eat potatoes, a little casserole of whatever's leftover in

the fridge, omelets, pomme frites. Everyday cuisine."

After three decades at Miramar, and numerous restaurants across Europe, Pérez could live anywhere. But he's happy to stay close to his first restaurant and in his beloved Catalonia. "I grew up in this magical place between the mountains and the sea," he says. "People eat food based on the environment around us: the mountains, sea, and garden. There is a sense of religion in cooking for oneself, family, and friends. My best experiences have been here."

1. **CHOCOLATE,** gifts from a customer, and a favorite of his son's

2. **BLACK TRUFFLE JUICE**

3. **STRAWBERRY JAM**

4. **SPANISH DATES**

5. **ARTICHOKES**

6. **SOBRASADA DE MAJORCA** (cured sausage)

7. **IDIAZABAL CHEESE**

8. **CHEESE,** from Gipuzkoa, San Sebastián

9. **SHEEP'S MILK CHEESE**

10. **FEVER-TREE MADAGASCAN COLA—** "My wife and I prefer it to Coca-Cola. At least it's less harmful."

11. **ANCHOVY-STUFFED GREEN OLIVES—** "Sometimes these are just for a snack or sometimes as a tapas in a meal."

12. **PICKLED GUINDILLA PEPPERS**

13. **JAMS**

14. **GREEN BEANS**

15. **FIGS—**"We used to eat figs around the table with Julia, the brave woman who started this dream of a restaurant called Miramar. There was a fig tree in the garden and we ate fig by fig in the afternoon until the end of the summer."

16. **MUSHROOMS,** from a local market to use in pickled mushrooms (see recipe page 175)

17. **DULCE DE MEMBRILLO** (quince paste)

Q & A

What do Catalonians eat? They eat vegetable stews, different kinds of fish, and olive oil with everything. Every season is fantastic and products such as sea cucumber, pigs' trotters, broad beans with fresh mint, and especially peas from Maresme are extraordinary. Unfortunately, now, with globalization, people also eat whatever they want.

What did your grandmother or mother use to make you? Open sea urchins with tomato bread.

What do you cook for your friends and family? Different kinds of rice, stews, fish over hot coals, Catalan-style green peas, and vegetables in a thousand ways.

What is your favorite food when coming home from a long day at work? Something simple in a crockpot. Almost every day I have a lunch cooked in a crockpot—could be rice (there are thousands of ways to cook rice), fish, meat, surf and turf. To be honest, I am always playing and exploring in the crockpot.

What foods do you hate? Hot dog with mustard and ketchup.

Looks like you love local cheese and sausages! Where do you get them? The charcuterie comes from my friend José, a high-quality butcher, and the fish, very fresh fish, is from my friend Xavi. I've known them both almost my entire life. Sometimes I'll just buy things to take out, and sometimes we'll all eat together. Most of the time we don't have a plan. They come to Miramar and say hello and last month I went with José to Manchester and visited Tast, the restaurant I am advising there.

What do you reach for when you are starving? Yogurt with cereals and fruits and honey.

What food could you eat every day without getting sick of it? Iberian ham with *pa amb tomàquet*, a rustic Catalan specialty of toasted bread rubbed with tomato and garlic.

Pickled Mushrooms

Our first time testing pickled mushrooms at the restaurant was an instant success. It was autumn and all of the chefs were gathered around the pot, battling over who was going eat them. I had to remind them to slow down: cooking is patience.

4½ cups mixed mushrooms—shiitake, porcini, button
1 garlic clove
⅓ cup extra virgin olive oil
2 shallots, sliced into rounds
½ cup sliced carrots
1 bay leaf
10 black peppercorns
1 sprig thyme
⅓ cup white wine vinegar

Carefully wash and clean the mushrooms with a dry towel. Smash up the garlic clove and sauté it gently in a pot with the oil over low heat for 10 minutes. Add the shallots and carrot slices to the garlic. Cook for another 10 minutes. Slice the mushrooms into 1-inch pieces. Add 4 cups of the mushrooms, the bay leaf, black peppercorns, and thyme to the pot. Continue cooking over low heat for 5 to 10 minutes.

Pour in the vinegar and cook for 5 more minutes. Add the remaining uncooked mushrooms and stir well.

Refrigerate the mushrooms for 24 hours before using them.

SERVES 4

NADINE LEVY REDZEPI

You might think that being the wife of René Redzepi, chef and owner of the world-renowned Noma, might be challenging if you also love to cook. But you'd be wrong—Nadine Levy Redzepi may well be the best chef in the Redzepi household. "René is not demanding at all. I just think he is appreciative of someone cooking for him, since he spends so much time cooking for others," she says. Not only does she help run the Noma franchise, she also runs the household, does all the shopping and cooking for six people, throws together last-minute dinners for guests with aplomb. She even managed to write a best-selling cookbook in her spare time.

Redzepi is the daughter of two street musicians. Her parents met in Paris—her Danish mother was an au pair, her father an English street busker. When they weren't bouncing from one capital to another and living out of cars and cheap hotels, they returned to Tavira, the tiny Portuguese coastal town where Redzepi was born and where her grandparents had bought them a house.

"Every day seemed to revolve around food and eating," she says. "I remember pomegranates, warm from the sun, their sweetness, the bitterness of the skin, and the bright pink juice running down my arms and hands." Neighbors would come to trade tomatoes in exchange for their olives, almonds, and eggs. When they were on the road busking, she would get treated to an ice cream. "I always chose rum raisin or mint chocolate, flavors that remind me of France, and that I don't eat elsewhere."

She started cooking early on, mostly porridge and scrambled eggs. But she really became obsessed with cooking at eight, when she happened upon the BBC show *Ready Steady Cook* as she lay sick in bed. "I was blown away that they could cook three dishes in twenty minutes, and I just grabbed my notepad and wrote everything down." She felt hungry for the first time in five days.

Back in Copenhagen, where her aunt lived, Redzepi started working as a waitress at Noma when she was nineteen and met René by chance when she got lost looking for linens on her third shift. He offered to help her. Clueless as to who he was, Redzepi asked how long he had been working there. "From the beginning," he replied. "You know this is my place, right?" She blushed, went back to work, and replayed the conversation in her head throughout that evening. A month later at a staff party, he threw a piece of bread at her from across the room. The rest is history, she says.

Influenced by her nomadic childhood, her cooking style is eclectic—she's a fan of big flavor and light ingredients, and not averse to experimenting with whatever her husband brings home. "I love playing around with things like chicken-wing garum and different ferments—they make everything taste so delicious and satisfying."

She does all this from the Redzepi household's warm, lived-in kitchen, with its wooden countertops, fireplace, brass sink, and exposed beams. And although her newfound fame has made her an instant celebrity, the guests who have been at their home have always known that Redzepi is much, much more than the wife of a great chef.

1. **SMOKED CHILI PEPPERS,** a gift from a Mexican friend

2. **CHEESE,** from Paul Cunningham, an English chef in Copenhagen

3. **ROYAL BELGIAN CAVIAR**—"I honestly like to eat it on really good potato chips with 50 percent full-fat crème fraîche."

4. **SUN-DRIED TOMATOES,** from a former Noma chef

5. **MORGENOST CHEESE**

6. **LEFTOVER CHICKEN**—"We probably have chicken once a week with roast potatoes."

7. **CHICKEN FAT**

8. **PUMPKIN SEED MISO**

9. **KELP SALT**—"It's great on steamed rice with some chili de arbol. I even like it on plain yogurt."

10. **EGGS**—"They're from a woman who used to be my mother's boss. She had a house in the country and would bring extra eggs to sell to the staff. My mom started buying them for us. René tasted them and wanted them at the restaurant."

11. **GARUM PROTEIN**—"René brings them home from the restaurant's fermentation lab."

12. **VEGETABLE GARUMS**

13. **VEGETABLE REDUCTIONS**

14. **NOMITE**—a Marmite experiment from Noma's Australia pop-up. "Being half English, I grew up with Marmite. When I feel a little nostalgic, I like to eat it on buttered toast with soft-boiled eggs. Actually, buttered toast with Marmite and caviar is also quite delicious."

15. **HOMEMADE HOT SAUCE**—"René and I made it together."

16. **EGG WHITES,** for the financier cake (recipe on page 180)

17. **APPLESAUCE**—"I always make homemade applesauce. The apples come from the communal courtyard where we live."

18. **SUJUK SAUSAGE**

19. **PHILADELPHIA CREAM CHEESE**— "I'm the only one who eats this."

20. **SLICED BACON**

21. **MOZZARELLA,** leftover from a playgroup—"I asked my daughter what she wanted to have for dinner and she wanted them all to make their own pizza."

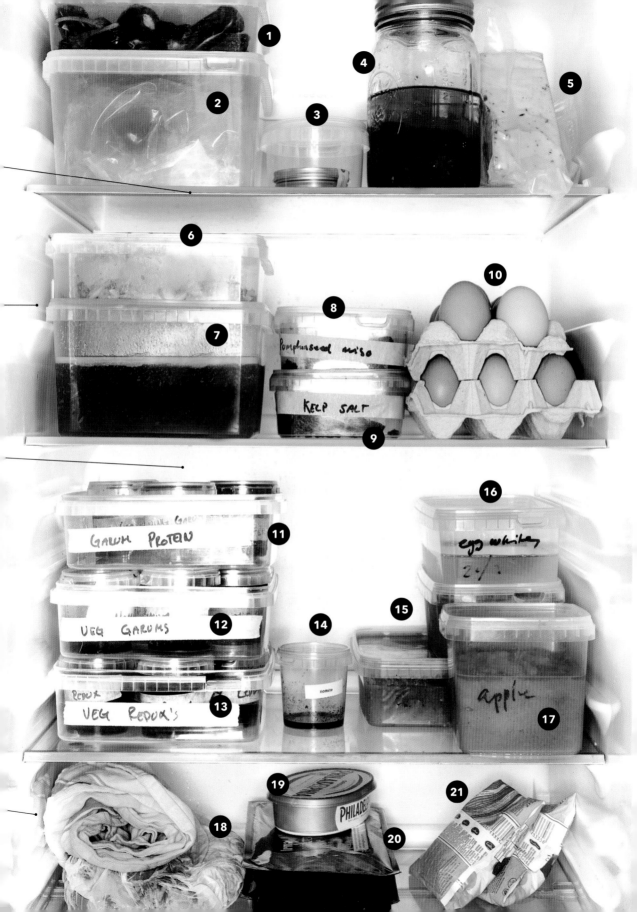

Large Financier Cake

I am quite obsessed with egg yolks in general, whether curing them in various ways or making pasta, so I was thrilled to have a recipe that not only allows me to use the leftover egg whites, but also just happens to be one of my favorite cakes.

1⅓ cups almond flour
1¾ cups sugar
⅓ cup all-purpose flour
Flaky salt (preferably Maldon)
1 vanilla bean
1½ cups egg whites
14 tablespoons butter

Preheat the oven to 350°F. Line a 8-inch square baking pan with parchment paper. Butter the sides of the pan.

Mix together the almond flour, sugar, and all-purpose flour along with a pinch of salt. Split the vanilla bean lengthwise and scrape out the seeds. Add the vanilla to the egg whites and then beat with an electric beater or stand mixer until stiff. Fold the dry ingredients into the egg whites and continue to fold until the dough has an even consistency.

Cut the butter into small pieces and melt in a saucepan over medium-low heat. Stir the butter with a whisk. Tilt the pot from side to side. As soon as you see golden-brown sediment at the bottom of the pan and the butter smells nutty, remove from the heat. (Butter can burn quickly, so be careful not to overbrown it.)

Pour the butter into the dough and stir until incorporated. Pour the dough into the baking pan, sprinkle with salt, and put in the oven to bake for 25 to 30 minutes.

Remove and let cool. The cake will fall once it starts to cool, but this is what you want. I prefer this cake when it has cooled completely. It's great with fresh berries and ice cream, but also just as fantastic on its own with a cup of tea.

SERVES 8

Q & A

What do you cook for your family? Do they have any favorites? The favorites vary. My kids, like all kids, go through phases of not wanting to eat certain things, but we always insist they taste everything properly. Everyone loves forest chicken with roast potatoes though!

What do you always have in your fridge? A lot! René and I work out five times a week with a trainer and a few friends, so afterward, I cook a decent breakfast for everyone. We also often have dinner guests drop by, so it's just very well stocked at all times.

Why do you have two fridges? There actually just wasn't space for a big fridge in our kitchen, so we have the big one in the pantry and the smaller pullout one in the kitchen with all the things that we use the most.

The large fridge is really well organized, almost like a refrigerator in a restaurant. How come? There are six of us living here and lots of people coming through on a daily basis, so it makes sense to have it organized restaurant style. I can cook faster when everything is where it's supposed to be. Between my mother and the kids, I often have to reorganize it, though.

What would we never find in your refrigerator? Ketchup and store-bought mayonnaise—it only takes two minutes to make mayo.

What foods would you never eat? I don't like processed foods. I like my produce to be as close to its natural form as possible.

What is your favorite junk food? None. I don't like the way junk food makes you feel tired and heavy after you eat it.

It looks like half of the larger refrigerator is a collection of garum and miso experiments! Do you use them at home?

Having the ferments makes it quite effortless to make vegetarian meals. Also making pasta with a few drops of chicken-wing garum and egg yolks takes no time at all.

How important is umami in your cooking? Very! Good food makes me happy.

Who does the food shopping in your house? And where do you shop? I do! I go to the market pretty much every two days, and then to the best supermarket and the best butcher. All my favorites are within a five-hundred-meter [about a third of a mile] radius. They're also in the same vicinity as our youngest child's kindergarten, so it works out perfectly that I can shop just before picking her up on the bike.

Did you have any strange cravings when you were pregnant? I was incredibly nauseous in the first term with all three girls, so the only thing I could think to eat was rye bread with cream cheese, sliced tomatoes, and lots of salt and pepper. This is still something I love to eat now.

What are some local products you love to use? Everything from the ocean is incredible. The vegetables also are delicious, and although we might not have lots of exotic fruits, we have a huge variety of greens, and root vegetables that are all really so tasty. When it's berry season, I think the Nordic berries are the best. The season is very short and sweet.

What is in your freezer? When I make curries and other simmer dishes, I like to make them in large amounts so that I can freeze portions, so that I have delicious food for days where I might not have time to cook. It takes hours for a curry to simmer into what I want it to be, and to be able to just take that out of the freezer and cook some rice and a few other things is quite amazing.

ANTHONY ROSE

To this day Toronto chef Anthony Rose admits he still gets nervous cooking while his mother is around. She penned the foreword to his book, *The Last Schmaltz*, and claims that he makes the best pastrami—ever—but that she never imagined him becoming a successful cook, despite his culinary school degree. Rose's cuisine is more akin to his grandmother's cooking than fine dining—with one major difference. In spite of undeniable guilt as a child when he first tasted forbidden bacon with his Uncle Irv ("I just ordered as he did," he recalls), from then on, he has never looked back. Now the owner of seven restaurants, including the famed Rose and Sons, he serves an eclectic mix of cuisines that are definitely not kosher.

Rose's career first took off as the head chef of Alias, a Manhattan bistro on the Lower East Side. After getting rave reviews, he "promptly moved to upstate New York where no one cared," he recalls. He returned to Toronto, his birthplace, became the head chef at the Drake Hotel for five years, and, afterward, began testing Jewish food. He opened his first place and hit it big: "Jewish food was so hot and I was the Canadian poster child. My mom is very proud," he says.

Rose isn't much of a stickler for orthodoxy. That's why he can serve up matzo ball soup from his mom's recipe at Rose and Sons, and then squeeze a barbecue joint, complete with pork ribs, into its backyard. He is unapologetic in his cultural mash-ups and comic overtures. His newest venture is a bakery, which turns out such over-the-top sweets as banana split layer cake. Rose's quick puns often leave him the butt of his own jokes. The translation of his newest restaurant, Fet Zun (Fat Son), isn't lost on Rose. Overweight and awkward as a child, he explains his love of food this way: "I can eat one patty melt every year, but the fat kid in me eats one per day."

Rose's kitchen is the kind of place where you don't know where to look first. Memorabilia, vintage concert posters, and framed photos—his girlfriend is a photographer—cover the walls; kilims blanket the wood floors; and photos of his son plaster the refrigerator door, spilling over to the cabinets.

His home fridge is equally eclectic, filled with easy takeout and convenience foods like potato salad and coleslaw. But root around and there's a hot sauce shelf to bring tears to your eyes, a noteworthy assortment of legalized marijuana goods, and a camouflaged box of fudge. Rose got excited when a Cabela's, the sporting goods store, opened about twenty minutes from his cottage in north Canada: "I started buying things that I didn't need—like little lures or camp equipment," he explains. "Then I noticed they make two dozen different types of fudge. So now I just go for the fudge." That same fudge made an indulgent addition to the bread pudding recipe he recently concocted with his son.

CURRENT HOMETOWN:
Toronto, Ontario

RESTAURANT THAT MADE HIS NAME: Alias, New York City

SIGNATURE STYLE: Comfort food with Jewish roots

BEST KNOWN FOR: Being dubbed the "King of Comfort Food" by *Toronto Life*; Rose and Sons, a diner turned deli and six other restaurants in Toronto; and his cookbook *The Last Schmaltz*

FRIDGE: Jenn-Air

1. **SOUR PICKLES**—"I fermented them for two months."

2. **HIS MOM'S MATZO BALL SOUP**

3. **SOOM TAHINI**—"I'm going to use it for a tahini ranch recipe which I'll pour over tomatoes with lots of red onions. I also like making club sandwiches with it."

4. **POTATO SALAD AND COLESLAW,** from Rose and Sons

5. **HENDERSON BEER**—"That was made specifically for Rob Wilder, my business partner, and has his face on it. It's absolutely delicious BUT the image is amazing."

6. **DATES**

7. **SMOKED TURKEY AND PASTRAMI**

8. **CABELA'S FUDGE**

9. **SAUERKRAUT**

10. **BLUE CHEESE**

11. **DRIED TUNA**

12. **AGED MIMOLETTE**

13. **JERK SPICE,** made by a friend

14. **SAUVAGINE RAW COW'S MILK CHEESE**

15. **CAULIFLOWER SOUP**—"My son's fave."

16. **HENDERSON BEER**

17. **LOCAL CIDER**

18. **BANANA SPLIT SCHMAKE,** from Rose's deli Schmaltz Appetizing

19. **TOMATO SAUCE WITH SAUSAGES**—"I make huge batches once a week and pull from the freezer to make dinners for my family."

20. **BRAISED HAM HOCKS**

21. **BREAD PUDDING**—"My son was eating French toast and he said this is like bread pudding. So we baked a bread pudding. We don't eat a lot of sweets. It's more about the process of making them."

22. **BEAN SOUP**

23. **STRAWBERRIES AND RASPBERRIES**—"I only buy fruits my son is actually going to eat."

24. **FLOUR AND CORN TORTILLAS**

25. **SAUSAGE,** from an agricultural exhibition—"I picked it up when I did a demo at the fair."

26. **ANCHOVIES WITH CHILIES IN OIL**

27. **HOT DOGS**

28. **DOUBLE-SMOKED BACON**

29. **CLEARLY CANADIAN SPARKLING WATER**—"This is what I drank as a kid."

30. **KARNATZEL** (dry aged beef sausage)

31. **PEAMEAL (CANADIAN) BACON**

Q & A

There seem to be a lot of Canadian specialties in your fridge. That is what Americans call Canadian bacon or what we call peameal bacon, as it used to be rolled in crushed yellow peas on the outside. We use it for the famous peameal bacon sandwich. That's breakfast around these parts. It's so good. And right next to that we have hot dogs, which I like to have with my Kraft mac 'n' cheese. Which is also very Canadian.

You literally slice up hot dogs and throw them in? It's one of my dirty meals. I would eat it with extra Kraft cheese slices, extra butter, and hot dogs on top. It reminds me of when I was a very fat kid.

How often do you eat this? I'd say once a year I go back to that place.

When did you lose weight? You seem to be in great shape. I had always fluctuated. But it's since I started yoga, the gym, and eating paleo.

Is paleo a big thing in Canada? I'm not sure. I do it most of the time, except when I'm around my son. We went to Baskin-Robbins once and he ordered peanut butter chocolate ice cream—which is also my favorite. And I ordered nothing. He got bummed and said it wasn't fun. He wanted to eat ice cream with me. So ever since then, when I'm with him I don't really say no—although he has started to eat healthier.

What don't you have in here? I use everything! I have too much mustard, though. Here is the mustard shelf, with a little bit of other things thrown in, including marijuana gummies. Those are a little intense; you just have to eat a little.

What's a little? Like a nibble, a quarter. It's funny, at the store they say take one, then you're like, what the fuck, man! Feel free to help yourself.

What is in your freezer? As of this morning I have absolutely nothing in my freezer. My sweet and lovely girlfriend left it open a crack and everything completely thawed. Usually I cook once a week and freeze the food for later. I am so mad—I was very much looking forward to tomato-braised beef shank. I babied this sweet meat for a good week with a beautiful marinade and then a crust before slow roasting.

Tell me the one premade item that is indispensable for you. Clamato—one of the most important things in the fridge. You can't make a Caesar cocktail without it.

Is that like a Canadian Bloody Mary? It's similar, but it has Clamato (clam and tomato juice blend) as well as vodka, Worcestershire, Tabasco. I like it shaken and then strained. I don't drink Caesars after two p.m. It's a morning or brunch cocktail. You know—when you wake up and you just need to drink something?

It looks like you also eat pretty healthily. Any superfoods in here? Dandelion greens. I think this is the most impressive product: it's the greatest thing for you. The more bitter, the better, and then you make that into a kimchi—that's a superfood right there.

What are the dates for? I was trying to make a granola bar or ball for my son to eat for breakfast. And this was holding it together.

Is this Mimolette [a cheese from France]? Check it out—it has black skin! For years it was the same way here as in Europe. Then there was a massive shipment of Mimolette that was infested with mites as well as fleas in the crevices. The government said, You can't send this cheese here. So they started dipping it in wax for export. The other cheese is a raw cow's milk—Sauvagine, that's a very sexy cheese.

Maple Bread Pudding

You can make the bread pudding and stop there or you can cut it up and turn it into French toast. To say that this "needs" anything extra would, frankly, be decadent but to elevate it to the realm of a serious brunch dish, some stewed seasonal fruit or fresh berries would not go amiss.

For bread pudding:

2 ¾ cups full-fat milk

¾ cup cream

1 orange rind, shaved into long strips

3 long cinnamon sticks, broken in half

1 vanilla bean, split lengthwise, seeds scraped

1 pound brioche, crusts removed, cut into eight 1-inch-thick slices

6 eggs

2 tablespoons maple syrup

¼ cup sugar

For the French toast:

¼ cup unsalted butter

8 teaspoons powdered sugar

1 cup sour cream

Maple syrup to serve

Preheat the oven to 375°F. Place the milk, cream, orange rind, cinnamon, and vanilla pod and seeds in a medium saucepan. Heat gently over medium-low heat and remove just before it comes to the boil, about 5 minutes. Set aside for about 20 minutes so the cream cools a bit and the flavors infuse.

Line a 9 x 13-inch rectangular baking dish with parchment paper and lay the brioche slices flat on top.

Place the eggs, maple syrup, and sugar in a medium bowl and whisk well. Pour the warm milk gradually into the eggs, whisking the whole time. Strain the custard. Pour two thirds of it over the brioche so that the pieces are fully covered. Place the remaining custard in a wide, shallow bowl and set aside.

Place the baking dish in the oven and bake for 20 minutes, until the custard is cooked through and golden brown. Set aside to cool. Then slice into eight squares.

To make French toast: Place half the butter in a large nonstick frying pan and place on a medium-high heat. Dip half the bread squares into the remaining custard mix, transfer to a plate, and sprinkle ½ teaspoon of powdered sugar over each square.

Put the bread squares immediately into the pan sugar side down, and fry for 30 seconds to 1 minute to caramelize the sugar. While the squares are frying, sprinkle another ½ teaspoon of powdered sugar onto each slice. Flip over and cook for the same amount of time, until the sugar is dark brown and crispy.

Remove from the pan, rest on a wire rack, and repeat process with the remaining butter and bread squares.

To serve, place a slice of French toast on each plate with 2 tablespoons of sour cream and as much maple syrup as you like.

SERVES 8

Smoked Turkey Reuben

Schmear as much or as little Russian dressing on each sandwich as you like. Or let people help themselves. I used to hate Russian dressing, but now I love it. This dressing should be chunky chunk-chunk, more of a relish or salsa than a condiment. It should be an important part of the sandwich, not an afterthought.

¼ pound Swiss or Emmentaler cheese, thinly sliced

8 slices rye bread with caraway seeds

¼ cup butter

1 cup sauerkraut, squeezed of liquid

2 pounds smoked turkey, shaved thin

½ cup Russian dressing (recipe below)

Evenly divide the cheese between four slices of rye bread, then top with remaining rye bread slices. Melt half the butter in a large frying pan over medium-low heat. Add two of the cheese sandwiches. Brown the sandwiches for approximately 5 minutes on each side until they're a crispy golden brown and the cheese has melted.

Remove the sandwiches, add the rest of the butter to the pan, and brown the remaining two sandwiches as above.

Open the sandwiches, divide the sauerkraut and turkey between them and place on top of the melted cheese. Spread the Russian dressing on one side of each. Close the sandwiches and serve immediately.

MAKES 4 SANDWICHES

Russian Dressing

½ cup mayonnaise

2 tablespoons ketchup

3 tablespoons finely chopped cornichons or dill pickles

2 tablespoons chopped tarragon

Splash of Tabasco

Splash of Worcestershire

Salt

Pepper

Mix the mayonnaise, ketchup, pickles, tarragon, Tabasco, and Worchestershire together. Season with salt and pepper.

MAKES 1½ CUPS

MARIE-AUDE ROSE

Marie-Aude Rose first tried to go to cooking school at age fourteen, but the director shooed her away, telling her "it was not a job for her." Little did he know, though, that she had been making *poulet au vinaigre* from her mother's cookbook forever and brioches with her grandfather from age nine. As a student at the Sorbonne in Paris, Rose majored in American culture, but on the weekends she studied the Parisian food markets and cooked French classics for her friends. For a time, she was an actor, but even that didn't make her as happy as cooking did, so she finally entered the Parisian culinary school, École Ferrandi.

After seven years working her way through Paris's Michelin-starred restaurants steeped in rigor and technique, Rose got an offer to work at Thomas Keller's French Laundry in California. But on the eve of her departure, she had dinner at a tiny restaurant in Paris's 9th arrondissement, and from there, her plans changed—the chef of Spring, an American from Chicago named Daniel Rose, needed a hand in his closet-sized kitchen.

When Rose started cooking at Spring in 2007, she was inspired by the young chef's irreverent manner; he had come to study in Paris and ended up cooking his way through France. The two worked side by side. At the end of each day they would discuss the next day's menu, "which would allow me to order and then of course things would change by the following day as he'd get inspired by something else." Rose liked the dynamic and found it refreshing. There was no pressure to live up to Michelin standards, and instead of perfection, she could create one prix-fixe meal a night

based on seasonal fare, working alongside the chef and connecting with the customers, who were sent home after dinner with thick slices of banana bread for breakfast the next day.

The duo worked well together—in and out of the kitchen. In 2012, Marie married Daniel Rose. From there a string of successes followed: a larger Spring, two new bistros, and, in 2016, a move to Manhattan with their two young children. There, Daniel opened Le Coucou, which won a James Beard Award for best restaurant a year later.

After a couple of years in the city, Rose, along with the architects who had designed her husband's restaurant, wanted to open a design store with a European-style restaurant. "Little by little the position appeared to be perfect for me and we started dreaming about it and then it became real," she says. La Mercerie, a French-style café just around the corner from Le Coucou, opened up in December 2017. There Rose delivers French classics, like her signature flaky croissants and roasted bone marrow with Bordelaise sauce and horseradish. Diners can take home not only pastries but also the cutlery, dishware, and even their table.

When Rose opened La Mercerie, she was there all day, every day, for the first five months, though now she works only days as well as a couple of night shifts every week. Between her and Daniel—whose schedule is quite flexible—one of them is often home at night to put the kids to bed. Still, two chef parents means you have to be organized, which is why Rose prepares dinners in advance for nights when she and Daniel both have to work—and then labels them.

CURRENT HOMETOWN:
New York City

RESTAURANT THAT MADE HER NAME: Spring, Paris

SIGNATURE STYLE:
Traditional and modern French

BEST KNOWN FOR:
Co-chef at La Bourse et la Vie (Paris) along with her husband, Daniel Rose; her crepes; and as the chef at La Mercerie in New York City

FRIDGE: Frigidaire

1. **COCONUT OIL**—"I bake with this as Daniel doesn't do well with dairy."

2. **AMARENA CHERRIES,** for cocktails

3. **PEANUT BUTTER**—"I discovered peanut butter when I was thirteen. I was bugging my mom to find peanut butter in France; it was hard to find."

4. **PARMESAN CHEESE**

5. **WHITE BREAD,** from Maison Kayser, a French-style bakery—"It's the closest to what we get in France and there is no other boulangerie around us, not like in France where there's one at every corner. "

6. **SHREDDED CARROTS WITH GREENS**—"A good appetizer we all like."

7. **CRÈME FRAÎCHE**

8. **GOAT CHEESE CRUMBLES,** for salads

9. **BABYBEL CHEESE**—"It's for the kids and myself, it carries a bit of nostalgia."

10. **PETIT SUISSE YOGURT WITH FRUIT**

11. **LEFTOVER LENTILS WITH SAUTÉED BRUSSELS SPROUTS**

12. **CREPE BATTER**—"I make crepes once or twice a week, and my kids also come for them at the restaurant; they love them so much."

13. **CARROTS**

14. **MINI TORTILLAS**

15. **PEELED ONIONS**—"I like to always have them for when I want to make something with meat, fish, or soup. Some-times I cut them and freeze them too."

16. **LEFTOVER VEGETABLE PIECES,** from a soup recipe and also for crudités

17. **FERMENTED CABBAGE**

18. **TOMATO SAUCE**

19. **BEEF PATTIES**

20. **CHICKEN THIGHS, VEAL CUTLETS**

21. **BABY SPINACH**

22. **CHIVES**

Q & A

In your opinion, is American sour cream almost as good as French crème fraîche? No, it's not. . . . I can find good cheese here, although it's expensive.

Who does the cooking at home? You or your husband? Daniel cooks at home on the weekends, although he is making Passover dinner tonight.

What do your French-American kids like to eat? They really like baby bok choy. You can definitely eat healthy here.

They don't like American kids' favorites like chicken nuggets and mac 'n' cheese? Not really. But they do like ketchup, either with a beef patty or rice.

What do you miss most foodwise from France? I miss the fishmongers and butchers. It doesn't seem as fresh here, and the whole fish at the markets just look sad.

What is an average weeknight dinner for you? I don't usually make it home in time to eat dinner with my kids. I eat the leftovers from their dinner. I keep it light, as most days I eat a late lunch at work around four p.m.

What are a couple of typical meals you prepped recently for your kids? Green peas *à la française* with breaded veal cutlets. That takes me about an hour to prep. Or I might make celery *en remoulade* with *hachis parmentier* (shepherd's pie), which takes me about thirty minutes.

Who eats the fermented cabbage? It's for Daniel. I make it for him. He has food restrictions—no gluten, dairy, or seafood. So the bacteria is good for him.

All these items in your refrigerator seem really healthy. We try not to eat processed food at home. If I can't prep dinner, I will order ahead at Sweet Greens. They have hot bowls and salads, quinoa, salmon, roast squash, walnuts—that's a good healthy meal. I set it up so the babysitter can pick it up. We generally eat balanced meals. We don't eat meat every day. We eat organic dairy except when it is French.

Do you remember what you ate the first night you had dinner at Spring? Vividly—there were little raw clams, followed by squab served with almond puree and cherries, and a strawberry dessert with a lemon curd and some cream. It was amazing.

Do you think lunch boxes are a good idea for school? Or do you think a lunch system like the one in France, where the kids all have a hot meal, is better? I like the French system. It's also getting better every year, I feel, because many public schools are going organic. It's always a balanced meal; I really think it's best. I did do lunch boxes for my kids for two years and loved it. But I had the time—I wasn't working at that time, and now that I work I would go insane if I had to do it.

What do you bring back from France when you go home? Sea salt, olive oil, chocolate, and little cookies called Petits Coeurs. You know what is missing here that I can't bring back? Chipolatas! All of the sausages here are too sweet.

A fridge mantra to live by? Use all perishables before going back to the store, meaning empty the refrigerator so we can start fresh and not waste.

Classic French Crepes

Crepes are delicious with jam, melted chocolate, or even the simplest filling of all—sugar and lemon juice. There is a lot of nostalgia attached to making and eating crepes. I remember afternoon gatherings around the kitchen table with my cousins at my grandma's house; she would make the crepes and we could never get enough of them. They were so good and we were starving kids!

1¾ cups flour

½ cup sugar

½ teaspoon sea salt

4 cups whole milk

4 large eggs

2 tablespoons unsalted butter, melted

1 tablespoon dark rum

Whisk together the flour, sugar, and salt. Warm the milk slightly and whisk in the eggs, butter, and dark rum.

Add the milk, eggs, and butter to the dry mix. Use an immersion blender to mix thoroughly. Strain the batter through a fine sieve into a bowl. Set it aside to rest overnight or for a minimum of 2 hours.

Spray an 8-inch frying pan with cooking spray. Wipe it clean, so the pan is barely coated. Turn the heat to high. Using a 2-ounce ladle, spoon out crepe batter into the hot pan. Immediately tilt the pan to spread the batter in an even circle.

Flip the crepe over after the top is dry, about 45 seconds. Cook the other side for 30 seconds, until lightly browned. Fold in half and store on a sheet tray. Cover with aluminum foil. Continue the same process for the rest of the batter. Stack the crepes on top of one another under the foil to keep them warm.

Serve warm with jam, melted chocolate, or sugar and lemon juice.

MAKES APPROXIMATELY 12 CREPES

CURRENT HOMETOWN:
Sant Pol de Mar, Spain

RESTAURANT THAT MADE
HER NAME: Sant Pau, Sant
Pol de Mar

SIGNATURE STYLE: Modern
Catalan with Asian
influences

BEST KNOWN FOR: Being
the only female chef to be
awarded seven Michelin
stars between her three
restaurants—San Pau (now
closed); San Pau, Tokyo;
and Moments in Barcelona

FRIDGE: Gaggenau

CARME RUSCALLEDA

When I was growing up, they didn't ask little girls what they wanted to be, but I knew I was destined to be an artist," says the Catalan chef Carme Ruscalleda. Looking for something to do with her hands, she started helping out in the kitchen at twelve, boiling vegetables and making *escudella*, a rustic local soup with rice and pasta. Sometimes she'd make cookies, crema catalana, and other sweet inventions while no one was looking.

Despite having so much fun in the kitchen, she never really considered a culinary career. She studied business because her parents were grocery store owners and, afterward, charcuterie making. After she married Toni Balam, the two of them took over her parents' store. There she stocked nontraditional herbs like lesser known varieties of thyme on the shelves and added spices to the cold cuts and blood sausages; her charcuterie soon became the talk of the town. She also began tearing through cookbooks, ambitiously testing all the recipes she could—eating, tasting, and exploring anything to do with food. New dishes such as fresh pasta and croquettes were added to the menu, and their grocery shop soon became a popular place to eat.

When the run-down villa just across the road became vacant, they bought the building and created Sant Pau. At first they served classic Catalan *platillos* (small shared dishes) of cheeses and local meats. But soon they were serving seafood and stews. Her confidence grew and she perfected her skills. "I wanted to do the highest quality cooking: a light, modern cuisine with personality," she recalls.

The dining room with its small garden overlooking the Mediterranean Sea, close enough to smell the salty air, added a fairy-tale dimension, as did the fantastic menu. Dishes quickly evolved—deceptively normal-looking fried parrotfish surprised the taste buds with licorice and curry, for example—as did Ruscalleda's presentations: a mini wooden crate brought to the table revealed a tiny masterpiece of cod brandade and black olives that mimicked a Mondrian painting.

The artistic plating and smaller portions were a new idea, and locals and critics alike panned the new venture. "There's nothing on the plate, but everything on the bill," Ruscalleda was once told. But she remained steadfast, and soon received accolades, drawing customers from all over to her tiny corner of Catalonia. And although the first ten years "were like crossing a desert," her highly personalized melding of traditional Catalan cooking and global influences brought her culinary fame.

Sant Pau closed in 2018, but she has two more restaurants, in Tokyo and Barcelona, also run by family members, and there are plans for pop-ups. She still lives across the road from the original Sant Pau. From the small terrace of her spotless, stainless-steel kitchen you can catch a sliver of the sea. That fits her culinary philosophy perfectly: "A cook is an explorer and should use what they learn however they wish. Cooking the same dishes as my ancestors through a modern lens and respecting the culture of this, my place, is my everything," she explains.

1. **IDIAZABAL RAW MILK CATALAN CHEESE**—"I eat this for dessert."

2. **HOMEMADE BLACK PUDDING**—"I add this to many vegetable dishes but I also eat it with omelets and for simple sandwiches that we make for breakfast or dinner with bread and tomato."

3. **HOMEMADE SALSA ROMESCO**—"I always have it in the fridge. It can be eaten on toast, with meat or fish, or in a soup."

4. **BLACK OLIVES**

5. **DRIED FRUIT CONFITURE**—"The dried fruit has vinegared nuts. I use them for appetizers or in a sauce for meat or even for dessert."

6. **CHOPPED COD IN WATER**

7. **MUSHROOMS**

8. **SUAU DE CLÚA CHEESE**

9. **AUSTRALIAN MACADAMIA NUTS**—"I buy them from a Barcelona artisan toaster that makes them with a unique smoked touch."

10. **DANONE NATURAL YOGURTS**—"I eat one for breakfast every morning with chia and at night sometimes I eat one with grated pear."

Q & A

Do you often eat at home? Even though the restaurant was just across the street, I always dined at home, and I eat mostly the same dishes. It could be a simple lentil stew, or local white beans with fish, or just a black pudding sausage.

Do you cook for friends and family? Normally, I just cook for my husband and myself. But if we have a little time off, we'll go with friends to a little spot of land we own overlooking the sea and have a nice barbecue or we'll make Catalan-style rice, my favorite! We'll make it with shrimp, mussels, and squid, maybe a bit of rabbit sausage, and just simmer it all down in a broth with tomatoes, onions, and mushrooms if they're in season. It's the ultimate surf and turf!

It doesn't seem like there are any markets in town. Where do you buy your produce? The market comes to me. This is a fishing village. There isn't really a market, more like small producers who deliver to your home, or sell their wares in specialty shops and bodegas. Sometimes we go directly to the boats when they come up on the beach with their daily catch. The local red prawns are some of the best in the world.

Are there any other interesting local products? Oh yes! Sant Pol de Mar is located in El Maresme, a region with very impressive vegetables and fruits and very delicious seafood. My favorites are the peas and the strawberries. In the restaurant all the dishes cooked with those ingredients were usually more elaborate, but at home I always go with more simple recipes.

I see some unfamiliar beige stuff in a jar. Is it cheese? Yes, it's called *tupí*, a local alcohol-infused condiment made with sheep, goat, or cow cheese. It has a strong character, with notes of anise and brandy liqueur. Tupí has many uses: It can be eaten as a fast dinner on a toast with a salad or it can be cooked as a sauce for meat or fish or as a dessert. I always make my own.

You have a few Japanese condiments in there as well. Yes, I have some red miso from Japan and some good soy, I think. The Catalan and Japanese people are similar in many ways. Both cultures respect seasonal produce, but they also like the sweet, salty, and spicy like us, and they love textures. Their condiments create amazing umami.

Do you like spicy food or sauces? There are none in your refrigerator. I do not use elaborate sauces; I like freshness and dishes served at the moment. But I do like black and white pepper and hot, spicy dried chilies.

And there's no junk food. I never eat junk food. But if junk food exists it's because there is a market for it. It's our fault because we buy it. If no one buys it anymore, they will change their ways. I understand, though—home cooking is good and healthy, but people don't have time anymore.

Soft Eggs with Vegetables and Goat Cheese

I consider this a very elegant and gourmet way to eat an egg— it's fragile and beautiful, very seductive. When I entertain friends at home, I add a spoonful of good caviar. For my husband, I cook the eggs longer and then I sprinkle them with some bread crumbs and a little cheese.

1 teaspoon white vinegar

4 large organic eggs

1 small white onion, diced into ½-inch pieces

¼ cup extra virgin olive oil

1 small red pepper, diced into ½-inch pieces

⅔ cup pear, peeled, cored, and diced in ½-inch pieces

½ cup crumbled soft goat cheese

1 tablespoon chopped parsley

Salt

Black pepper

In a small pot, heat 1 quart of water and the vinegar to 160°F. Carefully lower the eggs into the pot. Cook them for 15 minutes, turning every 3 minutes. Place the eggs in an ice bath to cool for 2 minutes. Carefully peel the eggs.

Sauté the onion in the olive oil over medium heat for 10 minutes. Add the red pepper and continue to cook for 4 more minutes. Add the pear and cook another 2 minutes.

To serve, divide the vegetables among shallow bowls. Place an egg in the middle and sprinkle the crumbled cheese and chopped parsley on top. Season with salt and pepper.

SERVES 4

Catalan Miso Soup

This soup is very versatile. On cold nights, I like to add chorizo and Manchego cheese. I feel that if you are tired and downcast a miso soup will heal you. Japanese and Catalan cultures are very wise and healthy, and this inspires me to mix the two together.

Dried kombu seaweed, 16 inches long

8 cups water, room temperature

2 teaspoons katsuobushi (dried bonito flakes)

1½ cups julienned leeks

3 cups julienned green pepper

6 ounces angel hair pasta

1½ cups chopped mushrooms

⅔ pound desalted cod, skinless 1-inch fillets

20 chives, minced

1 cup red miso

⅔ cup romesco sauce

With a pair of scissors, cut the kombu into 1 by ¼-inch strips. Fill a stainless-steel pot with the water and soak the kombu strips for 4 to 6 hours. Heat the pot over medium heat. Once the water boils, remove and set aside the kombu. Add the katsuobushi to the pot. Once the water boils again, skim off the katsuobushi.

Add the leeks, green peppers, and angel hair pasta. Cook for 5 minutes. Add the mushrooms and continue to cook for 3 more minutes.

Take the pot off the heat. Add the cod fillets and the julienned kombu to the pot along with the chives. Cover and let sit for 10 minutes in order for the cod to cook.

Pour ½ cup of broth into a bowl. Add the miso and the romesco and stir together. Pour back into the pot and gently stir into the soup. Serve immediately.

SERVES 4

NANCY SILVERTON

Nancy Silverton never set out to make pizza. Although it was on her to-do list, she started off her culinary career as a pastry chef because it was the "fastest route to the kitchen," as she says. That skill took her from Wolfgang Puck's Spago to co-owning, with her then-husband chef Mark Peel, Campanile.

First, though, came her bread. She opened La Brea Bakery next to Campanile at a time when most people were still buying bread at the supermarket. Her loaves, the recipe that she obsessed over for months, would often sell out before lunchtime. Living above the bakery was helpful. "I had two young kids then and I baked all night. It was easy for me to run upstairs to wake them up and then come back downstairs. I had always had a fantasy of living upstairs from the shop," she says. Silverton also had a knack for getting people to line up around the block or three deep at the bar for her "grilled cheese nights," when customers eagerly waited for sourdough bread spread with marinated peppers and caramelized onions and cheese.

In hindsight, it seems obvious that she'd put innate instinct for the good things in life—especially bread and cheese—all together and create a mini empire of Italian restaurants. After all, Silverton knows her California customers crave "simplicity, seasonality, and wine-friendly dishes," as she puts it, which is why her pizzas feature Fresno chilies and preserved lemons alongside salame and guanciale and cheese.

Italy has been an inspiration for Silverton forever—it's the place where she goes when she leaves one restaurant for another, opens up a new establishment, or, once, after her divorce. Why Italy? "Everyone was going to Provence, or if they went to Italy they went to Tuscany," she explains. "So we went to Umbria. It was a lot less expensive." Silverton even bought a house in the Umbrian countryside so she could search out local bread makers, the best tomatoes, olive oil, and anchovies for her restaurant.

If she has a mantra, it's this: "I know what I like to eat, and apparently it's what a lot of other people want to eat too." It's the same approach she takes to her restaurants and the backyard entertaining she does. When she recently got a new refrigerator—a high-tech smart one by Samsung—she knew that she had to hold on to the old one too: "Growing up, my friends' parents often had a refrigerator in the garage and that was their drink refrigerator." So she did the same thing and stocked it with beer.

The one in her homey kitchen, which is decorated with her prolific collection of rolling pins and whisks, is a shrine to condiments, which is fitting: Silverton wrote a cookbook with recipes that showcased canned and jarred items. Upgrading simple condiments is a favorite trick of hers—"often chefs I know give me tips about a certain item, and then I test it at home."

CURRENT HOMETOWN:
Los Angeles, California

RESTAURANTS THAT MADE
HER NAME: Campanile
and La Brea Bakery,
Los Angeles

SIGNATURE STYLE:
Italian-Californian

BEST KNOWN FOR: Her
artisanal breads; multiple
James Beard Awards,
including Outstanding
Chef (2014); cookbooks;
and her current ventures,
Pizzeria Mozza and
Osteria Mozza

FRIDGE: Samsung

1. **JARRED PEPPERS**

2. **CALABRIAN CHILIES**

3. **MEZETTA ROASTED BELL PEPPERS**

4. **RETINOL ANTI-AGING SERUM, ANTI-WRINKLE CREAM**

5. **RODOLPHE LE MEUNIER BUTTER**

6. **CALABRIAN CHERRY PEPPERS**

7. **HEINZ KETCHUP**—"I always use Heinz."

8. **LEFTOVER CHICKEN**—"It's from 'chicken time,' the staff lunch meal at Osteria Mozza. We call it chicken time because 95 percent of the time it's chicken thighs, which is just fine with me. I love chicken thighs."

9. **CHIPOTLE PEPPERS**

10. **OLIVES,** from her restaurant chi SPACCA

11. **ANCHOVIES IN CHILI OIL**

12. **OLIVES,** from chi SPACCA

13. **HOMEMADE PEANUT BUTTER**

14. **SQIRL STRAWBERRY JAM**—"It's so good, I like to eat it straight from the jar."

15. **MEYER LEMON JAM**

16. **CYPRESS GROVE'S PURPLE HAZE GOAT CHEESE WITH LAVENDER AND FENNEL POLLEN**

17. **FRESH GOAT CHEESE**

18. **VERMONT BUTTER**

19. **PICKLED GREEN TOMATOES**

20. **CHILI PICKLES**

21. **TACO TRUCK PICKLED PEPPERS,** a gift

22. **CAPERS**

23. **HOMEMADE TAHINI**

24. **SALT-PICKLED ANCHOVIES**

25. **PARMESAN**

26. **BACON**

27. **CHILI SAUCE**

28. **MUSTARD**

29. **STRAUS BARISTA MILK**—"It comes from Sonoma County. I like it with a Not Nutter cookie from La Brea Bakery."

30. **MEYER LEMON MARMALADE**

31. **KUMQUAT MOSTARDA**

32. **KROGER MUSTARD,** something a houseguest left

33. **ORANGE MARMALADE**

34. **SNAKE OIL HOT SAUCE**

35. **SALT-PACKED CAPERS**

36. **CAPERS IN BRINE**

37. **GREEN PEPPERCORN**

38. **PICKLED GREEN BEANS**

39. **BLACK OLIVE PASTE**

40. **PINOT NOIR MUSTARD**

41. **TARRAGON MUSTARD**

42. **VANILLA EXTRACT**— "I'm using these for some recipe testing."

43. **COFFEE EXTRACT**

44. **TOMATO PASTE**

45. **SMOKED SOY SAUCE**

46. **HOT SAUCE**

47. **PISTACHIO OIL**

48. **PERSONALIZED VODKA BOTTLE FILLED WITH WATER**

Q & A

Does your refrigerator tell you things like, don't buy more mayonnaise because you already have two bottles? I'll show you on my phone if I can figure out how to do it. Supposedly I have an app . . . . There is a camera that can show me what's in there. Aside from listening to music and watching TV on the screen there is a thing for notes, for like a housekeeper or kids. And you can put photos on it.

So gone are the days of putting up pictures with magnets? I put my magnets on my old refrigerator in the garage.

The first things I see in the refrigerator are condiments. Why so many? Condiments last—I have three grown kids but they no longer live with me, so I no longer have the responsibility of keeping food with a short shelf-life. When I'm home and ready to entertain, then I'll go out to shop for those items. I host half a dozen big parties here a year, and good condiments give you flavor with little effort. I often doctor things up and reseason. I use simple mayonnaise and then flavor it with chipotle to make a spicy mayo or use some fresh grated garlic, olive oil, and lemon to make an aioli. I use the condiments as a base.

When you have a food craving do you reach for savory or sweet? Savory.

What is your eating style at home? Snacking on anchovies and small plates? Sometimes after a shift at Mozza, I'll stand by the sink and eat a snack. Maybe some pistachios from Syria. Maybe some bread and Rodolphe butter. That with red wine? Heaven.

Something we'd never find in your fridge? I never have takeout containers. Don't get me

wrong, I love leftovers, but as soon as I come home from a restaurant, I take them and put them in a home container.

Anything else? Margarine. The French butter I have always in the fridge—Rodolphe le Meunier beurre de baratte with fleur de sel—would kick the margarine's ass. And would kick other butters' asses as well.

Have you ever had your own chickens? We used to have chickens in our backyard and then I put in a pool. That coincided with the dog eating the last chicken and my getting divorced. My youngest loved the chickens. They were heritage breeds and laid a gamut of different colored eggs. It was great, we would be baking and realize we needed eggs and we would just run out back to get some.

Do you enjoy shopping for food? I love going to grocery stores in Italy. It's an adventure. Half the stuff I don't know what it is. It's less fun here.

Do you bring back condiments from Italy? When I travel I bring back condiments, crackers, and cheese. I'm an anchovy fanatic. I love cured anchovies. But I can't bring those fantastic cured meats back. On the record I can't say I've ever smuggled back a large ham in my suitcase—I will leave that answer open-ended.

And your hot sauce collection? Lots of those are gifts.

There is also a vinegar theme here, between pickles and capers. Are you drawn to acidity? Definitely.

Would we ever find bread in your fridge? No, just bagels in the freezer.

Buttermilk Fried Clams with Chipotle Mayonnaise

Chipotle peppers, added to mayonnaise, make a wonderful condiment for many dishes.

For the chipotle mayonnaise:

1 cup mayonnaise

¼ cup finely chopped cilantro leaves

2 tablespoons extra virgin olive oil

2 tablespoons fresh lemon juice, or more to taste

4 large garlic cloves, minced, or more to taste

1½ teaspoons pureed chipotle peppers, or more to taste

1 teaspoon kosher salt, or more to taste

For the fried clams:

1 cup plus 2 tablespoons flour

¼ cup plus 2 tablespoons Old Bay Seasoning

¼ cup canola oil

Three 8-ounce jars of clams (about 30), rinsed and drained

1 cup buttermilk

To make the chipotle mayonnaise: stir the mayonnaise, cilantro, olive oil, lemon juice, garlic, chipotle peppers, and salt together in a small bowl. Season with more lemon juice, chipotle peppers, garlic, or salt to taste.

To make the clams: stir the flour and Old Bay Seasoning together in a small bowl. Soak the clams in the buttermilk and then drain. Heat half the oil in a large skillet over high heat until the oil is almost smoking, about 2 to 3 minutes. Dredge half of the clams in the seasoned flour and carefully lay them in one layer in the oil.

Fry the clams for 2 minutes until they're golden brown and crispy. Flip the clams and cook them for another minute, then reduce the heat to medium-high and cook the clams for 1 minute more, until the second side is golden brown and crispy.

Lift the clams out of the oil with a slotted spoon and place them on paper towels to drain. Repeat, heating the remaining oil over high heat and frying the remaining clams in the same way. Serve the clams with the chipotle mayonnaise.

SERVES 4

Open-Faced Omelet with Anchovies, Olives, and Onion Confit

The perfect meal when there is basically nothing but condiments in your fridge. The "open-faced" aspect takes away the intimidation of flipping or rolling an omelet. But if you want to roll it, it could easily become a closed omelet.

6 eggs

2 teaspoons cold water

½ rounded teaspoon kosher salt

2 tablespoons plus 1 teaspoon unsalted butter

6 to 8 anchovy fillets

⅓ cup pitted Taggiasca olives

¼ cup onion confit

¼ cup grated Parmigiano-Reggiano

1 tablespoon minced chives

Beat the eggs in a medium bowl with the water and salt until well combined. Heat half of the butter in a 10-inch nonstick skillet over medium-low heat until melted, 2 to 3 minutes. Be careful not to let it brown or sizzle.

Pour half of the eggs into the pan. Shake the pan very gently, without swirling, until the sides are set. Use a heatproof rubber spatula to draw the set edges of the egg away from the sides of the pan. Tilt the pan so the raw egg runs into and fills the space created. Continue gently cooking and pulling the eggs in this way until almost no egg runs off when you tilt the pan.

Immediately scatter half of the toppings over the eggs, and if the eggs seem to be setting, remove the pan from the heat. If the eggs are still runny, continue cooking over low heat another 30 seconds. Slide onto a plate. Repeat the same process to make the second omelet.

MAKES 2 OMELETS

CLARE SMYTH

Clare Smyth was smitten by the food world in her early teens. Even though she'd helped out around the house with various chores in the kitchen of their family farm in County Antrim, Northern Ireland, her early interest in cooking didn't really go much further than that. "My parents had respect for the food, but never considered it an art form. It was more quantity over quality," she says.

All that changed when she met some friends of friends who'd worked in Michelin-starred restaurants. She started to read up on chefs, finding the work so appealing she decided she could make some sort of career out of it. At fifteen, she began working part-time as a cook and waitress in restaurants near her home-town, learning new flavors and dishes. A year later, during a two-week holiday with friends, she enrolled herself at Highbury College in Portsmouth to study culinary arts. Smyth, who was always headstrong and focused (she was once a competitive horse rider), simply made plans to pursue her dream, despite her family's attempts to bring her back home.

After graduating from culinary school, at Highbury College at Portsmouth, Smyth landed a job at Restaurant Gordon Ramsay. Even though she was told she wouldn't last a week there, she worked her way up to sous-chef. Her quest for culinary knowledge was insatiable; rather than resting at the end of a long day, she stayed up reading classic French cookbooks such as Escoffier's *Le Guide Culinaire*. A few years later, she went to cook at Alain Ducasse's legendary Louis XV in Monaco for a couple of years, then returned to Gordon Ramsay as head chef and eventually chef/patron. "I wanted to work again for Gordon because I knew his was the best and toughest kitchen out there and I wanted the opportunity to head up a three 'Michelin' starred kitchen," she explains. Ramsay ended up giving her complete freedom: she became a partner in the business and maintained those three Michelin stars.

In August of 2017, after more than ten years at Restaurant Gordon Ramsay, Smyth opened Core, in London's trendy Notting Hill. She calls her restaurant an "informal luxury" one. "We are completely independent, cooking what we want, with no dress codes, no pretension, and no intimidation," she explains. It also celebrates all things British—not just British food and ingredients but everything else in the dining room, from dishware to the custom-made craft tables.

Diners are treated to potatoes slow cooked in seaweed, then topped with Scottish trout and herring roe, or the restaurant's signature carrot dish infused with braised lamb neck. "I want to show that simple ingredients can be luxurious, that a potato can taste as delicious as a lobster," says Smyth. It is, she says, a way of changing people's perspectives and showing them that sustainable local food can be haute cuisine too.

As she is at Core every shift, Smyth doesn't spend a lot of time in her kitchen at home, immaculate as it is. She even skips breakfast: "I prefer to stay hungry so I can taste things in the restaurant's kitchen," she explains. Coming home late at night from work, though, she

CURRENT HOMETOWN:
London, England

RESTAURANT THAT MADE
HER NAME: Restaurant
Gordon Ramsay, London

SIGNATURE STYLE: Modern
British fine dining

BEST KNOWN FOR: Being
the only woman chef in
the U.K. to gain and hold
three Michelin stars;
catering Prince Harry and
Meghan Markle's wedding
reception; and her two-star
Michelin restaurant, Core

FRIDGE: Miele

might snack on a piece of cheddar, some charcuterie, or Spanish olives or anchovies. "I really
love Spanish food," says Smyth, who spent
many summer holidays in Spain. If she has
a bit more time—for instance, on Sundays—
she'll do a typical British roast chicken or beef
for her husband, Grant, or herself, or "something Asian because it's different."

"Core means the core of me, my heart,"
Smyth explains, which is why she uses her
restaurant's reputation to help others, cooking
private dinners to raise money for charities.
And although the restaurant is an extension
of her, it does have a life of its own. "It's like
the evolution from a caterpillar to a butterfly.
We've only just begun," she adds.

1. **HOMEMADE PRESERVED LEMONS,** for salads and tagine

2. **PICKLED ONIONS**

3. **CORE BEER**

4. **PONZU**

5. **PICKLED HOT PEPPERS,** from Brindisa

6. **PRUNIER CAVIAR**

7. **WAITROSE BEEF DRIPPING**—"I use this with roast potatoes."

8. **PARMESAN CHEESE**

9. **FIVE-YEAR-OLD CHEDDAR**

10. **MORE PARMESAN CHEESE**

11. **COPPA**

12. **SALAMI**

13. **CHORIZO**

14. **SMOKED SALMON**

15. **BUDDHA'S HAND LEMON**—
    "Grating the zest is a great way to
    finish fish, and it's also good in a gin
    and tonic."

16. **OLIVES**

17. **RUTABAGA**

18. **HOMEMADE PICKLES**

19. **HERBS: ROSEMARY, THYME,
    CURLY PARSLEY**

20. **EL NAVARRICO BUTTER BEANS,**
    for salads, soups, and stews

21. **CHORIZO**

22. **PANCETTA**

23. **HAM HOCK**

24. **PASSATA TOMATO SAUCE**

Ploughman's Pickle

This is a British classic. In this version I put more vegetables than usual as it makes it more interesting. I like this pickle with cheese— it is also perfect in a sandwich or served as part of a ploughman's-style salad or lunch.

3 medium chopped carrots

1 medium cubed rutabaga or turnip

4 garlic cloves, peeled and finely chopped

1 cup chopped dates

1 small cauliflower head, cut into small florets

2 white onions, finely chopped

2 apples, unpeeled, finely chopped

2 small zucchini, finely chopped

1 large chopped cucumber (equivalent of 3 cups)

1¾ cups brown sugar

2 teaspoons salt

2 teaspoons allspice

1 teaspoon cayenne pepper

Put all the ingredients in a large saucepan and bring them to the boil. Once boiling, reduce the heat to a simmer and cook until the rutabaga is cooked but still remains firm, about 2 hours (depending on the size of the cubes). Stir well. Spoon the mixture into hot, sterile jars and seal them. Allow the pickle to age for a few weeks before using.

MAKES 1½ QUARTS

Q & A

What are your go-to condiments?
Definitely pickles, miso, and ponzu for a quick and easy salad dressing. I like tasty and easy-to-use things. I have an addiction to anything with acidity.

Is caviar a staple in your fridge? Yes! I do have a thing about luxury ingredients, I must admit. We cook so much of them, but don't eat much ourselves. At the restaurant it's all about everyone else.

There's no ketchup? We don't have ketchup. I don't use it. I don't like it. But we do have barbecue sauce, and we use French's mustard for things like burgers.

What do you never have in your fridge?
Things like Coca-Cola or fizzy drinks.

Do you cook at home? I normally try to cook at home at least once a week, and I like things that are all in one pot—stews, ramens, and curries.

Do your friends invite you for dinner, or are they sometimes too intimated to have a Michelin-starred chef over? I am always happy to have people cook for me, and my friends know that I like to eat simple food just like anyone else. I normally bring wine or Champagne.

What is a dish from your childhood you still love? I am still a big fan of hearty soups and stews such as Irish stew.

Where do you shop for food? Waitrose and Brindisa for Spanish foods.

Does Waitrose have good chef-approved products? They have a pretty good range of produce. I like the Duchy Organic: it is well sourced from British farms.

What do you crave when you are starving, sweet or savory? Savory—I love salt-and-vinegar crisps as a snack, but a roast chicken is one of my favorite meals as well as spaghetti Bolognese.

METTE SØBERG

Mette Søberg can give full credit to the Brussels sprout-and-apple dessert she concocted at Noma for landing her present-day job as its head of research and development. She'd begun as an intern at the famous Danish restaurant, quickly moving up to line cook. At one of the staff show-and-tells (dubbed Saturday Night Projects) she presented her dessert, which caught the eye of René Redzepi, Noma's chef and owner. "Fucking crazy!" he exclaimed, thinking, *This girl is creative and thinks deeply about food*. Some time later, Redzepi moved her to the R&D kitchen, where she now creates, under his watchful eye, the menus for the restaurant.

Noma, as just about everyone is aware of now, is the restaurant that put Denmark on the map. Redzepi concentrated on local, often unheard-of natural products, transforming them through fermentation and other experiments. He showcased vegetables, carefully preparing them so they'd be as satisfying as meat, and created food whose influence spread far beyond Copenhagen. He also discovered and invested in the talented people who found their way into his kitchen.

One of these was Søberg, who grew up in Rødovre, a suburb of Copenhagen. She first discovered the joy of cooking while helping her grandmother prepare copious family meals during Christmas and Easter: "It was the highlight of the year for me," she says, recalling plates of herring, shrimp, salmon, and eel, not to mention heaping servings of chicken, duck, and pork. "We just sat at the table eating and sharing. *All day long.*"

Even though she had planned to go to university to study, she wanted to cook and decided to take a gap year after high school to go to culinary school. After six months of classes she began an internship, and realized she'd made the right decision. "I just felt comfortable there, I loved that energy," she says. Her first job was at a seafood house, which was then followed by a yearlong gig at Marque, a fine-dining restaurant in Sydney, Australia. When her visa expired, the chef gave her the recommendation that landed her at Noma.

Søberg created the menus for the Noma pop-ups in Sydney and Tulum, Mexico. With her tireless team and her boundless curiosity, she found local products and produce to create such brand-new dishes as celeriac truffle shawarma, mounted on a spit and carved like meat, and pumpkin cooked with kelp and avocado fudge. Ever unassuming, she credits Redzepi: "He's taught me so many things, but I think the most important lesson is to trust your instincts and always be curious."

On the rare moments that Søberg has some downtime, she cooks at home in a small kitchen filled with Mexican baskets and handmade pottery, where meals can be anything from quick snacks to a mash-up of items that look as if they came from Noma's pop-ups—some foraged from her trips abroad. There are plenty of jars of fermenting fruits and vegetables as well as an impressive mother lode of condiments, including her homemade concoctions. Luckily for Noma and the future of foodies everywhere, Søberg keeps listening to the same inner voice that propelled her into her cooking career.

CURRENT HOMETOWN:
Copenhagen, Denmark

**RESTAURANT THAT
MADE HER NAME:**
Noma, Copenhagen

SIGNATURE STYLE:
Seasonal Nordic

BEST KNOWN FOR:
Being the head of
Noma's R&D kitchen

FRIDGE: Ikea

1. **MUSHROOMS**—"Some are from the market and some I forage in a forest north of Copenhagen. I like to go a couple of times when it's mushroom season, and even though you don't find many it's always nice to take a walk in the forest to clear your mind."

2. **CHICKEN STOCK**

3. **JALAPEÑO AND HABANERO SAUCES,** from Hija de Sanchez

4. **HOKKAIDO PUMPKIN**

5. **BACON**

6. **BLUEBERRIES**—"My niece loves them and they're good to have when I'm babysitting her on Mondays when I'm not working."

7. **SHEEP'S CHEESE**

8. **BÄHNCKE GROV SENNEP WHOLEGRAIN MUSTARD**

9. **SMOKY WHITE RIND CHEESE**

10. **SWEDISH *PRÄSTOST* (PRIEST'S) CHEESE**

11. **ROSEHIP BERRY JAM,** from her grandmother's recipe

12. **FRESH CHILI PASTE**—"I often make it with lemon, lime, salt, serrano and pasilla chilies, and oil."

13. **PASILLA CHILI OIL**

14. **PLUMS**—"I cook them in a syrup made from muscovado sugar and water and eat them just as they are or on top of vanilla ice cream."

15. **LEFTOVER COOKED PUMPKIN**

16. **MUSHROOMS COOKED IN GRAPESEED OIL,** for risotto or pasta

17. **FENNEL FLOWERS WITH APPLE VINEGAR**

18. **CHILI PEPPERS: HABANEROS, SERRANO**

Q & A

Holy moly, there is a boatload of chilis in there! I know! I brought a lot of dried chilis home with me from Mexico, when we did the Noma pop-up there. And I make sure to always have at least one type of chili oil in the fridge because you can put it on almost everything and it will make it better.

What do you eat when coming home from a long day at work? If it's quick I always eat rye bread with something on top, whatever is in the fridge. Otherwise rice with fried egg, chili oil, and maybe some leftover vegetables from the night before.

What do you cook for your boyfriend and friends? Mexican food! Simple pasta dishes. Whenever I go food shopping I always take my time and end up buying way too much stuff, without knowing what I'm going to do with it! This is nice, but when you're in a hurry and don't have much time, it's better to have a plan. I love cooking dried pasta and throwing in just chorizo, tomatoes, and chili, or just some sushi rice with different greens and maybe some mushroom and eggs with a broth. Otherwise, my boyfriend is crazy for Mexican flavors. I'll get some of the amazing corn tortillas from Hija de Sanchez [a taqueria in Copenhagen] and make some kind of salsa, and then stuff them with avocados, fresh cilantro, and chilies, or chorizo, pork, or chicken.

What do you always have in your fridge? I always have the basics—yogurt, milk, eggs, and chili oil.

There is a lot of cheese in there too. I often have cheese in my fridge—it lasts long, you can use it for a lot of dishes. And it's also great to serve if you have guests coming over unannounced.

What would we never find in your fridge? Sodas, unless maybe if we have guests.

What foods do you hate? Or what foods would you never eat? I can't think of any! I eat everything!

What is your favorite junk food? Chocolate. The Mexican chocolate that we have at the restaurant is the best. We found it when we were traveling around Mexico before the pop-up in Tulum, and it is made from native Jaguar cacao, sometimes mixed with chili. And when I run out of that, I get some delicious little almonds covered in chocolate and cinnamon from a little shop around the corner from me.

Who does the food shopping in your house? Your boyfriend? And where do you shop? We normally do it together, and it's usually a mix between the food markets in Copenhagen, supermarkets, and small greengrocers.

What are some of the lesser known, more surprising Danish specialties? We have amazing apples in autumn. A very classic (and quite easy) dessert is made from layers of apple compote, whipped cream, and macaroons—my grandmother would make this dessert every time we came to visit.

What is a favorite food from your childhood you still love to eat? One of my favorite meals as a kid was fjord shrimps. Both because the season starts in late spring so it reminds you that summer is close, but mostly because they are just boiled and served with the shell on. So you sit together at the table and peel your shrimps, and it's such a satisfying feeling once you've finally peeled enough shrimps to fill your slice of bread and add mayonnaise, lemon, pepper, and dill. And in my family there would always be the added excitement that you couldn't possibly leave the table, because then somebody would steal your already peeled shrimps.

What is in your freezer? Summertime berries, all kinds; homemade chicken stock; and ice cream.

Wait—is that a wedding cake in there too? Yes, it's the cake from my sister's wedding last year. I made it for her, and here it's tradition that you save the top and eat it for your one-year anniversary. So it's still in my freezer.

Does your boyfriend like to cook? He does like to cook but I probably end up cooking most of the time. He makes a very good lasagna. And I love it when he makes me pancakes.

Tell us about something special in your fridge. I have a jam made from rosehip berries and apples that I make every year. It's something my grandmother always used to make.

Apple-Rosehip Jam

I make this jam in the late summer when the rosehip berries are in season and plentiful. My grandmother used to always make a big batch and give some to everyone in the family. I think it's particularly good in the morning with yogurt and granola or on a piece of toasted bread. It's also great with cheese.

3 cups apple chunks with skin left on (sweet red-skinned apples work well)

1 cup rosehip berries, stems and seeds removed

1½ cups cane sugar

½ cup water

Two 8-ounce jam jars

Sterilize two jars by washing them thoroughly and putting them in a pot of water and boiling for 10 minutes. Put the lids and bands in a pot, and let the water simmer. Dry everything thoroughly with a clean paper towel.

Cook all the ingredients together in a pot and let simmer for about 1 hour, until the texture turns jammy and there are still chunks of fruit left. Pour into the jars and store in the fridge for up to 2 months.

MAKES TWO 8-OUNCE JARS

Rice with Mushrooms, Kale, Pumpkin, and Egg

I started making this when we were traveling around Scandinavia the summer before opening the new restaurant. We would bring rice and chili oils on our journeys and then find some eggs. Right now we start every morning at the restaurant with a bowl of rice, with egg yolks cured in soy sauce, and lots of different condiments to choose from, like seaweed, different types of pickles, or fresh chili.

For the rice:

2 cups rice (I normally use sushi rice)

For the vegetables:

3 tablespoons grapeseed oil

2 cups mixed mushrooms (wild if possible)

1 tablespoon butter

1 clove garlic, finely chopped

1 teaspoon chopped fresh ginger

4 teaspoons chicken glacé (reduced stock made from leftover chicken carcasses)

2 cups chopped mixed kale, including cavolo nero, green, or purple kale

2 teaspoons chopped parsley

1 teaspoon chopped lovage

Zest of 1 lemon

Salt

For the pumpkin:

½ Hokkaido pumpkin (or butternut squash)

2 tablespoons grapeseed oil

Salt

1 teaspoon toasted black pepper

3 teaspoons toasted mustard seeds

3 teaspoons dried ginger or ginger powder

1 teaspoon toasted cilantro seeds

1 teaspoon dried juniper berries

3 tablespoons butter

For the fried eggs:

4 eggs

1 tablespoon grapeseed oil

2 tablespoons butter

Pasilla chili oil

Wash the rice thoroughly in cold running water until the water is clear then cook the rice on the stovetop or in a rice cooker according to instructions.

For the vegetables, place a frying pan over high heat until it's very hot; add grapeseed oil. Fry the mushrooms and cook for 5 minutes. Add the butter and finely chopped garlic and ginger. Add the chicken glacé. Add the kale. Cook until the kale starts to wilt a bit, about 2 minutes. Add the chopped parsley, lovage, and lemon zest and cook another 2 minutes. Season with salt.

For the pumpkin, take the seeds out of the gourd and carve it up into thick wedges. Brush with grapeseed oil and season with salt. Put in the oven at 200°F for about 40 minutes, or until tender. Let the pumpkin cool down before you scrape out the flesh and cut it into small pieces. Then, in a small bowl, blend all the spices together for the spice mix. Melt the butter and add in 1 tablespoon of the spice mix (store the rest). When the butter foams, add the pumpkin pieces to warm them up, about 2 minutes.

To make the eggs, fry them in grapeseed oil in a pan over medium heat. Add the butter and baste it onto the eggs so the egg whites are thoroughly cooked, approximately 2 minutes. Spoon the rice into bowls and top it with the mushroom and kale mix, the pumpkin, and an egg. Serve the dish with the pasilla chili oil.

SERVES 4

CURRENT HOMETOWN:
New York City

RESTAURANT THAT MADE
HIS NAME: Empellón,
New York City

SIGNATURE STYLE:
Mexican-inspired food

BEST KNOWN FOR:
His creative desserts
at Alinea and wd~50;
making the James Beard
Best Chef semifinalist
list since 2013; and being
named Best New Chef
by *Food & Wine* (2013)

FRIDGE: Avanti

ALEX STUPAK

Alex Stupak has come a long way from his Old El Paso eating roots. Sure, the thirty-something chef was cooking from an early age, but he ate Mexican food the way most people from the suburbs of Massachusetts did—out of boxes and cans. Now of course he's a groundbreaking iconoclast who's changed people's perceptions of what Mexican and American cooking can be.

He's from a family of cooks: his grandfather was a chef and his dad was the head of the kitchen at home. After having gone through a recipe book when he was eight, he made his mother red cabbage salad with Russian dressing. At twelve, he lied about his age to get a dishwashing job as a way to break into food prep, and at fourteen he was cooking Thanksgiving dinner for his entire family. By the time he won a scholarship to the Culinary Institute of America, he had "worked every food industry job you can imagine," he says.

His professional life started at the Boston restaurant Clio, where chef Ken Oringer offered him a pastry chef position. Stupak, who had never been interested in pastry before, resisted, until Oringer basically threw Albert Adrià's cookbook *Los Postres de el Bulli* at him. Stupak was fascinated by Adrià's creativity and embraced the possibilities of pastry.

From there, Stupak went to Chicago as the head pastry chef at Alinea. In Chicago, he met the two loves of his life: his (now) wife, originally from California, and Mexican food. "I was cooking Mexican food in secret for over seven years, checking out the humongous Mexican population in Chicago, flying off to Mexico any chance I got, studying masa corn.

I fell in love with Mexican cooking in my spare time," he recalls.

Next up were a few years as the pastry chef at Wiley Dufresne's wd~50. With that kind of background, Stupak could have easily created a modern fine-dining place: "I was pedigreed to be the fucking third coming of molecular gastronomy, but nothing could have interested me less. You could watch some asshole on *Top Chef* make liquid nitrogen ice cream, and I didn't want to be a part of it," he says.

And so he opened a taco place in the East Village, Empellón Cocina, and from that restaurant, four more. The dish that first turned him on at East L.A.'s La Parrilla became the vehicle for luxurious high-end products and high-brow mishmashes like A5 Wagyu beef fajitas with black pepper mole, and crab nachos with Hokkaido sea urchin "queso." "*Empellón* means 'push out of the way,' and I'm always pushing to the next level," Stupak explains. "The name is a constant reminder. What is Mexican food anyway? It's always been changing, influenced by outside forces. What I do is not authentic and not traditional. It's cultural exchange."

On the day of this interview, Stupak was at the front door, whispering a greeting because his youngest son was down for a nap. His kitchen looked like a typical one belonging to a family with young kids—there were bottles drying on the counter—except for the *Food & Wine* Best New Chef of the Year Award hanging on the wall next to the sink. Over some homemade Mexican pasta and a little tequila, he talked about the last thing he bought on a whim and the virtues of using his home as a test kitchen.

1. **WHITE SAUCE**—"It is my favorite condiment and I always have some in my fridge."

2. **YUZU MARMALADE**—"The last time I used the marmalade was to give some sweet potatoes some edge at Thanksgiving."

3. **PICKLED TURNIPS,** for any Middle Eastern–inspired sandwich

4. **PARMESAN CHEESE RINDS,** to infuse in a soup or sauce

5. **PICKLED HABANEROS**

6. **AMERICAN CHEESE**

7. **WHITE MISO**

8. **CHIPOTLE PEPPERS IN VINEGAR**

9. **MEXICAN CHORIZO**

10. **KASHKAVAL CHEESE**—"Super mild and melty. What's not to love?"

11. **CORN TORTILLAS**—"I always prefer to take these from my restaurants. I never buy them elsewhere. Once you have had fresh masa it is hard to go back."

12. **STRING CHEESE AND YOGURT POUCHES,** for the kids

1. **YUZU JUICE**—"Use it in the same way you would use lemon juice. My wife, Lauren, puts it in her vodka soda."

2. **KEFIR CHEESE LABNE**—"I add raw garlic to it and use it as a spread."

3. **GEORGE WATKINS MUSHROOM KETCHUP**

4. **KEWPIE MAYONNAISE**

5. **TONIC WATER**

6. **VERMOUTH**

7. **WHOLE MILK**

Q & A

What are we going to find in your fridge? You will always find a lot of convenient, highly preservable flavor bombs, such as pickled chilies. I buy fresh chilies, put them in a jar, and drench them in vinegar to preserve them. They will last a lifetime. That way you can buy more than one chili, because if you buy ten chilies and you don't use them right away, they will rot. I hydrate chipotles in vinegar too; it increases their shelf life. I also use some of those chipotles in the Mexican pasta I make (see page 237). It's very homey but intriguing.

Is this something you learned from your wife's family? That's a misconception about me—people don't get it because it's not a neat little package. My wife is actually American. The same ingredients in the hands of a Mexican chef taste different than they would in any other culture. The first time I heard about the Mexican pasta dish I was fascinated, it sounded odd to me. When you see it, you start to understand. Spaghetti gets broken, and then toasted. Tomatoes are blackened and burned and so is the garlic, and that gets pureed with chilies and gets absorbed into it. The topping is crema, coriander, and avocado.

What do you do with all that mayo?! I have a very unhealthy relationship with it. I think mayo is the only mother sauce. Well, okay, Duke's is king, but other than that if I see interesting mayo in a store I pick it up or I shop for it on Amazon. I'm not a health nut—I will always have American cheese, yellow mustard, and four to five different types of mayonnaise. When you get life insurance you get a blood test—they were like, 'You're only 150 pounds but . . . .' I still got the life insurance but with a slight risk assessed. At home, we are really comfort-food driven: We like carbs, we like fried egg sandwiches at three in the morning, that type of thing.

Ok, let's say it's 3 a.m. and you're going to make an egg sandwich. What goes in it? It's a sunny-side-up egg cooked hard on the bottom so it's really crispy. I'm a fan of Martin's potato rolls, so it would be on one of those, with mayo, American cheese, and then anything to further embellish, whatever I have around, maybe a can of Spam or some ham. I'm also obsessed with shawarma from halal carts. Ordering a gyro from a street cart was something I never did until I moved to New York City. Now it is a regular habit in my life.

They always ask if you want white or red sauce—whatever the friggin' white sauce is—it's my favorite thing on earth! I'm experimenting with my own white sauce.

It sounds like your home kitchen is a test kitchen. It is. I'm not cooking as much at the restaurant but I've never cooked more, I've never created more. I test either at home or downstairs in the smaller restaurant where I can hide in the basement. The problem with being a creative person is that when you get known for something it's part of the success but it also is when boredom sets in, the idea of grinding the same thing out in perpetuity.

Do you make pastry at home? Never.

What is it you are testing? Persian food.

What did you last buy on a whim? Kashk, a fermented dehydrated milk. It tastes like nutritional yeast. I bought it at Kalustyan's, which is such a fun place to shop. Kashk adds its own Parmesan-like funk to things. I found it to be particularly great in a light tomato sauce.

Persian Cucumbers with Sumac and White Sauce

Ordering a gyro from a street cart was something I never did until I moved to New York City. Now it is a regular habit in my life. I've never been able to find a recipe for that white sauce so once upon a time I attempted to approximate my own. Cucumbers are my crunchy snack and even though it is a healthy one, this sauce makes it feel hedonistic.

2 garlic cloves

4 egg yolks

Pinch of salt

Pinch of MSG

1 lemon, juiced

2 tablespoons white soy sauce

¼ cup water

1 teaspoon black pepper, cracked

⅛ teaspoon ground cumin

¼ teaspoon ground cardamom

½ teaspoon ground caraway seeds

1½ cups vegetable oil

8 Persian cucumbers

Coarse salt, to taste

Sumac powder, to taste

Blend the garlic and egg yolks in a food processor. Add the salt, MSG, lemon juice, white soy sauce, water, black pepper, cumin, cardamom, and ground caraway. Blend. Slowly pour in the vegetable oil to emulsify. Transfer to an airtight container and store in the refrigerator.

To serve, cut the cucumbers in half lengthwise and arrange on a plate cut side up. Season with a sprinkling of salt and sumac. Serve with a container of white sauce on the side to dip.

SERVES 4 AS AN APPETIZER OR SNACK

Sopa Seca de Fideo (Mexican Spaghetti)

This is the type of dish I eat when I'm in need of something comforting. We all have dried pasta in the house, but the treatment here makes it feel a bit more interesting and special. Cooking pasta with smoky chilies gives the dish an edge, and by dressing it lavishly with crema, Mexican cheese, and avocado it becomes a late-night pasta dish that you would be proud to serve to other chefs if you happen to have some over.

2 cups vegetable oil

2 cups fideo cut spaghetti

2 cloves garlic, peel left on

3 tomatoes

2 chipotle chilies (previously hydrated in white vinegar)

6 ounces crumbled Mexican chorizo

1 cup chicken broth

Salt

4 tablespoons Mexican-style crema

1 avocado, peeled and cubed

½ white onion, thinly sliced

4 ounces Cotija cheese, grated

Handful of cilantro leaves, roughly chopped

Heat the oil in a shallow braising pan. Add the pasta and toast it until golden brown. Drain the pasta and allow the oil to cool before storing for reuse.

To make the sauce, heat a dry cast-iron skillet over a medium heat. Place the garlic cloves and tomatoes in the skillet and roast them. The garlic is ready when it is soft and fragrant and has black spots. The tomatoes are ready when they are blackened in spots and the juice is bursting out of them. Peel the garlic and place in a blender with the tomatoes. Cut the chipotles in half, scrape out and discard the seeds, and add them to the blender. Puree the mixture until smooth.

Fry the chorizo in the skillet until it is well done. Add the pasta along with the tomato puree. Cook the mixture until the puree is reduced. Add the chicken broth and continue to cook until the pasta is tender. Turn off the heat and season with salt. Stir in 2 tablespoons of the crema.

To serve: Dress the pasta with the avocado and onion. Drizzle over the remaining crema and sprinkle with the Cotija cheese and cilantro.

SERVES 4

CHRISTINA TOSI

Christina Tosi always dreamed of opening her own bakery. Of course, the dessert dynamo and CEO of the ever-expanding Milk Bar chain of bakeries has done way more than that, but her childhood is never far from her mind. "I wanted to build something that would inspire ten-year-old me growing up in Ohio and Virginia," she explains.

Her earliest memories involve cooking with her grandmother. "Her oatmeal cookies had this gorgeous crackled texture, the perfect balance of chewy middle and crispy shell," recalls Tosi. She pined for an Easy Bake Oven, but her mom, who didn't understand the fuss over a toy stove, told her, "Just cook in a real kitchen." So she did, attending the French Culinary Institute in New York after college, and then working in restaurants to support herself. "I wanted to be in the most highly regarded and intense kitchens in New York, even when the risks were challenging, exciting, and downright terrifying," she says.

She ended up making high-end desserts at Bouley. Later, she got her foot in the kitchen of wd~50 after dining there and on a whim calling Wylie Dufresne to tell him how he could do dessert better. Dufresne admired her chutzpah, and eventually recommended her to his friend David Chang, who needed help creating a food safety program at his newly opened Momofuku restaurant. "It meant that I was always tinkering with recipes, tasting thoughtfully, setting up our station better than the shift before, looking for ways to improve every step of the way," she recalls.

As she was becoming tired of making fancy desserts, the job seemed a perfect fit. She also brought homemade cookies to work every day, which caught Chang's eye. One day, he challenged her to make a dessert for that evening's dinner, and the strawberry shortcake with heavy cream, sour cream, and sherry vinegar she baked blew them all away.

Tosi continued evolving her confections. "I like to take the flavors and feelings of childhood memories and turn them on their head, creating something brand-new and familiar enough to make you feel at home, but with enough range to give you a sense of newness and excitement. I channel nostalgia in my cooking because food is the best vehicle for memory that I know," she says. The result were such Momofuku classics as Crack Pie, Compost Cookies, and cereal milk.

Tosi got her bakery when the space next door to Momofuku's came up for rent. Now she lives what she calls a "healthy/unhealthy" lifestyle, eating as much sugar as she can. She also does a lot of prerecipe tasting at home—on the day of this interview she was hard at work eating a large slice of chocolate cake at her dining room table.

"It's hard to capture lightning in a bottle in my eleven-thousand-square-foot test kitchen at the bakery," she explains; and the enviable amount of counter space in her home kitchen lends itself perfectly to trying out new concepts. Her refrigerator is organized on the basis of flavors that might go together. "I'm thinking as I put things back, and I put them back in an interesting way," she says. One idea that may be coming to a location near you: "To make Milk Bar cookie dough that you can buy at the grocery store."

CURRENT HOMETOWN:
New York City

RESTAURANT THAT MADE HER NAME: Momofuku, New York City

SIGNATURE STYLE: Genius desserts

BEST KNOWN FOR: Crack Pie; the Milk Bar bakeries; being named James Beard Rising Star Chef (2012); and her cookbook *All About Cake*

FRIDGE: Gaggenau

1. **BEER**—"For my husband or if I'm out of bread, I will use it to make a quick beer bread."

2. **MAPLE SYRUP**

3. **STRAWBERRY PICKLE JAM,** from Milk Bar—"It's good whipped into yogurt for breakfast. "

4. **BIRTHDAY CRUMBS**—"This is the textural layer in our birthday cake and confetti cookies. At home we use them as the crunchy granola in a parfait."

5. **SSÄM SAUCE**—"It's great on pizza. We also use it to amp up takeout foods."

6. **LEFTOVER HALLOWEEN CANDY**—"My husband is a Snickers guy, I'm a Take 5 girl."

7. **COCA-COLA**—"We are big fans in this house. I grew up in a family where my mom was worried about sugar and would only let us drink diet soda. I couldn't wait to be a grown-up and have the right to drink normal soda."

8. **JAMS, FROM A FRIEND IN THE U.K.**—"I always try to figure out what to do with jellies and jams beyond the obvious: add in between a cake layer or when I'm out of duck sauce and I need to fashion a dipping sauce on the fly. It's also great on grilled cheese."

9. **NUTELLA**—"I eat it with a spoon! When I was thirteen I stayed in northern Italy with my extended family. My favorite part of the day was at 3 p.m. We would get fresh rolls and we would smother them with Nutella."

10. **VINNY WINE**—"I'll add basil to it as a wine cocktail. I like effervescence. It probably takes me back to the soda ban of my childhood."

11. **FERRERO ROCHER CHOCOLATE**—"Hazelnuts are my kryptonite."

12. **COMPOST COOKIE DOUGH**

13. **SPRITE,** for non-Coke-drinking guests

14. **DULCE DE LECHE**—"It's one of the greatest things in the world. I spread it on cookies."

15. **CONFETTI COOKIE DOUGH**—"It's a project that I'm playing around with. This is a good one with dulce de leche. It probably explains why they are so close together in the fridge."

16. **ACQUA PANNA SPARKLING WATER**—"I drink a lot of bubbly water; the acidity balances out my stomach."

17. **SAUVIGNON BLANC AND CHARDONNAY,** from New Zealand

18. **CHAMPAGNE**—"One of my husband's best friends works for Krug, so it's nice to know we will always have Krug in our lives."

19. **PICKLED JALAPEÑOS,** for late-night snack attacks along with the salsa con queso and chunky salsa—"Sometimes chips are boring and I need the jalapeños for dipping in the salsa."

20. **SEVAROME PISTACHIO PASTE**—"If you like PB&J, pistachio and apricot jam is the next level. I also like to bake with it, not in a Milk Bar layer-cake way but in a more homespun fashion."

Q & A

How do you drink your cereal milk these days? It's really good if you froth it up. I've become obsessed with cereal milk lattes.

Other cereal milk fetishes? My aspiration is to buy a soft-serve machine for our deck. Cereal milk is pretty mellow on its own, and it's also good in panna cotta.

Do you have any "aha" cooking moments at home? I put stuff in my refrigerator and stare at it long enough until it surprises me. For instance, if I look at milk or bubbly water, and I'll be like—ah!—and I'll hit on something. I'm currently trying to convince our marketing director that there should be a birthday-flavored sparkling water.

There are a lot of sauce packets in your fridge door. I'm a little bit of a cheap old lady at heart. I always ask for extra sauces with deliveries—extra ranch dressing, soy sauce, duck sauce . . . . I play the leftover game and I'll add stuff, like with vegetable soup or stew. I like to season with soy, duck sauce, and apple cider vinegar. They always give it to you, so why would you throw it away?

With miso—do you tend to go sweet or salty? One of my favorite things to do with miso is to spread it on a sheet pan, basically burn it in the oven. Then blend with sherry vinegar, light brown sugar, some butter, and make a butterscotch sauce with it. It's great for an ice cream sundae or folded into things, or in an apple pie or just for dunking apple slices.

And the basil? When I'm in desperation mode or to spruce up leftovers or water I use fresh herbs like basil. I'm not good at drinking water, so I feel like I'm my own parent trying to make it fun to drink. On virtuous mornings, I blend coconut water with fruit and veggies for a smoothie. It masks the vegetal taste. It's the cleanest thing that comes out of this fridge.

There is milk—that feels wholesome. I use a splash of vinegar in whole milk to make buttermilk. It's for me the best way to not have to keep six different kinds of dairy in my fridge. We eat a lot of cereal too. I have coconut milk for when someone doesn't drink milk. It's nice to have it, and it lasts forever.

Your top three breakfast cereals? Honey Bunches of Oats, Cinnamon Life, and then it depends, Cap'n Crunch or Lucky Charms. Golden Grahams, sometimes. Honey Bunches of Oats because it makes you feel like a grown-up, eating healthy. It's a good study in texture. Some stay soft, some stay medium. The big pieces are super crunchy. It keeps my brain engaged as I'm eating the cereal.

But with all this sugar you seem super fit! I run almost every day. It's my happy place. It's my sanity.

Have you ever tried making any of those sports energy bars? No, I'm like grab a fistful of cookie dough and go. I keep it very simple.

Do you have a stomach made from steel? I must! If I've eaten way too many baked goods or stuffed myself to the gills, a cup of warm ginger tea is all that I need.

Like if you've eaten too much of that massive cake in the center of your refrigerator? This is our German Chocolate Jimbo Cake. We made it for the birthday of *GQ*'s editor in chief and put it on the menu. I have an ongoing joke with my husband. We both travel a lot for work. When I'm in recipe-testing mode or when I'm auditing a cake, I'll bring the cake home. And he'll be like, "Stop leaving me home alone with all this cake!" I live with it every day so I think I have self-control most days. He will just take a fork, and in a day or two from now, there will be fork carvings all over it.

What are you checking for? Moisture, height, dispersion of fillings, and texture. It's also eating it and wondering if it's as good as we can possibly make it. Do I still feel as passionate about it with my morning coffee? Because if not, I'll tweak. It's a gut check.

On average how many do you taste a week? I was in L.A. last week and I audited twelve cakes.

Do you have any secret family recipes? I have a family favorite called Gooey Butter Cake, which is cream cheese, butter, a pound of confectioners' sugar, and a box of cake mix. Growing up, it was a family standard in my house. If I'm going somewhere that is supposed to be fun and easy, bringing that is a good way to disarm. People assume that it has to be a fancy dessert to meet my approval. No, it just needs to be down-home delicious. I don't care about anything else.

No meat in your refrigerator? Life is such that if I'm going to make a roast chicken, I will shop for it the day of. I like to get my proteins the day I need them. I don't like raw chicken hanging out with my cake truffles.

Anything you're snobby about in your fridge? I always keep really good unsalted butter. The snobbery comes in when it comes to unsalted butter. I want to control the salt after the fact. If possible, European style, as it's cultured and has a greater depth of flavor. Non–European style is surface-level flavor.

Is your midnight snack sweet? Always. Sometimes I will eat something salty just to ramp into the indulgence of sweet.

Any particular refrigerator-hygiene habits you want to share? I wrap up take-out like a crazy person. I don't wrap the cake, because I'm worried it will damage the sides.

But if there is Indian or Chinese food in there it gets wrapped six times! I rotate the baking soda in my fridge a lot too!

You have boxed wine? There are actually cans inside. My husband is a restaurateur. They started making wine called Empire State, using all upstate New York grapes. It's a fun grab-and-have bubbly white wine. It always feels like a celebration.

Are you anti-artificial sweeteners? They taste really chemical to me. I try to keep it pure. But I don't hate on it. I'm going to eat real sugar all day long so I'm not gonna fool myself.

What's in the freezer? My husband loves Crack Pie so I always keep some in the freezer. I like to have some birthday cake in case I have a kid's birthday party or for other baking. We always keep some sort of ice cream. Never a solid flavor, always lots of flavors. These are ripe bananas that I buy to ripen, then freeze. It's when bananas taste like bananas to the max.

Compost Cookie Dough Cookies

What, might you ask, is a cookie dough cookie? It's a confection made in a very hot oven, so that it looks like a perfectly baked cookie on the outside, but on the inside you have a gooey, unbaked cookie dough center. My. Dream. Come. True. The weakest of weak nights requires a minimum of one cookie dough cookie.

For the graham crust:

1½ cups graham cracker crumbs

¼ cup milk powder

2 tablespoons sugar

¾ tablespoon kosher salt

4 to 5½ tablespoons butter, melted

¼ cup heavy cream

For the cookie dough:

1 cup butter, at room temperature

1 cup granulated sugar

⅔ cup light brown sugar, tightly packed

2 tablespoons glucose or 1 tablespoon corn syrup

1 egg

½ teaspoon vanilla extract

1⅓ cups flour

½ teaspoon baking powder

¼ teaspoon baking soda

1 teaspoon kosher salt

¾ cup mini chocolate chips

½ cup mini butterscotch chips

⅓ cup old-fashioned rolled oats

2½ teaspoons ground coffee (see Note)

2 cups potato chips (see Note)

1 cup mini pretzels

For the graham crust: in a medium bowl toss the graham crumbs, milk powder, sugar, and salt with your hands to evenly distribute your dry ingredients.

Whisk 4 tablespoons of the butter and heavy cream together. Add to the dry ingredients and toss again to evenly distribute. The butter will act as a glue, adhering to the dry ingredients and turning the mixture into a bunch of small clusters. The mixture should hold its shape if squeezed tightly in the palm of your hand. If it is not moist enough to do so, melt an additional 1 to 1½ tablespoons of butter and mix it in. Stored in an airtight container, graham crust will keep fresh for 1 week at room temperature or for 1 month in the fridge or freezer.

For the compost cookie dough: combine the butter, sugars, and glucose or corn syrup in the bowl of a stand mixer fitted with the paddle attachment and cream together on medium-high for 2 to 3 minutes. Scrape down the sides of the bowl, add the egg and vanilla extract, and beat for another 7 to 8 minutes.

Reduce the speed to low and add the flour, baking powder, baking soda, and salt. Mix just until the dough comes together, no longer than 1 minute. Scrape down the sides of the bowl with a spatula.

Still on low speed, add the chocolate chips, butterscotch chips, graham crust, oats, and coffee and mix just until incorporated, about 30 seconds. Add the potato chips and pretzels and paddle, still on low speed, until just incorporated. Be careful not to over-mix or break too many of the pretzels or potato chips.

Using a 2¾-ounce ice cream scoop (or a ⅓ cup measure), portion out the dough onto two parchment-lined sheet pans. Pat the tops of the cookie dough domes flat. Wrap the sheet pan tightly in plastic wrap and freeze for 1 hour or until fully frozen.

Preheat oven to 500°F. Put individual frozen rounds on a greased or lined baking sheet and bake just until the cookies begin to spread and the thinnest of golden-brown skins forms on the surface but before the bottom of the cookies begin to burn, 4 to 5 minutes.

Remove from the oven and immediately refrigerate until cool and set, about 15 minutes.

MAKES 15 TO 20 COOKIES

Note: Don't use instant coffee; it will dissolve in the baking process and ruin the cookies. And never use wet, sogalicious grounds that have already brewed a pot of coffee. We use Cape Cod potato chips because they aren't paper-thin, and so they do not break down too much in the mixing process.

Molten Chocolate Mug Cake

Sometimes it's 11:30 p.m. and I realize there is no dessert in the house. Enter mug cakes! They come together in less than five minutes and are dangerously indulgent. I like to scoop my favorite ice cream atop this gooey masterpiece and drift peacefully to sleep, like you just had a boring old glass of warm milk, but better.

2½ tablespoons unsalted butter, melted

2 tablespoons buttermilk

1 tablespoon plus 1 teaspoon grapeseed or other neutral oil

¼ teaspoon vanilla extract

1 large egg

½ cup sugar

⅓ cup plus 2 teaspoons cake flour

2 tablespoons cocoa powder

2 teaspoons baking powder

½ teaspoon kosher salt

3 tablespoons mini chocolate chips

Whisk the melted butter, buttermilk, oil, vanilla extract, and egg together in a bowl. In a separate bowl, whisk the sugar, cake flour, cocoa powder, baking powder, and salt together. Pour the wet ingredients into the dry ones and stir to combine. If the batter looks lumpy, use a whisk to break up all the lumps. Stir in the chocolate chips.

Find your two best 11-ounce mugs and divide the batter evenly between them. Microwave the mugs for 1 minute. If the cake looks too raw, continue to microwave in 15-second increments up to 2½ minutes, until the sides and top have set, leaving hot gooey cake batter hidden inside. Remove the mugs from the microwave. Let the mugs cool for 1 minute before serving.

MAKES 2 MUG CAKES

JEAN-GEORGES VONGERICHTEN

If he hadn't been a wastrel first, Jean-Georges Vongerichten may have never become a chef. Vongerichten grew up in a suburb of Strasbourg. His bedroom was located above the family kitchen, so he woke up every day to the smells of the pork-and-cabbage lunches that his grandmother and mother prepared for the employees of the family's coal company. As the eldest son, he was expected to take over the business, but engineering trade school proved to be a bust—he was kicked out after a year. "I had no idea what I wanted to do," he says of this period. "Pretty much all I learned was how to drink and smoke!"

That changed when he was sixteen. His parents invited him for a meal at Auberge de l'Ill, then a three-star Michelin restaurant. The service and classic dishes transfixed him, and much to his father's surprise, for the first time Vongerichten was interested in *something*. When chef Paul Haeberlin approached the table to see how things were going, the elder Vongerichten asked if he could find a job for his "useless son." The three-year apprenticeship at the legendary restaurant was the beginning of Vongerichten's illustrious cooking career. "It just happened," he says.

After learning his trade at Auberge d'Ill, Vongerichten did his military service on an antisubmarine destroyer as the captain's personal cook. They were based in Brest, but traveled from port to port from England to Morocco. "I had to shop in each city so I really got a flavor for the local markets," he recalls. His travels continued as he worked his way up

the restaurant business, learning from such masters as Louis Outhier, one of the founders of nouvelle cuisine, and Paul Bocuse. Thanks to Outhier, he became a consultant with a hotel group, and opened restaurants in Thailand, Singapore, Hong Kong, and Japan. He studied each country's cuisine, and began to evolve his own style that mixed East and West.

Outhier then sent him another mission, this time to the Drake Hotel in New York, and Vongerichten found his niche. He put the lessons he had learned in Asia to good use and transformed his cuisine, cutting out heavy sauces and replacing them with vegetable broths, introducing lemongrass, ginger, and other exotic ingredients that New Yorkers were unaccustomed to finding outside of Chinatown. He drew an influential clientele, including one Phil Suarez, a media tycoon. One day Suarez handed over his business card. "If you ever strike out on your own, give me a call," he told Vongerichten.

Vongerichten remembered that card when he walked past a restaurant with a "to rent" sign and learned it was available if he paid a month's rent the following day. He dropped Suarez a line, and a day later, check in hand, became his own boss. He named his new restaurant with his childhood nickname, JoJo.

JoJo was just the first in a string of restaurants that Vongerichten and Suarez opened together. Next came Vong, a Thai/French fusion restaurant, followed by dozens of others, including the flagship Jean-Georges, and outposts as far away as South America

CURRENT HOMETOWN:
New York City

RESTAURANT THAT MADE
HIS NAME: Restaurant
Lafayette in the Drake
Hotel

SIGNATURE STYLE: Seasonal
French-American nouvelle
cuisine

BEST KNOWN FOR: His
flagship Jean-Georges and
many other restaurants;
numerous James Beard
Awards; his cookbooks;
and a memoir, *JGV: A Life
in 12 Recipes*

FRIDGE: Viking

and Asia. As Vongerichten says, "Opening a new restaurant is easier than changing the menu in an old one."

A self-confessed health freak who boxes every morning, Vongerichten has an industrial chic Viking refrigerator that contains mostly produce and is very neatly organized. There's also a lot of water, chilled bottles of beer, and charcuterie. He has them on hand for evenings when friends come over to hang at his immaculate Greenwich Village pad with its white minimalist kitchen and views of the Hudson River. "Where I grew up, it was black everywhere," he recalls. "We'd be playing on mountains of coal in the backyard and we were always filthy. I've come a long way from the coal pits of Alsace. Not bad for a simple cook and high school dropout!"

1. **FIJI BOTTLED WATER**—"I knew the guy who started the company way back before they became well known. I agreed to stock his product, and he began to send me three or four boxes a week. So I always have tons and give it away to friends and family!"

2. **CROWN MAPLE SYRUP,** from the Hudson Valley—"I always have maple syrup for plain yogurt or pancakes on the weekend."

3. **FEVER-TREE TONIC,** for gin and tonics at aperitif time

4. **BUTTERMILK,** for making pancakes

5. **SPANISH OLIVES,** for snacks and entertaining

6. **JUICES, FROM ABC**—"I drink one before or after the gym."

7. **CHIA PUDDING**

8. **MIRABELLE JAM**—"My favorite flavor."

9. **SALTED BUTTER**

10. **ALMOND BUTTER**

11. **PEARS**

12. **PEANUT BUTTER**—"I eat it by the spoon!"

13. **SAKE**—"I like to drink it straight up."

14. **PERONI BEER**

15. **CHARCUTERIE**

16. **FRENCH SAUCISSON SEC**

Organic Chia Seed Pudding

Since I can make it easily the day before, I often make chia pudding to eat for breakfast during the work week. We serve the same at ABC for breakfast—it's very energizing.

½ cup organic white chia seeds

One 15.5-ounce can organic light coconut milk

One 15.5-ounce can organic coconut cream

½ lime, juiced

1 tablespoon maple syrup

2 drops vanilla extract

Dash of salt

Cardamom or cinnamon, to taste (optional)

Whisk together all the ingredients. Let sit overnight, covered, in the refrigerator. Serve with seasonal fruits, dates, nuts, and seeds.

SERVES 4

Q & A

What's your fridge style? My fridge is always organized with lots of fruit.

There is a lot of empty space in there—do you live alone? Yes, I'm separated. I have three kids and three grandkids.

This is a very healthy fridge for a bachelor. Do you eat healthy all the time? Even late at night? Yes, mostly. I come home round 11:30 p.m. or midnight. I've already had dinner so maybe a persimmon for a late-night snack. Or maybe a yogurt or some milk chocolate before I go to bed. I know, the last is the worst just before bed!

Anything we would never see in your fridge? Anything with genetically modified ingredients.

That sounds a little less virtuous, though you seem to drink a lot of water. I drink two to three Fiji each day. It has lots of silica. I also have lots of juice from ABC.

What types of juice? A green juice of green apple, kale, spinach, jalapeño, and celery. The red is beet, carrot, ginger, and orange. And a turmeric tonic with fresh turmeric, water, sea salt, lime juice, and honey. With the stress we have in the kitchen, the last one is a good remedy when I come home.

What is always on tap in your fridge? Some Champagne, tonic water for gin and tonics—I always have vodka, gin, and Campari. But we had a lot of Negronis last night!

What do you serve when you entertain? Most often it's ham or saucisson sec.

Any food you really miss from Alsace? My mother's cooking, especially her *choucroute*. And my favorite childhood dish, *baeckoffe*.

What do you cook on the weekends? I pick up seasonal fruits and vegetables at the farmers market before going to the country, where I spend most of my weekends with my family. Being that most of us are in the industry, everyone gets involved with the cooking. My son Cedric is usually at the grill, Philippe helps me in the kitchen. We serve everything family style. They all love my breakfasts, especially my pancakes.

Do you ever order takeout? I am not really one to order takeout. I sometimes order from Perry Street and bring it up to my apartment.

ALICE WATERS

I was a very picky eater as a kid and my mother wasn't a very good cook," recalls Alice Waters. While most fussy eaters don't necessarily grow up to become chefs, let alone pioneer an entire food movement, Waters has done just that, thanks to her early education in California, France, and England.

She went to the University of California, Berkeley, in the sixties and started cooking for her friends and housemates. That's when she realized that if she could cook for ten people, she could cook for twenty—and first conceived of opening a restaurant.

But before that came a junior year abroad in Paris, where she skipped most of her classes at the Sorbonne to educate herself in the cuisine of the small bistros in the French countryside, eating buckwheat crepes, Brittany oysters, and, of course, baguettes. And then, after graduation, a stay in London to study the teachings of Maria Montessori. The Montessori principle of learning through your senses and by doing felt like a hopeful way to enact change, she explains.

Even though she lived on a shoestring budget and with no heat in London, Waters still managed to cook tarts and steam mussels. She also went frequently to the kitchenware store run by Elizabeth David, the famous English food writer whose cookbooks Waters also used for learning to cook. Another influence was Lulu Peyraud, the proprietor of the Domaine Tempier, whom Waters met during a trip to Provence.

All of those forces fed into the restaurant she opened in Berkeley in 1971, Chez Panisse. From the beginning, she based the menu upon the freshest seasonal ingredients available, just like the bistros in Paris. During the restaurant's early days, Waters was often invited to New York to cook for events, and she brought her mesclun salads on the plane direct from California—still in the soil. She only cut them just before serving. Waters stood out from the other male chefs but her salads were what everyone spoke about.

Waters famously mixed a salad with her bare hands, vinaigrette and all, on fellow Francophile Julia Child's cooking show, and she has continually learned by using the Montessori way. "I think that when you dress a salad with your hands, it's easier to tell when you have the right amount of oil and vinegar on the leaves," she says. Waters still feels especially indebted to Child, who made French cooking more acceptable in the United States. These days, though, Chez Panisse is more than just a French restaurant, as the daily menus can go from French cooking to Moroccan, Indian, or Russian.

Aesthetics are important to Waters: "Beauty is the language of care" is something she says often. There's a purpose behind each object in her home kitchen—in the well-worn butcher block island, the carefully chosen handmade pottery, and the iron-forged egg spoon hanging above the fireplace. Her refrigerator door is green. "I didn't want a big white or stainless-steel thing in the kitchen. I want real materials like wood, colors that harmonize with food. I like lighting that makes the food look good, at Chez Panisse and at home," she explains. "Same for cooking equipment—it doesn't need to be all stainless steel. I use cast-iron and copper pots. I want to have a kitchen that is warm and cleanable. I resist the sanitized kitchen."

CURRENT HOMETOWN:
Berkeley, California

RESTAURANT THAT MADE HER NAME: Chez Panisse, Berkeley

SIGNATURE STYLE: Market-fresh cuisine made with local ingredients

BEST KNOWN FOR: As a pioneer in farm-to-table organic cooking; as an advocate for free, nutritional school lunches via the Edible Schoolyard; numerous awards, including a National Humanities Medal; four cookbooks; and a memoir, *Coming to My Senses*

FRIDGE: Sub-Zero

7. **SWEET-AND-SOUR PICKLES**

8. **LEMON CURD**

9. **ANCHOVIES**—"These are special. I found these myself in Spain. We were using the salt-packed anchovies from Italy in the first years at Chez Panisse. Now we use these delicious Spanish ones and I always have them in my own fridge as well!"

10. **CRAB APPLE JELLY**—"I wrote divine on it, because it is."

11. **BLENHEIM APRICOT JAM**—"I am very stingy about this so I usually put it way in the back so no one can grab it."

12. **PICKLED PEPPERS**

13. **HOT PEPPERS**

14. **PRESERVED LEMONS FROM A FRIEND**—"I do a lot of things with them, but I love to make Moroccan dishes, lamb or chicken, with the preserved lemons."

1. **UME WINE**—"This is a Japanese plum wine, *umeshu*, that someone gave to me. I've been sipping it for about six months now."

2. **SHERRY**

3. **DESSERT WINE**

4. **FERMENTED APPLE CIDER**

5. **APPLE SHRUB**—"I add it to sparkling water as a drink."

6. **SWEET ITALIAN BAROLO**

15. **TORTILLAS**—"I get my tortillas from Primavera because they are organic and they're small and very thin. And they always label the package with the date that the tortillas were made on!"

16. **PARMESAN AND MONTEREY JACK CHEESE**

17. **SALADS**

18. **POMELO**—"It signifies Chez Panisse's connection with Chino Farms, one of our longtime purveyors. It's a very special fruit within the Japanese culture for the New Year. And they are really rather delicious."

Q & A

There's lots of green inside your fridge.
And many bottles of wine. The Bandol rosé comes from the domaine of my mentor, Lulu Peyraud, who is now one hundred and one years old. So I have a glass of rosé wine and toast to her every night. I keep a bottle or two in case friends come over.

What about some of the other bottles?
I have lots of gifts; most everything in here was a gift. When we don't finish a bottle, especially of sweet wine like the Italian Barolo, I love to save it. Sometimes it can moisten fruit compote or it can be drizzled over a cake. It has lots of purposes. I just keep those in the back in case. It's a beautiful way to keep people in your life every day.

Your refrigerator looks almost like a still life painting! Is there a purpose to the way you organize it? It's important that the refrigerator looks beautiful. I think about that all of the time. I don't want any plastic in here.

What about the overturned bowls that serve as lids? This technique—it's desperation. I'm waiting for some glass containers, old ones; I'm waiting for them to arrive. I keep tortillas and cheese inside the bowls, as well as my salad.

What do you always have in your fridge?
I always have greens, cooking greens and other greens. Always. I always have onions, carrots, and celery too, for a mirepoix. Everything is organic. That's very important to me.

Where do you shop? There is a farmers market about a block from Chez Panisse and then there is shopping at Chez Panisse! On Saturdays I go to the farmers market at the San Francisco Ferry Plaza. I desperately try to not buy too much, even though it is such a temptation. But you can't really calculate who will come to dinner. Sometimes we have unexpected dinner guests. On Sundays when I'm in town I get the food and we cook together, usually family and friends. We don't know what we will cook until we start cooking.

Does your daughter, Fanny, live here?
She is in and out.

You have lots of Japanese condiments— do they each have a story? We have many gifts from Japan. Some I have to taste to know what they are. I don't even know what it is. Maybe I should taste it [she sips]. It's sesame oil. We also have a number of hot sauces.

There is quite an important collection of little jars in here. This is a strange one. It's a spicy pickle. My friend's husband David drew a picture on the front of their parrot Ortle. Even though it's ancient—I can't throw it out.

And there seem to be lots of jams . . .
I always buy from the farmers—what they make or can in the winter. The things I have the most of are citrus jellies and marmalades. This is sweet quince relish from my tree. Over here is crab apple jelly—our pastry chef made it from crab apples from the Edible Schoolyard garden.

What do you do with leftovers? I often make simple tacos with leftovers. It's so easy when you just have a little bit of something.

Do you have a trick for Thanksgiving leftovers? Yes—I send them home with my guests.

What would we never find in your refrigerator? I hope you would never find anything that I didn't know where it came from. I hope that I know about all my food.

What is your guilty pleasure food?
Very bitter dark chocolate and salty organic potato chips.

Marinated Beet Salad with Anchovies

Beets of different colors make a very beautiful salad when paired with anchovies, which I always have in my fridge.

1 pound beets

1 teaspoon salt plus more to taste

1 teaspoon red wine vinegar, plus more to taste

2 teaspoons olive oil

1 tablespoon anchovies, minced

Preheat the oven to 350°F. Trim the beet greens to ½ inch from the beets. Wash the beets thoroughly. Put them in a baking dish with a little water (enough to cover the bottom of the dish to a depth of ⅛ inch) and sprinkle with 1 teaspoon of salt.

Cover tightly and place the beets in the oven and bake until they can be easily pierced with a sharp knife, 30 minutes to 1 hour, depending on their size.

Uncover and cool. Cut off the tops and roots and slip off their skins. Cut the peeled beets into small wedges or ¼-inch dice and sprinkle with red wine vinegar. Let stand for a few minutes to allow the beets to absorb the flavor. Taste and add more salt or vinegar as needed.

Toss with olive oil and anchovies, and serve.

SERVES 4

MOTHER
IN LAW'S
KIMCHI
NAPA
CABBAGE
16 FL OZ · 1 Pt
of Jang Mo Gip
Restaurant.
Est.1989.

6

7

8

1. SESAME OIL

2. JALAPEÑO HOT SAUCE

3. SOY SAUCE

4. PIRIPIRI SAUCE

5. HOT UMAMI PASTE

6. MISO PASTE

7. KIMCHI—"My daughter,
   Fanny, loves this kimchi."

8. SALTED PLUM

Organic Garden Salad Tortillas

My salad garden is the inspiration for a delicious lunch: fresh greens folded into a warm tortilla with Monterey jack cheese. I make these differently each time, depending on what is available and what I choose to pick—tender spring lettuces, winter rocket, sweet cucumbers, bittersweet frisée, mint leaves, cilantro sprigs, or sliced radishes. A little slice of leftover roasted meat is good too.

8 corn tortillas

3 to 4 cups grated Monterey jack cheese

8 cups washed salad greens

Fresh herbs, such as cilantro and mint

3 tablespoons olive oil

Sprinkle of salt

1 lime, quartered

Preheat a broiler at 375°F. Heat the tortillas directly over a gas burner or in a hot pan, then place on two baking sheets. Sprinkle the cheese over the warm tortillas and place the baking sheets under the broiler. Melt the cheese quickly, for less than 30 seconds, and remove from oven. Add the greens and herbs and finish with the olive oil and salt. Serve immediately with lime wedges.

SERVES 4

BIBLIOGRAPHY

Acheson, Hugh: Personal interview, December 1, 2018; email correspondence, February 5 and April 26, 2019.

Andrés, José: Personal interview, November 28, 2018; email correspondence, January 31 and May 1, 2019.

Andrés, José. *We Fed an Island: The True Story of Rebuilding Puerto Rico, One Meal at a Time.* New York: Anthony Bourdain/Ecco, 2018.

Barber, Dan: Personal interview, November 13, 2018; email correspondence, March 1, 2019.

Barber, Dan. On *Chef's Table*, Season 1, Episode 2. Netflix, 2015.

Barbot, Pascal: Personal interview, October 29, 2018; telephone interview, May 25, 2019.

Baumann, Kristian: Personal interview, October 1, 2018; telephone interview, May 2, 2019.

Boulud, Daniel: Personal interview, November 12, 2018; email correspondence, December 21, 2018.

Brock, Sean: Personal interview, November 16, 2018; email correspondence, March 5, 2019.

Brock, Sean. *Heritage.* New York: Artisan, 2014.

Cohen, Amanda: Personal interview, November 30, 2018; email correspondence, February 28 and March 31, 2019.

Crenn, Dominique: Personal interview, January 10, 2019; email correspondence, February 26, 2019.

Dufresne, Wylie: Personal interview, November 14, 2018; email correspondence, February 27 and May 20, 2019.

Essig, Kristen, and Michael Stoltzfus: Personal interview, January 24, 2019; email correspondence, February 19 and May 9, 2019.

Gagnaire, Pierre: Personal interview, January 18 and April 29, 2019.

Hall, Carla: Personal interview, January 22, 2019; email correspondence, February 20, 2019.

Hereford, Mason: Personal interview, January 24, 2019; email correspondence, February 18 and May 6, 2019.

Kahn, Jordan: Personal interview, January 11, 2019; email correspondence, February 12 and May 12, 2019.

Kitchin, Tom: Personal interview, December 14, 2018; email correspondence, February 22 and June 3, 2019.

Koslow, Jessica: Personal interview, January 11, 2019; Email correspondence, February 27 and May 21, 2019.

Lefebvre, Ludo: Personal interview, August 8, 2017; email correspondence, October 6, 2017, and February 28, 2019.

Lynch, Barbara: Personal interview, January 25, 2019; email correspondence, February 1, 2019.

Lynch, Barbara. *Out of Line: A Life of Playing with Fire.* New York: Atria Books, 2017.

Marchand, Gregory: Personal interview, December 11, 2018.

McMillan, David: Personal interview, January 23, 2019; email correspondence, January 30, 2019.

McMillan, David, Frédéric Morin, and Meredith Erickson. *Joe Beef: Surviving the Apocalypse.* New York: Knopf, 2018.

Olvera, Enrique: Personal interview, June 5, 2015, and January 8, 2019; email correspondence, May 14, 2019.

Orkin, Ivan: Personal interview, January 22, 2019; telephone interview, May 13, 2019.

Orkin, Ivan. On *Chef's Table*, Season 3, Episode 4. Netflix, 2015.

Pérez, Paco: Personal interview, October 16, 2018; email correspondence, March 14 and March 16, 2019.

Redzepi, Nadine Levy: Personal interview, February 5, 2019.

Rose, Anthony: Personal interview, November 16, 2018; email correspondence, December 16, 2018.

Rose, Anthony, and Chris Johns. *The Last Schmaltz: A Very Serious Cookbook.* New York: Appetite by Random House, 2018.

Rose, Marie-Aude: Personal interview, December 3, 2018; email correspondence, March 22 and May 9, 2019.

Ruscalleda, Carme: Personal interview, October 16, 2018; email correspondence, May 3 and May 6, 2019.

Silverton, Nancy: Personal interview, January 9, 2019; email correspondence February 27 and May 22, 2019.

Silverton, Nancy, with Carolynn Carreño. *A Twist of the Wrist.* New York: Knopf, 2007.

Smyth, Clare: Personal interview, February 5, 2019; telephone interview, February 13, 2019.

Søberg, Mette: Personal interview, October 1, 2018; email correspondence, September 30, 2018.

Stupak, Alex: Personal interview, November 14, 2019; email correspondence, December 10, 2018, and February 18, 2019.

Stupak, Alex, and Jordanna Rothman. *Tacos: Recipes and Provocations.* New York: Clarkson Potter, 2015.

Tosi, Christina: Personal interview, November 29, 2018; email correspondence, May 20, 2019.

Vongerichten, Jean-Georges: Personal interview, December 4, 2018 and March 21, 2019,

Waters, Alice: Personal interview, January 10, 2019; telephone interview, February 11, 2019; email correspondence, May 21, 2019.

Waters, Alice. *Coming to My Senses: The Making of a Counterculture Cook.* New York: Clarkson Potter, 2017.

INDEX OF RECIPES

Restaurant Addresses

Some of these chefs have small local eateries, others far-flung empires that span the globe. Wherever they may be, these are the places where names were made and reputations forged.

HUGH ACHESON

Hugh Acheson's Five & Ten restaurant in Athens, Georgia, has helped to define the new Southern cuisine—a blend of Southern-style dishes with Mediterranean influences. At Acheson's flagship restaurant, you'll find light-handed takes on Georgia classics such as collard greens with ham broth and beer mustard, and frogmore stew (shrimp, sausage, corn, and potatoes in a light tomato broth). At his cozy, saloon-styled Empire State South in Atlanta, Acheson turns out unabashedly Southern plates like shrimp and grits in a relaxed light-wooded dining room overlooking a tree-lined bocce court. www.hughacheson.com

FIVE & TEN
1073 S. Milledge Avenue
Athens, GA 30605
T: +1 706 546 7300

EMPIRE STATE SOUTH
999 Peachtree Street
Atlanta, GA 30309
T: +1 404 541 1105

JOSÉ ANDRÉS

José Andrés, the man who turned America on to tapas, has built up an empire of twenty-seven establishments, ranging from experimental Spanish-inspired cooking to food truck sandwiches. To see where it all began, get a table at Jaleo in Washington, D.C., and dig into classic snacks like cured Ibérico ham croquette or *pan con tomate* (tomato bread), a deceptively soothing term for an intense experience combining bread, tomato, garlic, olive oil, and salt. His two-star, Michelin-rated minibar is an avant-garde spot where Andrés pushes the limits of traditional Spanish cooking. Plan far ahead for a seat at this tiny counter for mind-bending small dishes such as spot prawn and nasturtium *leche de tigre*, and beef tendon churros. www.joseandres.com

JALEO
480 7th Street NW
Washington, DC 20004
T: +1 202 628 7949

MINIBAR
855 E Street NW
Washington, DC 20004
T: +1 202 393 0812

DAN BARBER

Influential chef, writer, and maven of the farm-to-table movement, Dan Barber has two addresses where he serves his deliciously elegant and sustainable tasting menus. The first Blue Hill, opened in Greenwich Village in 2000, show-cases produce from local artisans in a below-street-level speakeasy. The second, opened in 2004, and less than an hour away in Pocantico Hills, has a similar menu, and is located at the Stone Barns farm that provides much of the food for both establishments. Diners delight in dishes such as locally caught pheasant with eight-row flint corn polenta, and parsnip schnitzel. www.bluehillfarm.com

BLUE HILL
75 Washington Place
New York, NY 10011
T: +1 212 539 1776

BLUE HILL AT STONE BARNS
630 Bedford Road
Pocantico Hills, NY 10591
T: +1 914 366 9600

PASCAL BARBOT

Hidden on a tiny cul-de-sac, Astrance, chef Pascal Barbot's two-Michelin-starred restaurant, offers ever-changing tasting menus using the best of French produce combined with Asian techniques and flavors. In the twenty-five-seat duplex dining room, guests experience dishes often thought up by the chef after he's received the morning delivery of food. The light and largely butter- and cream-free cuisine has been celebrated for dishes such as a millefeuille "tart" of thinly sliced mushrooms, apples, and verjus-marinated foie gras, and lightly poached langoustines with a crunchy satay sauce. www.astrancerestaurant.com

ASTRANCE
32, rue de Longchamp,
75016, Paris, France
T: +33 1 40 50 84 40

KRISTIAN BAUMANN

Located on the waterfront in aformer warehouse, Kristian Baumann's 108 is often considered the younger sibling of René Redzepi's Noma. But this place has its own vibe. 108 is all dark wood and metal, with the original exposed brick and beams, embracing the materials of its past. Much of the produce for the kitchen comes from a biodynamic farm, and Baumann is a fan of pickling, curing, and fermenting techniques. Dishes from the small plates menu follow the seasons and include such favorites as raw lamb tartare with last year's pickles, and roasted kelp ice cream with hazelnut oil and caviar. www.108.dk

108
Strandgade 108
1401 Copenhagen, Denmark
T: +45 32 96 32 92

DANIEL BOULUD

Daniel Boulud has a constellation of highly admired restaurants throughout the world. His flagship, eponymous restaurant Daniel is the epitome of fine dining, serving luxurious classics like Dover sole au citron and flambéed Hudson Valley foie gras. For a more affordable Gallic experience, head to Bar Boulud for homey dishes that range from country style pâté to fluffy lobster-filled omelets. www.danielboulud.com

DANIEL
60 East 65th Street
New York, NY 10065
T: +1 212 288 0033

BAR BOULUD
1900 Broadway (at 64th Street)
New York, NY 10023
T: +1 212 595 0303

SEAN BROCK

Chef, heirloom seed activist, and part-time TV star, Sean Brock is the South's most famous food celebrity. Until recently, he was a consultant for the Husk restaurant group, and served as executive chef at the original Charleston, South Carolina, restaurant. There he created a new style of Southern cuisine, like cornmeal-crusted catfish with heirloom beans and chowchow. He quickly opened three other branches throughout the region. In 2020 he will be opening a new restaurant in East Nashville focused on Appalachian cuisine. www.chefseanbrock.com

AUDREY
809 Meridian Street,
Nashville, TN 37207

AMANDA COHEN

Dirt Candy, Amanda Cohen's Lower East Side vegetarian restaurant, was a game changer when it opened in 2008. Her philosophy was to make vegetables delicious by any means necessary. That creative approach resulted in such dishes as Brussels sprouts tacos and broccoli "hot dogs" (micro broccoli served inside a toasted bun with a secret mustard-vinegar sauce). It's no wonder Dirt Candy's light and airy dining room has never lacked for customers, even if they're the most dedicated meat eaters. www.dirtcandynyc.com

DIRT CANDY
86 Allen Street
New York, NY 10002
T: +1 212 228 7732

DOMINIQUE CRENN

One of the U.S.'s most highly respected chefs and kitchen activists (she is a staunch enemy of restaurant machismo), Dominique Crenn moved to San Francisco from her native France, serving up whimsical French-inspired cuisine made with products from her Sonoma Valley farm. Atelier Crenn (*atelier* means "workshop"), her tasting-menu-only restaurant, has inventive dishes as the Kir Breton, her cider-and-cassis take on the classic aperitif of her beloved Brittany, and "seed and grain," an exercise in textures using smoked buckwheat, quinoa "soil," bottarga, and bonito dashi broth. Bar Crenn, and Petit Crenn, her other, more casual establishments, offer, respectively, her luxe take on classic French bistro dishes and seafood cooking inspired by her Brittany youth. www.ateliercrenn.com

ATELIER CRENN
3127 Fillmore Street
San Francisco, CA 94123
T: +1 415 440 0460

Petit Crenn
609 Hayes Street
San Francisco, CA 94102
T: +1 415 864 1744

Bar Crenn
3131 Fillmore Street
San Francisco, CA 94123
T: +1 415 440 0460

WYLIE DUFRESNE

Wylie Dufresne, the chef who put New York's Lower East Side on the culinary map with genre-bending establishments such as Clinton Fresh Food and wd~50, left that all behind to create Du's Donuts and Coffee, a doughnut shop in Brooklyn. Still using all of his imagination and scientific wizardry, he makes cake doughnuts in all sorts of flavors, and enthusiasts make the trek to Williamsburg to sample the banana graham cracker and brown butter key lime ones. If you aren't into these baked goods, his scrambled egg grilled cheese sandwich has attained legendary status. www.dusdonuts.com

DU'S DONUTS AND COFFEE
107 N. 12th Street,
Brooklyn, NY 11249
T: +1 718 215 8770

KRISTEN ESSIG AND MICHAEL STOLTZFUS

Coquette, located in a historic 1880s building in New Orleans's Garden District, is known for its updated farm-to-table Southern cuisine. Popular dishes include black drum fish with Brussels sprouts and cauliflower, and Louisiana long-grain rice with crabmeat popcorn and jalapeño peppers. For the full effect, order the five-course surprise tasting menu, for which chefs Essig and Stoltzfus choose the season's best. www.coquettenola.com

COQUETTE
2800 Magazine Street
New Orleans, LA 70115
T: +1 504 265 0421

PIERRE GAGNAIRE

Master chef Pierre Gagnaire has come a long way from his famously failed first restaurant and now owns a collection of diverse establishments across the globe. His gourmet flagship, located off the Champs-Élysées in the Hôtel Balzac, has held on to its three Michelin stars for more than thirty years. His dining room, decorated with pieces from his own private art collection, is a temple to Gagnaire's poetic, spontaneous cuisine, which includes such masterpieces as langoustine in five variations (raw, steamed, grilled, in bouillon, and sautéed) and cacao-powdered duck. www.pierregagnaire.com

PIERRE GAGNAIRE
6 rue Balzac
75008, Paris, France
T: +33 1 58 36 12 50

MASON HEREFORD

Mason Hereford blasted onto the scene when his Turkey and the Wolf sandwich shop was named *Bon Appétit's* Best Restaurant of the Year in 2017. Locals and visitors line up daily outside of the squat cinderblock building in New Orleans for reinvented classics such as the fried bologna sandwich, with farm-raised Mississippi pork, Duke's mayo, cheese, homemade mustard, and shredded lettuce, and a gut-busting collard green melt that may have you rethinking vegetarian sandwiches. His newly opened Molly's Rise and Shine offers a more understated, yet always funky, menu of breakfast sandwiches, including a tweaked McMuffin with farm-raised pork and sweet potato burritos.
www.turkeyandthewolf.com
www.mollysriseandshine.com

TURKEY AND THE WOLF
739 Jackson Avenue
New Orleans, LA 70130
T: +1 504 218 7428

MOLLY'S RISE AND SHINE
2368 Magazine Street
New Orleans, LA 70130
T: +1 504 302 1896

JORDAN KAHN

Jordan Kahn's two L.A. restaurants offer up cutting-edge food presented in creative, theatrical ways. At Destroyer, his futuristic breakfast-and-lunch café, the standout dishes include raw oatmeal with red currant, almond milk, and vanilla; dense rye bread topped with preserves; and a reinvented avocado toast confit. Vespertine, his fine-dining restaurant, is located just across the road in a glass-and-steel building. There, Kahn delights and confuses diners with a lengthy tasting menu, complete with its own aromatherapy and soundtrack, that can include beautifully sculpted scallops with yucca, walnut, and white currant and teff salad with halibut.
www.vespertine.la
www.destroyer.la

VESPERTINE
3599 Hayden Avenue
Culver City, CA 90232
T: +1 323 320 4023

DESTROYER
3578 Hayden Avenue
Culver City, CA 90232
T: +1 310 360 3860

TOM KITCHIN

Tom Kitchin trained at some of the best restaurants in the world before opening The Kitchin in Edinburgh, and then, at twenty-nine, went on to become the youngest Michelin recipient in Scotland. Kitchin uses the best Scottish seasonal produce for such dishes as Rockpool local shellfish and sea vegetables in a shellfish consommé, and crispy veal sweetbreads. His gastropub, The Scran & Scallie, combines Scottish charm (aged tartans and textiles) updated with a bit of Scandinavian design sense and serves up a menu of revisited pub grub like Highland Wagyu beef burger and chips, and smoked haddock rarebit.
www.thekitchin.com
scranandscallie.com

THE KITCHIN
78 Commerical Quay
Leith
Edinburgh EH6 6LX, Scotland
T: +44 131 555 1755

THE SCRAN & SCALLIE
1 Comely Bank Road
Stockbridge
Edinburgh EH4 1DR, Scotland
T: +44 131 332 6281

JESSICA KOSLOW

Jessica Koslow's healthy eating mecca Sqirl is a boundary-breaking spot that helped popularize all-day breakfasts. Locals line up for simple, satisfying, and delicious dishes such as sorrel pesto rice bowl, with preserved lemon, hot sauce, feta, and poached egg, and next-level avocado toast topped with a za'atar spice mix, pickled carrots, and garlic crème fraîche. Then there are Koslow's famous homemade jams, which come in such flavors as strawberry rhubarb and Cara Cara with grapefruit juice and hibiscus. They top both the brioche and the ricotta toast at the restaurant and are for sale from the website.
www.sqirlla.com

SQIRL
720 Virgil Avenue, #4
Los Angeles, CA 90029
T: +1 323 284 8147

LUDO LEFEBVRE

Burgundy-born chef Ludo Lefebvre trained with some of France's culinary masters before coming to Los Angeles and wowing Angelenos with a series of pop-ups in the back of a friend's bakery. His tasting-menu-only Trois Mec, located in a former strip mall pizzeria (the sign is still hanging), is one of the city's most popular fine-dining spots and features such wonders as avocado sushi with salted cod and lime vinaigrette. Next door, the twenty-seater Petit Trois has a walk-in-only policy and delicious versions of classic French bistro food like steak tartare. There you can also order what many consider the best omelet in the city—perfectly smooth and filled with Boursin cheese.
www.troismec.com
petittrois.com

TROIS MEC
716 North Highland Avenue
Los Angeles, CA 90038
T: +1 323 484 8588

PETIT TROIS
718 North Highland Avenue
Los Angeles, CA 90038
T: +1 323 468 8916

BARBARA LYNCH

A high-school dropout turned successful restaurateur, Barbara Lynch now owns six restaurants in Boston. No. 9 Park, her flagship restaurant, located in Beacon Hill, is still going strong twenty years later. Well-heeled guests come for classic French- and Italian-inspired fare, especially the seafood entrées, and dine in

a polished-wood and white-linen dining room overlooking Boston Commons. Her other gourmet establishment, Menton, offers reliable revisited French fare such as seared Hudson Valley foie gras and steak tartare.
www.barbaralynch.com

No. 9 Park
9 Park Street
Boston, MA 02108
T: +1 617 742 9991

MENTON
354 Congress Street
Boston, MA 02210
T: +1 617 737 0099

GREGORY MARCHAND

Gregory Marchand's restaurant Frenchie started as a bare-bones, affordable bistro on a forgotten street at the edge of Paris's garment district. Now it's become an elegant fine-dining establishment with a newly minted Michelin star. In the intervening eleven years, the rue du Nil has become a foodie hotspot, with Frenchie Bar à Vins, a perpetually busy organic wine bar, and Frenchie FTG, a takeout shop with high-quality versions of fast-food classics like lobster rolls. Marchand has recently taken his concept abroad to London with Frenchie Covent Garden.
www.frenchie-restaurant.com

FRENCHIE
5 rue du Nil
75002, Paris, France
T: +33 1 40 39 96 19

FRENCHIE COVENT GARDEN
16 Henrietta Street
Covent Garden
London, WC2E 8QH,
United Kingdom
T: +44 207 836 4422

FRENCHIE BAR À VINS
6 rue du Nil
75002, Paris, France
T: +33 1 40 39 96 19

FRENCHIE FTG
9 rue du Nil
75002, Paris, France
T: +33 1 42 21 96 92

DAVID MCMILLAN

With its stick-to-your-ribs country cooking, David McMillan's Joe Beef has been Montreal's most emblematic restaurant since it first opened in 2005. Located in the pleasant, residential Little Burgundy neighborhood, this temple to Rabelaisian eating has been a magnet for locals as well as chefs and food writers. Inside the funky tavernesque digs, patrons tuck into fresh seafood platters, smoked meats, and the famous lobster spaghetti. McMillan co-owns several other establishments lining the same street, with Liverpool House offering fare similar to Joe's in a more relaxed setting, and wine bar Le Vin Papillon with lighter, less protein-heavy dishes and natural wines.
www.joebeef.ca

JOE BEEF
2491-2501 Rue Notre-Dame Ouest
Montréal, QC, H3J 1N6
Canada
T: +1 514 935 6504

LIVERPOOL HOUSE
2501 Rue Notre-Dame Ouest
Montréal, QC, H3J 1N6
Canada
T: +1 514 313 6049

LE VIN PAPILLON
2519 Rue Notre-Dame Ouest
Montréal, QC, H3J 1N4
Canada
T: +1 514 439 6494

ENRIQUE OLVERA

Mexico's most well-known chef became famous after opening the groundbreaking restaurant Pujol in Mexico City. Now Enrique Olvera has a small empire of restaurants, including a few north of the border. Cosme, named after the food market where he went as a child, is located in New York City's Flatiron district, and offers modern Mexican shared plates and exceptional mezcals. Atla, located in trendy NoHo, is an all-day café with such light, contemporary fare as flaxseed chilaquiles and mushroom quesadillas. For the full-on Olvera experience, however, book well ahead of time for a meal at Pujol, which, since opening in 2000, has consistently been ranked among the world's best restaurants, thanks to visionary dishes such as a five-year-old mole madre and *huitlacoche* (corn fungus) coupled with black truffles.
www.enriqueolvera.com

PUJOL
Tennyson 133
Polanco V Seccion,
C.P. 11560
CDMX, Mexico
T: +52 5545 4111

COSME
35 East 21st Street
New York, NY 10010
T: +1 212 913 9659

ATLA
372 Lafayette Street
New York, NY 10012
T: +1 347 662 3522

IVAN ORKIN

After years of breaking the rules and finding success in Tokyo, American-born Ivan Orkin closed up shop and moved back to his New York home, opening two different noodle-centric outlets, Slurp Shop in Hell's Kitchen (2011) and the eponymous Ivan Ramen on the Lower East Side (2013). Both places draw dyed-in-the-wool enthusiasts for bowls of exceptional ramen bathed in his homemade dashi broths, and small plates such as Japanese fried chicken and pork buns. But the especially hardcore swear by the Spicy Red Chili Ramen, a pilgrimage-worthy delicacy definitely not for the faint of heart.
www.ivanramen.com

IVAN RAMEN
25 Clinton Street
New York, NY 10002
T: +1 646 678 3859

SLURP SHOP
600 11th Avenue
New York, NY 10036
T: +1 212 582 7942

PACO PÉREZ

One of Spain's most highly respected chefs, Paco Pérez works with his wife and son at Miramar, offering such masterpieces of Catalan cooking as cockle "Bloody Mary" and hake cheeks with smoking pil-pil sauce.
www.restaurantmiramar.com

MIRAMAR
Passeig Maritim, 7
17490, Llançà
Girona, Spain
T: +34 972 38 01 32

ENOTECA
Hotel Arts Barcelona
Marina 19-21
08005, Barcelona, Spain
T: +34 93 4838108

ANTHONY ROSE

Although all of Anthony Rose's establishments are unique, they have a common theme: his Jewish heritage and food he likes to cook for himself. His deli Rose and Sons does delicious classics such as smoked turkey sandwiches and matzo ball soup, but also tasty mishmashes like pastrami fried rice with scallions and peanuts. His newest establishment, Fet Zun, goes full-on Middle Eastern, with homemade flatbreads and a vast selection of meze, including classics like chicken shawarma and the more unusual beetroot tahini on challah bread.
www.roseandsons.ca

ROSE AND SONS
176 Dupont Street
Toronto, ON M5R 2E6
Canada
T: +1 647 748 3287

FET ZUN
252 Dupont Street
Toronto, ON M5R 1V7
Canada
T: +1 647 352 3337

MARIE-AUDE ROSE

Located inside a hybrid florist/ furniture store/restaurant created by the design firm Roman and Williams, La Mercerie is as close to a perfect little French café as it is possible to get. Marie-Aude Rose serves up impeccably comforting Gallic food from an eclectic dining room where everything, from tableware to furniture, is for sale. Her textbook cheese omelets are the talk of the town and her sugar-coated crepes the best this side of Normandy.
www.lamerceriecafe.com

LA MERCERIE
53 Howard Street
New York, NY 10013
T: +1 212 852 9097

CARME RUSCALLEDA

Carme Ruscalleda's sophisticated take on Catalan cuisine draws diners from around the world to her Barcelona and Tokyo restaurants. Decorated in golden hues from the ceiling to the carpet, Moments, the Barcelona outpost, is overseen by her son Raül Balam. From the open kitchen, dishes such as "green pearl" peas from Maresme and sea cucumber delight guests. Tokyo's Sant Pau offers a similar menu of Catalan foods, but with local niche products such as Akaza Ebi langoustine shrimp or monkfish with salsa verde.
https://www.ruscalleda.cat/es

MOMENTS
Mandarin Oriental, Barcelona
Passeig de Gaàcia, 3, 40
08007, Barcelona, Spain
T: +34 931 51 87 81

RESTAURANT SANT PAU, TOKYO
Kitano Hotel Tokyo
2-16_15 Hirakawachon Chiyoda-ku
Tokyo 102-0093
Japan
T: +81 03 3511 2881

NANCY SILVERTON

From her days as a pastry chef at Spago, baking bread at La Brea Bakery, and creating the Cal-Italian cuisine with her restaurant Campanile, Nancy Silverton has had her finger on the pulse of Angeleno appetites for more than thirty years. Her drool-worthy pizzas topped with squash blossoms or handmade fennel sausage get customers quickly conversing at the bar of Pizzeria Mozza. Around the corner at the Osteria Mozza, in a chic room that's all dark wood and white tablecloths, diners feast on ricotta and egg ravioli and other creative pastas. For those in a rush, Mozza2Go has a pared-down menu of quality pies and antipasti.
www.mozzarestaurantgroup.com

PIZZERIA MOZZA
641 North Highland Avenue
Los Angeles, CA 90036

OSTERIA MOZZA
6602 Melrose Avenue
Los Angeles, CA 90038
T: +1 323 297 0100

MOZZA2GO
6610 Melrose Avenue
Los Angeles, CA 90038
T: +1323 297 1130

CLARE SMYTH

Clare Smyth, Gordon Ramsay's former head chef, has struck out on her own at Core, a charming converted Notting Hill townhouse serving up British ingredients in exciting new ways. Take, for instance, her lamb carrot: the root vegetable is braised in lamb-neck fat and topped with an intense meaty garnish, turning it into the main star. And her Charlotte potato is served with a generous dollop of herring and trout roe bathed in a luxurious beurre blanc sauce.
www.corebyclaresmyth.com

CORE BY CLARE SMYTH
92 Kensington Park Road
London, W11 2PN
United Kingdom
T: +44 203 937 5086

METTE SØBERG

Located in a former munitions warehouse in Copenhagen, Noma has been blowing minds in the Danish capital since it opened in 2003. Mette Søberg creates, with chef and founder René Redzepi's help, menus based on Scandinavian products, the ebb and flow of the seasons, and cutting-edge techniques that were invented at the restaurant. The lucky few who are able to obtain one of the precious reservations, feast on dishes unlike anywhere else, such as a decadent celeriac shawarma with truffle, and a Japanese mold-and-plum-seed ice cream sandwich.
www.noma.dk

NOMA
Refshalevej 96
1432 Copenhagen K, Denmark
T: +45 3296 3297

ALEX STUPAK

Alex Stupak, who was originally trained as a pastry chef, found his calling when he discovered the taco. Empellón, his first restaurant, plays on traditional Mexican dishes with a twist—like his octopus tacos or his sticky rice tamal. At first those dishes shocked people who were expecting more traditional Mexican food, but now Stupak is considered one of the best of contemporary American chefs. At Taqueria, a homey neighborhood spot in the West Village, the emphasis is on a small selection of tacos and ceviche, while Al Pastor focuses on reinvented bar food (think achiote hot wings and jalapeño poppers with bacon cream cheese filling) with a well-curated selection of East Coast and Mexican beers.
www.empellon.com

EMPELLÓN
510 Madison Avenue
New York, NY 10022
T+1 212 858 9365

TAQUERIA
230 West 4th Street
New York, NY 10014
T+1 212 367 0999

AL PASTOR (East Village)
132 St. Marks Place
New York, NY 10009

AL PASTOR (Murray Hill)
145 East 39th Street
New York, NY 10016
T+1 212 865 5800

CHRISTINA TOSI

Christina Tosi opened her first business in a tiny former laundromat next to Momofuku Ssam Bar, at the insistence of chef and boss David Chang. The first Milk Bar was an immediate success, with oddball sweets like compost cookies, a hodgepodge of oats, chocolate and butterscotch chips, ground coffee, potato chips, and pretzels. Now that there are multiple Milk Bar locations throughout the United States, everyone with a sweet tooth can delight in such whimsical treats as cereal milk soft serve ice cream and ooey gooey butter pie.
www.milkbarstore.com

MILK BAR East Village
251 East 13th Street
New York, NY 10003
T: +1 646 692 4154

Chelsea
220 8th Avenue
New York, NY 10011
T: +1 917 475 1187

West Village
74 Christopher Street
New York, NY 10014
T: +1 646 678 5189

Los Angeles
7150 Melrose Avenue
Los Angeles, CA 90046
T: +1 347 577 9504 ext 15

JEAN-GEORGES VONGERICHTEN

Widely recognized as a culinary genius, French-American chef Jean-Georges Vongerichten is a self-confessed restaurant junkie, owning dozens of unique establishments around the world. Jean-Georges, his restaurant overlooking New York City's Central Park, is rated two Michelin stars, and serves prix-fixe and tasting menus with dishes such as diver scallops with caramelized cauliflower, and young garlic soup with sautéed frog legs and thyme. If you are in the mood for something simpler, try his first restaurant, JoJo, which has recently reopened in an Upper East Side town house. There you'll find deliciously comforting food such as spicy yellowfin tuna tartare cups with avocado and shiso, and Wagyu beef tenderloin with salsa verde and lime.
www.jean-georges.com

JEAN-GEORGES
1 Central Park West
New York, NY 10023
T: +1 212 299 3900

JOJO
160 East 64th Street
New York, NY 10021
T: +1 212 233 5656

ALICE WATERS

When she opened Chez Panisse in 1971, Alice Waters wanted to create a dining space that made guests feel as if they were attending an intimate dinner party at the home of a good friend. In the wood-paneled-and-beamed dining room, a nightly four-course set-dinner menu features seasonal locally grown produce in such dishes as fresh pea, asparagus, and black truffle risotto, and juicy Full Belly Farm rack of lamb with Meyer lemon and thyme.
chezpanisse.com

CHEZ PANISSE RESTAURANT AND CAFÉ
1517 Shattuck Avenue
Berkeley, CA 94709
T: +1 510 548 5525

Acknowledgments

As anyone knows, inviting strangers into your home can be awkward. Letting them rummage through your refrigerator, all the way to the back of the shelves, where maybe you yourself haven't been in some time, is, well, intimate. We deeply appreciate the trust these chefs and their families gave us— and thank them for letting us into their kitchens.

We apologize if we put your favorite condiment back in the wrong spot. Thank you for finding the time (in between two shifts) not only to show us your fridges but to also feed us when we arrived jet-lagged and starving, for letting us discuss your family's dislikes, for teaching us how to whip up a sauce with a few leftover vegetables or how to freeze rice. Thank you as well for your honesty about shopping at the occasional big-box store and for understanding when our flight was late.

We are especially grateful to the amazing teams and PR companies who found our project insightful and worked hard to schedule us in and respond to follow-up questions. Thanks as well to all the friends and family who hosted us on couches or in guest rooms.

We are also incredibly thankful to those who believed in this book and made it possible: Sarah Smith, and the team at David Black, who championed our project; our editor Elizabeth Viscott Sullivan at Harper Design for her patience and vision; Linda Rodgers for her incredible attention to detail and sharp ideas; and Lynne Yeamans and Tanya Ross-Hughes for their work on the book design.

First published in 2020 by
Harper Design
An Imprint of HarperCollins Publishers
195 Broadway
New York, NY 10007
Tel: (212) 207-7000
Fax: (855) 746-6023

harperdesign@harpercollins.com
www.hc.com

Distributed throughout the world by
HarperCollins Publishers
195 Broadway
New York, NY 10007

ISBN 978-0-06-288931-7
Library of Congress Control Number: 2018965718

Book design by Lynne Yeamans and Tanya Ross-Hughes
Printed in Korea
First Printing, 2020

About the Authors

Carrie Solomon is an American photographer and writer who lives in Paris. Since moving there in 2002, she has become one of France's most celebrated culinary photographers. She is the coauthor, with Adrian Moore, of *Inside Chefs' Fridges, Europe*, and the author and photographer of *Une Américaine à Paris*. She also writes about and photographs food for *Elle* France.

www.carrie.paris; Instagram: carrie_in_paris

Adrian Moore is an award-winning palace concierge by day and a food and culture writer by night. When he is not keeping the secrets of food world luminaries and international jet-setters, he writes for publications like *Condé Nast Traveler*, *Travel + Leisure*, and *Monocle*. Canadian-born but raised in the United States, he lives in Paris.

www.theadrianmoore.com; Twitter: majormoore;
Instagram: adrianelvn